NEVER ALONE

NEVER ALONE

A SOLO ARCTIC SURVIVAL JOURNEY

WONIYA DAWN THIBEAULT

TIMELESS
WAYS

NEVER ALONE
A Solo Arctic Survival Journey
First Edition

Timeless Ways
3495 Lakeside Drive PMB 221
Reno, Nevada   89509

Cover & Layout Design: John van der Woude, JVDW Designs
Cover Images: Gregg Segal (author photo) and iStock.com
Interior Maps & Illustrations: Nathan B. Peltier

Library of Congress Control Number: 2023907247

ISBN   978-1-960303-00-4   *Hardcover*
        978-1-960303-01-1   *Paperback*
        978-1-960303-02-8   *Ebook*
        978-1-960303-03-5   *Audiobook*

Dedicated to the land, plants, and animals of my little slice of paradise on the shores of Tu Nedhe; and to the Alone family—the participants and show staff. It's not often that a solitary wilderness immersion makes you part of a community that understands intimately what you've been through. I'm grateful to the Alone family for being that community.

CONTENTS

ACKNOWLEDGMENTS

My *Alone* adventure would never have happened if a love of nature hadn't been instilled in me at a young age by both of my parents.

From the time I could carry a daypack, my mother brought me on Sierra Club hikes most weekends. Throughout my life, she has supported everything I have ever done, even when it included hauling dead animals home to tuck into her freezer. Thanks for seeing the beauty beneath the weird, Mom, and for always having my back, no matter what.

My father dragged me out to dusty trails any weekend I wasn't already hiking with my mom. A lot of people would never consider it possible to run 100 miles in one go, but I spent my childhood watching my father and his running-club friends do just that—and up and down steep mountains and canyons to boot. This shaped my faith in the capacity of the human body and spirit, and their will to persevere.

My love of nature wouldn't have blossomed into the skills I used in the Arctic if I hadn't found my way to the ancestral skills community early in life. I am deeply grateful to Dave Wescott for his devotion to those skills and to both Dave and Paula for the Society of Primitive Technology and Rabbitstick Rendezvous. I can't imagine my life without them. Thanks also to my early mentors in the skills community: Tamara Wilder, Margaret Mathewson, Jim Riggs, Alice Tulloch, Norm Kidder, Dave Holladay, and many more too numerous to name.

I had no idea what I was doing when I began this book, just a thousand potent memories pushing to get out, the capacity to write descriptive scenes, and a promise to share my story with the world. I poured those memories out, describing everything in exquisite detail. At the end of a multi-month marathon writing session, I had a manuscript of over 450,000 words. *And I had only reached day twenty-one of my seventy-three-day adventure.* I consulted a book coach, who had the honesty and grace to tell me that, while well written, my manuscript was utterly unpublishable. That was when I learned that there was a difference between *writing* and *telling a readable story*. Between that feedback and the onset of the coronavirus pandemic, in the spring of 2020 I dropped the book project like a hot potato.

Thus, *Never Alone* was written in two very distinct phases—the year after I came out of the Arctic wilderness and wrote like my hands were on fire, and three years later, after I participated in a second *Alone* adventure on *Alone Frozen*. Returning from *Alone Frozen* prompted me to finish *Never Alone*, the story of my first *Alone* journey on Season 6, so I could get started on the sequel! Had I not had a big pause in the process, and learned a lot through it, this book might have been over 1,200 pages. Thank goodness for small failures, huh?

Phase One of *Never Alone* received tremendous support from two households. The first was that of Marie McCree. I began the book in her beautiful home, perched on the rim of a chaparral canyon, listening to mountain lions yowl in the lowlands below. Marie voraciously read my first draft and begged for more, which helped me see that this book was worth writing and that it mattered. I wrote the rest of Phase One on a very special farm by a river, where I spent many long winter days holed up in a tiny house made of clay and straw, glued to my laptop with a hot water bottle in my lap. I am grateful for the support and encouragement I received there, while I was a bad landmate, emerging only for meals, farm chores, river walks, and an occasional dip in the wood-fired hot tub.

Phase Two came years later, and I'm grateful to Anne Alexander for the nudge to dust off my manuscript and get it finished. Thanks, Anne! That summer, advice from writing coaches Emily Gindlesparger and J.C. Sevcik kept me from abandoning the project in frustration.

Peregrine and Genevieve, whose own book projects inspired and encouraged me, were also a huge help. Sharing triumphs and woes with trusted friends as we each muddled our way through story-craft kept me going. Keep after it, you guys. I want to see those books in print!

My editors, Lisa Caskey and Anya Szykitka, helped make this book polished and readable. I'm grateful for their support and all I learned from them, and to my beta readers, Anne, Kirsten, and Meghan, for their wonderful feedback.

I received tremendous support from my Patreon team. They allowed me to pay the rent while I dropped everything to write, write, write. Regularly running progress reports and ideas by them helped the book feel more like a team effort and kept me motivated. Extra special thanks to my "Buckskin Pillars" Joanne, Alice, Jenny, and Shannon. You guys are miracle makers— thanks for your role in this one!

And huge thanks to another pillar in my life. Thank you, Taylor, for cooking and cleaning so I could keep my fingers on the keyboard, for your tremendous love and support, for your patience with my crazy work hours, and for tolerating the constant glowing light of the monitor—so out of place in front of this outdoorsy nature-woman. You believed in me from the get-go and helped me do the same.

PREFACE

I knew from the moment I left my wilderness home on *Alone Season 6* that I needed to write this book. While I understood that, as a televised event, the world would eventually get to watch some parts of it, there is far more to a solitary survival experience like mine than can ever be captured on film or shared in a few short episodes. Most people see the show as a competition or a wilderness adventure, but it's infinitely greater than either of those—a true rite of passage.

For many participants, our time on *Alone* is like stepping into a crucible—everything we think we know about ourselves, our skills, and our lives is thrust into the fire and melted down. It's hard to know what shape we'll take when we emerge from it.

The intention of this book is to give you a glimpse into that crucible and to share the heart of my journey in a deeper way than is possible from simply watching the show. It aims to help you vicariously experience not only the discomfort, deprivations, and struggles but also the beauty, magic, and joy that made it all worthwhile.

As I signed a non-disclosure agreement (NDA) to participate in the show, I'm very grateful for the generosity of The HISTORY Channel™ for agreeing to let me write this book at all. Because of that NDA, there are some limits on the details I can share. This is the story of *my journey*, not a behind-the-scenes look at the inner workings of the show itself. If you find yourself wondering why you aren't hearing more details about a specific aspect of the story, my contract restrictions are probably why. More important than describing the little details is sharing the profound nature of an extreme wilderness immersion like the one I experienced and the beautiful transformation it can elicit when one gives oneself to it fully—body, mind, and soul.

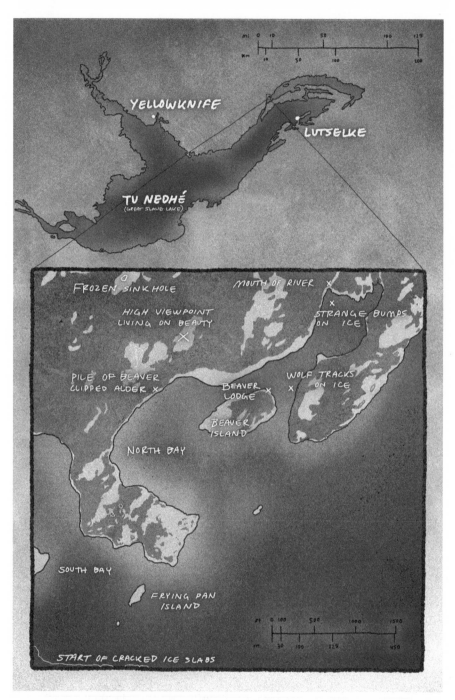

ABOVE: Map of Tu Nedhe (aka Great Slave Lake) and my area within it.
OPPOSITE: Map of my home peninsula.

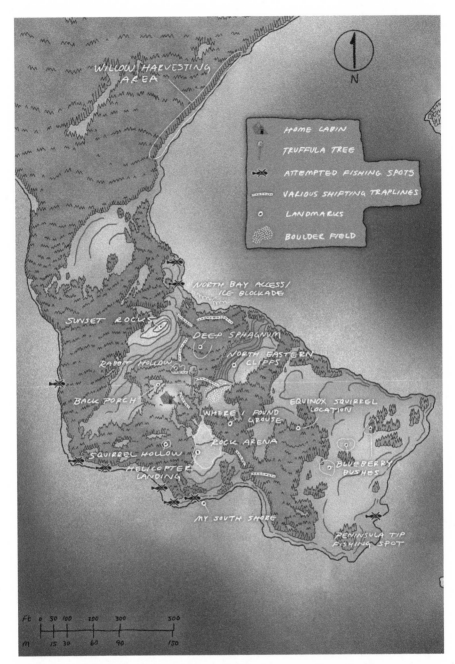

A Note About Scale: While it's important to include scale on maps, it can also be very misleading as the map is a flat surface. Besides the lake's surface, the land of the Tu Nedhe region is anything but flat, therefore what appears on the map as 50 feet might actually be several hundred feet once one accounts for switchbacks up tall cliffs or going down into deep crevices and up the other side. Add thick forest, foot-sucking sphagnum moss, and the cumulative effects of starvation to the equation, and the distances seem infinitely greater again than those reflected on the scale on the printed page.

PART ONE

PROVING
I CAN

ON THIN ICE

I heave a deep sigh and watch the water vapor from my breath—a small white cloud against the backdrop of heavy, dark clouds—float out across the ice. It makes it about ten feet before freezing solid and drifting down to the lake's surface.

The cramping of my shrunken stomach has become such a fixture in my world that I barely register it anymore. This time as it twists inside me, I'm deeply aware of the ache and how long it's been since I had anything to fill that empty hollow.

I ventured onto the frozen lake tonight to hunt, only to discover the game I was after was far out of my reach. But that wasn't my only motivation. The Arctic has taught me I can be fed by more than just food—beauty, adventure, and wildness are powerful sustenance as well.

An island blocks my view to the west, so I can't tell if the sun has dipped beneath the horizon yet, but I know it must be nearly down. At this latitude, just south of the Arctic Circle, there are about four hours of solid daylight this time of year, with another hour of hazy, low light at dawn and dusk. The smart choice would be to turn around and head back to the cabin, get the fire going, and make another pot of the coffee-colored chaga tea that serves for dinner (and breakfast, and lunch) these days. I know that. My body may be failing, but my reason is still intact. I know too that once the sun goes down, the temperature out on the ice is going to plummet.

Back toward camp and safety, or the open lake ice and adventure—*what's it going to be?*

I cup my palms to catch my warm breath and direct it over my cheeks until I can feel them again. I give my rabbit fur scarf a quarter turn to find a spot for my face that isn't crusted with my frozen breath, turn away from the island—and my little arctic home on the peninsula beyond it—and head out across the lake.

How did a woman like me, born and raised in northern California, a member of PETA at age sixteen, come to be out here, my survival hanging on my hunting prowess, making my way alone in the arctic wilderness? In some ways, it seems absolutely incredible, and in others, like a natural extension of my life's path.

I was nineteen and vegan the first time someone offered to roast up road-killed meat to share with me. The year was 1995, and I was attending the Rabbitstick Rendezvous, a weeklong event focused on teaching and learning primitive skills.

I was a student at the University of California, Santa Cruz, studying biology and environmental science. I felt increasingly depressed and disenfranchised in college, especially as I learned more about the impacts of modern society on the planet and its ecosystems. I'd spent as much of my sophomore year roaming the dirt roads of the forests near campus as I had in class. Studying the natural world in books wasn't enough for me. I was desperate to learn the deeper skills, the ones my long-ago ancestors had lived by, to know how to feel at home in the woods and gather and make the things I needed from the resources wild places offered.

I tried to teach myself. I studied the tracks in the dusty trails, harvested berries and wild greens, and bought cheap, chemically tanned leather and tried to make moccasins with it. It was better than nothing, but it didn't satisfy me—there was too much I didn't know, and I had no idea how to learn it.

I felt determined but also isolated and lonely. I read about a field program with academic instructors who also taught ancestral skills like friction fire and others. I signed up and spent the summer between my sophomore and junior years on their eight-week backpacking field course, voraciously absorbing all I could. At the end of the course, the instructors told me I should check out Rabbitstick Rendezvous, and I signed up as soon as I could.

The event is a primitive skills conference, and I was utterly entranced from the moment I stepped out of the car. Here were people teaching not only how to make but how to use stone and bone tools, as well as how to weave baskets, harvest wild foods, tan deer hides, and much more. The days were filled with learning new skills and the evenings with sharing songs and stories around the glowing coals of the central fire. It was everything I'd ever wanted and felt like coming home to a family I didn't know I had.

The offer of roadkill came on night four of that incredible week. I'd already been so changed by my time there and the new possibilities I'd been exposed to that I didn't bat an eye at the offer, I just grabbed a plate. The first course was a gray squirrel from a street in a Portland suburb. After years of working hard to deny my inner carnivore, the smell alone awakened something primal in me. Sinking my teeth into a leg and gnawing the juicy meat off the bone fed me in a way no veggie burger ever had. I felt nourished all the way down to my toes, and I sat around the fire and talked and laughed with my new friends until near dawn, as a selection of other critters that had been in the wrong place at the wrong time made their way onto the grill.

It might seem like a significant leap to go from strict vegan to eating roadkill, but I didn't see it that way. While I had been adamantly against hunting in high school, that was no longer true. I was vegan, but I wasn't opposed to eating meat; it was the way meat was raised and processed in the US that I took issue with. I had even started making a wooden bow on my field course, hoping to hunt with it one day myself, but the idea of making use of "roadside resources" had never occurred to me.

That night, and the rest of Rabbitstick, changed my life forever. They awakened me to the fact that, while the contemporary world wasn't going away, it was still possible to live a wilder life within it—one of a "modern hunter-gatherer"—harvesting food and raw materials from the roadways, the wilds, and everything in between.

It was a huge turning point in my life. I came home with new teachers and friends, more skills, armloads of projects, and a sense of hope and purpose I desperately needed. I also came home with pneumonia, probably from running around barefoot and underdressed in temperatures that dipped into the teens. The fever of pneumonia eventually passed, but the fever for the skills of my ancestors never left me. I poured myself into them, heart and soul, from that moment on.

Soon, I was picking roadkill myself and learning to butcher it through trial and error. In less than a year, I was sporting an entire outfit of clothing I'd made from deer hides I'd tanned and working on gear for a stone-age expedition.

There were ebbs and flows, as life, with all its joys and challenges, had its way with me, but only a few years passed between attending my first Rabbitstick Rendezvous and becoming an instructor there. Before long, I was making a name for myself in the field of ancestral technology.

Even so, I never would have predicted that my passion for ancestral skills would one day take this California-born, once-upon-a-time teenage vegan to the far reaches of the continent for a solitary arctic adventure.

Not all the way, I promise myself, as I head directly away from the small peninsula in the wilderness where I've been making my home for the past two and a half months.

I'll just go to the eastern shore, only a few hundred yards away, not the far-off northern shore. A few more minutes won't hurt. I can still make it back by dark.

With my legs pumping, I don't feel cold anymore. I feel lit from within, hungry to fill my senses with all I can of this place in the time I have left. The drive to see and explore is a fever not unlike the one awoken in me at my first Rabbitstick Rendezvous, so long ago.

I'm almost to the shore when I see something weird happening with the surface of the ice ahead of me. What has been flat white as far as the eye can see is now bumpy and ridged. The strange bumps aren't white like the rest of the ice, they're marbled with brown swirls. *What the heck?*

I turn around to check the light and judge how much time I've got. My impulsiveness is starting to catch up with me. I can feel the fatigue in my legs and the effort it's taken them to carry me here. This is too damn far from home for this hour of night, but I'm intrigued, and it'll only take me a minute to explore this new mystery. A minute more isn't going to make a difference in the light.

I creep cautiously toward the bumps, and I'm only a few steps from the closest one when I freeze.

It takes me a second to register what I'm sensing. *I hear something.* In all this vast, frozen wilderness there has been almost no sound for hours, except for the high-pitched calls of one chickadee on the island, and my own breath in my ears. This is totally different. Faint, low, and ever-changing. There's something familiar about it—something I know but can't quite place. And then I'm hot all over, my chest tight against the furs of my parka—my body registering what it is a second before my brain does.

It's gurgling. I look down at the ice below my feet. There, not far beneath my toes, I see an amoeboid white shape fly past under the ice, and then another. Air bubbles. My heartbeat thuds in my ears. Suddenly it all makes sense.

The shape of the land in front of me—a narrow valley pointing right toward the lake.

The irregular shapes on the lake surface.

The roar of sound I heard so often out of the north before freeze-up.

Not wind through the trees as I'd imagined, but a wide and rushing river, loud enough to hear from all the way back at the peninsula. The strange shapes are foamy water and standing waves frozen in place, the brown swirls are the muddy water they carry. I'm not standing on the lake anymore; I'm standing on top of an enormous, fast-moving river, and the ice beneath me is only inches thick.

Adrenaline clouds my thinking like the descending darkness clouds my vision. Months of careful risk avoidance while living on my own in one of the wildest, most remote places on earth amidst wolverines and wolf packs, and never a second of serious danger or deep, visceral fear. Now, in one foolish moment, I've hiked myself smack on top of the biggest hazard imaginable.

I take a few deep breaths to choke down my panic. Ice over moving water is soft and weak, full of air and irregularities. One wrong step and I could go down in a heartbeat, sucked under the lake's surface by the flowing current. It's already too dark for the rescue helicopter to fly. Even if it could, if I go through the ice and manage to stay on the surface, the crew would never get to me before the hypothermia does.

Think Woniya, think.

My eyes dart to the shore, so close I can almost feel it, solid and reassuring beneath my feet. Every animal instinct tells me to go there—run like hell for the shore and solid ground, faster than the ice can give way. But that leads me closer to the river's mouth, where the ice is likely more rotten than where I stand now.

As tempting as it is, I know heading for shore is a death wish. I force my feet to obey my will as I turn away from the perception of safety and back toward the open lake ice I just came from. I slowly plant one foot in my own closest track. *Solid—thank god.* I take another step, and another. The ice holds. I release my held breath.

With every step I feel a little more confident, a little less panicked. Finally, I'm back on clear white ice and snow, and flat feels like the most beautiful texture in all the world.

By the time I'm halfway home, I know I'll be okay, but my whole body is still shaky. I'm clammy with sweat inside my clothes, even in these subzero temperatures.

Then I hear a loud beep from my hip bag. *Oh god, right—my GPS device!*

YOU ARE OUT OF BOUNDS AND LATE FOR CHECK-IN. HEAD BACK IMMEDIATELY

In my excitement, I hadn't even stopped to think how far out of my assigned area I'd wandered. This far north, the satellites are so low in the sky that the signal doesn't send often, so I'm only getting the message now that

I'm well on my way back. I scared the hell out of myself, but at least I didn't know how much danger I was in until I was halfway through it.

Not true at production base camp, where there's a staff person watching my GPS signal day and night. Somewhere, many miles away, there's probably a group of frantic people yelling at a flashing blip on a screen, wondering if they'll be doing their first ever body retrieval tomorrow.

2

BE CAREFUL WHAT YOU WISH FOR

The invitation to my arctic journey came when I least expected it. At that moment, my life was more domestic than it had been in over a decade—indoor plumbing, electric lights, and all. It was also more highly scheduled than I was used to. I knew where I would be and what I would be doing that fall—living in the mild climate of coastal northern California, finishing the program that had brought me there.

And yet, there were unseen forces at play that were part of a larger chain of unpredictable, yet somehow perfect, events already set in motion.

At that time, I was studying at the Weaving Earth Center for Relational Education. The program I was enrolled in offered a unique, immersive style of learning that combined mentoring skills, nature connection, community-building, and land-based living skills. I and the other second-year students were out on a four-day "surthrival" trip—like backpacking only without modern gear or store-bought food. The goal wasn't to *survive* the wilderness but to do our best to *thrive* there. With a few metal tools brought along, it was a departure from the stone-age trips I used to do in the years after my first Rabbitstick, and with a very different kind of group. While I and a few others were seasoned outdoor people, some were sleeping in the wilderness for the first time.

The biggest difference between this trip and my prior ones wasn't the kind of gear, nor the experience level of the participants, it was the intention.

For decades I'd focused on the skills themselves, with the idea that leaving the modern world and its trappings behind would automatically lead to a deep connection with the land. As often as not, that hadn't been the case. On this Weaving Earth trip, such connection was the primary focus—the skills, gear, and food were secondary. The difference was palpable. Listening to and trusting in the land and being there in a reciprocal way—giving back as much or more than we were taking—changed everything. After so many years of practicing and teaching ancestral, land-based, and wilderness skills, I couldn't believe how profoundly approaching it with different goals affected my experience. It felt like something I'd spent my adult life looking for, yet that had always eluded me, had been dropped into my lap. It rekindled the coal of a fire—the one that ignited my fever for ancestral skills long ago—that had recently lost some of its brightness.

On the last evening of our trip, I was aching to experience everything I could before we headed back home, so I left the rest of the group for a solo wander, hoping to connect more deeply with the place.

I had been shedding layers, literally and figuratively, since arriving here. I'd left all plastic gear and tarps behind, though a huge rainstorm—an "atmospheric river"—was predicted to hit. I'd slept out in an open meadow under a buffalo skin—though the sky above was heavy with clouds—and the rain had held off for another day. When the sky had finally opened up and the rain had poured down, I'd sheltered in a rock crevice, warm and dry, while the water careened down the cliffs all around me.

I'd felt hunger and mild panic at the tiny portion of acorn meal that was breakfast, and at one daily walnut as a snack, but had adjusted to getting by on so little. At the start of each meal, one of us would scoop up a small portion, create a lovely plate on a leaf or rock, and lay it out as an offering to the land and the ancestors while speaking our deep gratitude aloud. Even though it meant less food to go around, I loved our practice of sharing some of every meager meal with the sacred and other-than-human community before we ate from our own plates.

It was almost sunset and I'd had little to eat or drink since morning, but as I headed out on my solo wander, I carried no flashlight, snacks, or water bottle. Nothing but the knife on my belt and the thin clothes on my back.

It was an exercise in trust, just as the whole trip had been, and that trust had so far been rewarded with the most beautiful wilderness venture I could remember.

The storm the day before had left puddles in the hollows of the granite ledges I walked on. When I got thirsty, I sucked up water from the rocks, unfiltered, just as the resident animals do. It tasted of the minerals of the bedrock, the storm clouds, and the very sky itself. With every drink, I felt wilder, more connected. Eventually, I meandered up toward the cliff edge, intending to look out over the open vista toward the distant river, when something closer caught my eye. The land below me was a gray and green patchwork of rocks and vegetation, but one gray was different—textured. *Fuzzy lichen perhaps?* But then what were those striking black and white patches?

My breath sucked in convulsively as it registered—the fuzzy texture was fur. *I was looking at a bobcat.* It was nestled on its stomach, paws crossed under its chin and head tilted to one side, like a house cat in front of a warm fire.

I can't believe I'm seeing this!

I hunkered down onto the rocks, watching it in stillness and silence, marveling at its intricate spotted pattern and the way the sunshine glistened in its tawny fur. Finally, I had to shift my cramping legs. The sound of my movement alerted it and it whipped its head up toward me. Our eyes met and we both froze.

I was locked in a staring contest with one of nature's most elusive predators. The remarkable thing, though, wasn't the eye lock we had going, but the fact that partway through it, the bobcat began to relax. *Really* relax. Its eyelids drooped and its head nodded. It caught itself and came back to alertness, like a sleepy toddler at the dinner table catching itself just before a faceplant, then it nodded off again, its chin falling onto its paws.

In that moment I knew—I didn't just *feel* wilder, I *was* wilder. Having this shy predator feel comfortable enough to fall asleep while staring me full in the face was proof of it.

When I got back to the group, my eyes were brimming with tears, and though part of me wanted to scream, "You'll never believe what just happened," I didn't. I couldn't.

It was too personal, too deep.

The moment had changed something in me—recalled me to the places in myself that knew they were part of the wild. Those places had been dead to me for too long, and with their awakening, I was beginning to remember what it had felt like to be whole.

While I'd been teaching people how to use wild resources to make the substance of their lives—food, shelter, clothing, and more—for decades, I wasn't a leader on this trip, I was just one of thirteen fellow students.

When I decided to join the Weaving Earth program, one similar to the kind I myself had been running not long before, I'd been at a crossroads. The drive I'd always had toward a more earth-based life remained, but there had been bumps along the way when it seemed I couldn't pursue it without losing other things I loved. Recently, I'd lost hope and become so depressed and dejected after watching all my dreams fall apart, one by one, that I wasn't sure how to carry on. I was mourning big losses when I came to the program. I'd spent my thirties living on a community owned, off-grid homestead in northern Oregon. While there I'd grown, gathered, and preserved my food without refrigeration, tanned deer hides for clothing, woven baskets from the willow shoots I harvested, and practiced and taught innumerable other ancestral and homesteading skills.

After many years of feeling like I was building the community land project of my dreams, over the course of two years group dynamics there had grown increasingly intolerable. Then my marriage to my second husband, Bryon, ended when he developed an autoimmune disease with complications that made our off-grid lifestyle untenable. Finding ways to meet his shifting needs took over our lives and led to his deciding he didn't want to start a family together after all. The decision was more than I could bear. Finally, I came to terms with the fact that the skills school I had been running was unsustainable. After all these blows, at thirty-eight years old and terrified I would never become a mother, I'd eventually met someone new, moved elsewhere, and started over. It had gone poorly and ended in a miscarriage and more heartbreak.

Knowing I needed a big change and some reprieve from my struggles, I bought a one-way ticket to Thailand and spent four months traveling around Southeast Asia by myself. Experiencing something so completely different—ecologically, culturally, and in all other ways—was a breath of fresh air and helped me feel again the joy and excitement I'd been missing.

When I returned to the US, one of the first things I did was visit a friend enrolled in a Weaving Earth immersion program. I was intrigued by what I saw, and though I'd never previously thought of applying, when I heard the program was accepting applications for the following year, I turned one in. I wanted to do the program for professional reasons, to learn how the instructors worked together to run it and what made their program successful when I had struggled so much with mine.

Deep down, I knew that was only part of my motivation. The collapse of everything I cared most about had leveled me, and though I'd regained some of my former happiness, my inspiration and drive to start over had taken a big hit. Signing up for something that reminded me of what mattered, and that gave me a year or two with fewer responsibilities so I could lick my wounds and regroup, was exactly what I needed.

The surthrival trip was the final project of my second year in the program. I'd learned so much in those two years as a student—not solely about the subjects taught, but about myself and the need to shift how I approached my teaching and my life. I better understood how to honor myself and the land around me, and what it feels like to be embedded in a community that supports and nurtures, rather than one enmeshed in conflict like the one I had left behind.

But I'd been growing restless. As I healed, I recognized my growing need to return to my work in the world. I couldn't be a student forever. I needed to teach and felt a desire to do so in new and bigger ways that reached the deeper goals of helping students feel more connected to the world around them. I didn't know what that would look like or when it would begin, but I knew it was coming.

Somehow, that moment with the bobcat was a catalyst. I could feel a new future beckoning, and I knew I wanted longer, deeper wilderness immersions to be a part of it.

As I shrugged into my pack basket the last morning of the surthrival trip to hike back to the cars, I wasn't ready to leave. Our time out had been too brief. It had awakened a hunger it hadn't satisfied.

I let the rest of the group filter out and stood in the grassy amphitheater that had been our camp. I threw my arms back, surrendering myself to the meadow and the rocks, and to the feelings of both joy and deep longing churning inside me.

"This right here," I called to the cliffs and the gray pines, the bobcat and the canyon wrens. "More trips like this, but longer and wilder, with fewer people and less modern gear." The ring of my voice bounced back to me off the granite and I heaved a deep sigh. *May it be so*, I thought, as I slung the strap of my buffalo hide sleeping bag over my shoulder and hurried off to catch up with the others.

Be careful what you wish for. I would never have guessed that the world would start working on that request right away, or the form that the answer to my prayer would take, but I was about to be reminded that magic works in mysterious and unpredictable ways.

3

DESTINY CALLS

omething in that wild and beautiful place had been paying attention. In the universe's own brand of ironic humor, my prayers for a deeper wilderness immersion were answered the moment I re-entered the technological world after our trip and fired up my computer to check my email.

"Hello from the *Alone* Casting Team," the subject line read.

It wasn't the first inquiry I'd received from a television show. Given the growing popularity of these shows and my reputation in the field of ancestral skills, I'd been contacted by a fair number of survival "reality" shows. I once even went so far as to let a film crew come out to the homestead to see about casting me in one. The experience had only affirmed what I already suspected: the show seemed forced and ingenuine. It was something I wanted no part of.

This one though? *This one was different...*

I'd heard of *Alone* and had even watched an episode when teaching a buckskin sewing course for the Boulder Outdoor Survival School (BOSS). My friend Randy, a BOSS instructor, had been on the show, and his season happened to air during my visit to BOSS's southern Utah campus. A group of instructors crowded around the television in the cramped staff trailer to watch it, complete with Randy's narration of what we were seeing on the screen. I learned from him that the show was a legitimate and extreme survival experience, not staged in any way, where contestants were dropped into the wilderness with minimal gear.

After that, I hadn't given it any more thought.

But the timing of this email was uncanny.

Had the request to chat with their casting director come at any other point in my life, I would probably have deleted the email, as I had done with similar requests in recent years. Receiving it now, immediately following a life changing trip and my fervent prayer that last day, was too much for me to ignore.

But seriously—*television*? I didn't think I could do it. Okay, okay—yes, I knew I needed a big change and a lot more wild time. And I had to admit that I'd actually said the words "I am ready to be seen" just before our trip.

I remembered the moment well. Several of the students had expressed interest in making their own gear for our expedition, so I'd decided to offer them a felting class to make wool vests for it. They would be our warm layer, our "rain gear," and our sleeping pads. I spent a full day sorting and carding wool and setting up the space. When the scheduled day arrived, I got a phone call from one person saying something had come up, then another from someone who didn't feel well. Over the course of an hour, every person who had committed to being there pulled out for one reason or another. I wasn't charging for the class, it was my gift to my fellow students, and I had put a lot of time, effort, and materials into preparing for it. I felt rejected, disappointed and unappreciated.

The group convened the night before we left for the trip to discuss logistics, but as I sat in the circle, I couldn't be present. My frustration about the unattended workshop was simmering within me and blocking my ears, so I finally spoke up.

"I have something I need to say," I said. "I worked hard to prepare for that class. After two years of letting my teaching career go, I was excited to finally be able to bring my work and passions to this program. Being asked to teach it and then not having a single person show up was really upsetting."

My voice was squeaky with emotion. I knew I was talking too fast and on the verge of tears, but I didn't want to lose my nerve, so I let it all pour out.

"It felt disrespectful of my offering. This stuff isn't just a hobby for me, you guys. It's who I am and what I do. I'm feeling really unseen and unappreciated and I'm frustrated about it. I want to be seen. *I'm ready to be seen.*"

There it was: I hadn't just asked for deep wilderness immersion, I'd also asked to be seen. I had meant *seen for the skills I have to offer*, not *seen on television by several million people*, but it wasn't the universe's fault I hadn't been specific.

I couldn't just ignore an invite that offered all the things I'd asked for, but this was television we were talking about, and I hated television. I'd always considered it gross—some of the worst aspects of our culture put together, then overly dramatized and commercialized.

And yet, who was I to question the inner workings of life's mysteries? I had spent the last two years setting aside my own teaching and other projects to become a caterpillar again.

When a caterpillar gets the internal message that it's time, it literally melts into goo inside its skin as its body remakes itself in the form of a butterfly. Hadn't I just done something similar—let go of my former ideas of self and surrendered to the magic of transformation? Was this part of that magic? The caterpillar doesn't know the form it will take as a butterfly; it only knows it's time to shrug off its useless old legs and grow new wings. Maybe television exposure could give me the wings I needed for whatever was coming next.

I wasn't convinced, but I wasn't going to deny the possibilities before me. My fingers shook a little as I drafted my response agreeing to meet with the *Alone* casting team, but I steadied myself, held my breath, and clicked "send."

4

NO EXCUSES

From my first conversation with Quinn, the casting director, it felt as if I had stepped onto a ride I couldn't step off. It wasn't like I didn't have a choice in the matter—of course I did. But the more questions I asked, the more of my excellent arguments against doing the show dissolved away, and the more the universe intervened and let me know this was all part of its plan.

I learned from Quinn that the show involved no predetermined story arc, where the producers make it seem they merely follow participants around when in fact they determine their actions. The producers wouldn't interfere in any way with the participant's experience or choices. In fact, they wouldn't even know about their choices until watching the footage much later, because everyone would literally be on their own out there, filming everything themselves.

The premise was simple: ten people would be hand-picked from amongst tens of thousands of applicants. Each would select ten gear items to bring, plus the permitted clothing, and be equipped with a case full of camera equipment. They'd be dropped off, by helicopter, in the wilderness. Alone. The goal would be to survive for as long as possible, or as long as they could stand it, until only one person was left.

I thought back to the countless afternoons I'd spent in my youth stalking along dusty trails barefoot, a knife on my belt and a sling in my hand. My goal had been to run off into the woods with nothing else and to harvest and make everything I needed to live. This show sounded like the closest I was likely to get to that long-cherished fantasy.

A wilderness adventure in parts unknown with limited gear? Hell yes, sign me up!

But broadcasting that adventure to a world of strangers? My insides quivered nervously at the thought. While excited on some levels, I was still looking for excuses not to go. *Why?*

I brainstormed answers.

I could do poorly, embarrassing myself in front of millions of viewers. But I'd poured my whole life into these skills, and I was excited, not afraid, to demonstrate them. I could lose, but I didn't care about that—the competition wasn't my goal, the experience was. The attention was intimidating, but I also knew I was ready to reach the world in new and bigger ways than I had managed thus far with my teaching.

My hesitation, I knew, wasn't coming from a place of logic—it was something deeper. Something I didn't want to look at. The truth was, it was plain fear. If I was honest with myself, I knew the insidious doubts were a matter of basic self-worth.

Do I really deserve this opportunity?

Am I good enough, important enough, to do such a thing?

Who do I think I am to appear on hundreds of thousands—probably even millions—of television screens?

I'd worked for years on my patterns of self-doubt, self-denial, and subtly punishing myself. I had come so far. I no longer bent over backwards to prove my worthiness to the world, my loved ones, and myself. Yet here were my old challenges and doubts, still staring me in the face.

Saying yes wasn't only about an amazing adventure or a good career move; it was a commitment to believing in myself, truly and utterly.

Okay, Woniya, step up or step off. Here's your chance to do the real work.

Being willing to step in front of a camera and show my biggest adventure and deepest heart to the world would be a tremendous expression of self-worth and a monumental act of empowerment.

Can I commit to that?

I didn't know.

A reprieve from finding the answer came a couple of days later during my next phone call with Quinn, in the form of some handy logistics that made it undoable.

"One week—*are you serious?*" I asked.

"Well, more like a week and a half," she relented.

They'd reached out to me late in their casting process. Though my reputation preceded me, I still had to jump through the necessary hoops by submitting footage of myself doing a variety of survival-related skills. I'd also need to clear my schedule for the next eight months or so. The footage was due in a week, but I was booked for the next two weeks, including many days camping with no access to computers. I didn't even have a video camera, much less any filmable projects lined up.

I was incredulous. Who could clear their schedule for eight months with less than two weeks' notice? I planned on doing three years at Weaving Earth. Year two was ending soon, but we started up again in the fall, exactly when the *Alone* participants were supposed to launch. My program or *Alone*? It would be an either/or call.

"I see. Well, that's too little time and too many conflicts for this year," I told her. "And I don't have a camera to record myself. Let's be in touch again about the next season."

I secretly heaved a deep sigh, preparing to write it off and return to life as usual.

But the universe had its own plans for me, and excuse after excuse dried up and blew away.

"Most people just film with their phones," Quinn had said.

Damn, I have a phone!

No camera, not a problem. Bang! One excuse shot down.

That was just the beginning. When I got to school for the next five-day session, the instructors had a big announcement for us. After much deliberation, they'd decided to shift our school year from starting in the fall, as it had always done, to the following spring.

My stomach jumped, then sank as excitement and trepidation wrestled for control over it. The eight months I needed to do the show, and had been holding as "scheduled," were now *completely free*.

The universe blew smoke from the barrel of its proverbial gun. Two excuses down.

I had the filming capacity. I had the time. A slew of interesting and impressive projects to document on a moment's notice though? No way, that wasn't going to happen.

But the night after our class session let out was a friend's birthday, and I'd offered to make him an all-wild-foods dinner to celebrate. It was hardly a whole application's worth of footage, but it wouldn't hurt to film it.

I did my best to hold the phone steady to record myself as I harvested succulent native greens to the sound of the trickling creek behind my house. I unpacked the clay cooking pots I'd made for our surthrival trip and used one to cook elk stew from meat I'd canned last fall and seaweed I'd collected at the coast. In the other, I prepared wild rice. As I poured in the rice grains, I remembered the smooth feel of the cedar sticks I'd used to knock them from the tall grass stalks into the canoe and the swish of them echoing against its aluminum sides. As I rinsed them, the faint scent of the smokey fire, over which we'd parched them before dancing the chaff off with our buckskin moccasins, wafted up at me. The sensations grounded me and helped quiet the countless questions that had been swirling around my mind ever since my first call with Quinn. From that calmer place, my body knew what my mind had yet to accept. *You can do this Woniya*, it told me. *Actually, it's exactly what you need.*

The ringing of the phone jarred me out of my wild rice reverie. It was a friend in town—a doe had been hit crossing the road in front of her house and was lying dead in her yard. She was vegan and didn't know how to handle it, so she called me.

She needed help, and I could use the meat, but I hovered on the edge of no. I had a guest arriving momentarily and dinner bubbling on the stove. "I'll ask," I told her.

When my dinner guest, the birthday boy, arrived, he was thrilled at the idea of learning to butcher a deer. My housemate Randall was excited too, so we left dinner where it sat and the three of us loaded up into Randall's pickup truck.

Magical gifts and messages from the wild. My third and final excuse not to apply, blown out of the water.

Okay, okay, universe! I get it already!

The rest was video history. It took a while to scrub the bloody fingerprints off all the crevices of my phone, and I had to shift my schedule around a bit to do it, but before the application window closed I submitted footage of myself harvesting wild plant foods as well as butchering a deer, tanning its hide, and processing its forelegs for bone tools and sinew.

5

THE MESSENGER

The second bobcat arrived just before my invitation to "Alone Boot Camp," the final stage of the casting process. If the first bobcat was a wake-up call, the second was a messenger.

I was packed up and ready to head out to teach at a weeklong ancestral skills event when my period hit early. Rather than hopping behind the wheel, I crawled into bed with a hot water bottle pressed against my aching belly.

If I hadn't, I would have been 100 miles away when a text came through telling me about an injured bobcat a friend had seen on the side of the road near our tiny town. *Thank you, uterus.*

The cramps all but disappeared as I headed out to search for it, not sure what I could do to help it but determined to try. By the time I got there, the bobcat, a female, was far beyond any suffering. She had apparently been hit broadside and probably died as soon as she reached the side of the road. Fleas hopped from her like popping corn as I scooped her up in my arms. I brushed them off, too in awe to pay them much mind. The bobcat encounter in the wilderness had been amazing, but though I grieved for this one's death, the wonder of being able to hold her—to feel the silky softness of her fur and cradle her small paw in my hand—was a whole new level of incredible.

The gravel crunched under my bare feet as I laid her on the streambank behind my backyard. I used my shirt tail to wipe the frothy blood from her nostrils. Other than that, she had no visible signs of injury. I lay down on the rocks nose to nose with her and stared into her fixed eyes. We were two bleeding females lying there together, one hoping to enter the wild, one having just left it. The synchronicity of that fact wasn't lost on me. Nor, as I could tell when I peeled back her skin and butchered her, was the fact that she too appeared never to have given birth to young.

Butchering an animal isn't gory and macabre to me; it's beautiful and incredibly intimate. How often do we get to know an animal from the inside out, to watch the sunlight dance in rainbows over the iridescent fascia that overlays each muscle and organ?

Instead of rushing off to the gathering, I gave over the afternoon to just being with her in every way—feeling the way her bones glided past each other as I worked her joints, removing and blowing up her lungs to reveal a three-dimensional map of the contours of her chest cavity.

I felt she had come to me for a reason, to give me strength for my journey and the hunting ability of a wild predator. Naturally, taking her into me was part of the gift, part of the transformation.

I could taste and feel the richness of her life and vitality as I ate her organs, and her raw power as I ate her muscles. I wanted to share in her keen senses too, to see through her eyes, but I couldn't bring myself to eat her raw eyeballs, so I baked them. One popped in the oven, the hot liquid scorching on the baking sheet. The other puffed up huge from the steam inside, so I pierced that one with the tip of my knife. A jet of boiling liquid shot straight back at me, burning my eyelids and forehead. I jumped back in pain, horrified, then realized that perhaps it was perfect, a blessing from the outside as well as from within.

Finally, as full as I could be, I cleaned her intestines for cordage and her skull for my altar. A dear friend heard about the encounter and texted me a photo of the bobcat page from a book about animal medicine. I read it as I got into bed that night.

"The bobcat is a solitary animal," it read. "Its medicine is that of learning to be alone but not be lonely."

Whoa! I felt so uncannily seen and spoken to that I was too shaken to fall asleep for hours.

When I rose, bleary eyed, to go to the bathroom one more time, I looked in the mirror and saw that the scab from the eye juice burn was on my brow between my eyes. It lined up almost perfectly with my third eye, believed to be the seat of our sixth sense and intuitive knowing. And finally, I did know. I no longer questioned whether I wanted to be on *Alone*—I now believed it was my destiny.

6

BOOT CAMP

estiny or not, as I sat in the sticky vinyl chair in the Sacramento International Airport on my way to *Alone* boot camp, waiting for my boarding group to be called, my stomach twisted inside of me.

Boot camp was the final selection hurdle for *Alone*. My invitation had arrived while I was away teaching at the ancestral skills gathering I'd been headed to when I got the call about the bobcat. The top *Alone* picks from amongst a sea of 20,000 applicants were being flown to New York state for the final round of tests. I wasn't worried about being tested on my skills, but New York? Modern hotel? Meetings with television executives? *Yikes!*

I wasn't sure what to expect from boot camp, but I certainly didn't expect that it would be both fun and bonding.

We were a group of twenty-two people competing for ten coveted spots—five women and seventeen men—plus all the show staff. As is often the case with me in large groups, I felt like the token weirdo right away.

Feeling like an outsider in clean, fancy places like hotel lobbies isn't a new thing for me. I tend to smell of woodsmoke no matter how clean my clothes are, and it isn't unusual for me to drip with little scraps of buckskin, plant fiber, or just straight-up dirt, even when I'm making an effort not to. Still, I'd hoped there might be some other dirty, woodsy folks there who seemed as out of place as me. No such luck. Most were clean-cut and well groomed, and I was the only one wearing animal parts I'd processed myself.

There are all kinds of people interested in "survival," and a lot of different ways to approach it. There are preppers, military survivalists, bushcrafters, outdoor hobbyists, and more. It's a small percentage that strives to live a wild lifestyle out of preference, not fear of catastrophe or societal collapse. The skills might be similar, but the mindset is very different. Survivalists tend to have the "grit your teeth and tough it out" mentality. Military survival is aimed at getting out of rough situations as soon as possible or at lasting until rescue is achieved. Bushcrafters tend to be more my style—crafty and skill oriented. Outdoor hobbyists can come from a lot of different angles: high-tech modern gear, primitive skills, and everything in between—but generally they are going back to their comfortable modern homes after their weekend in the woods.

There's nothing wrong with any of these approaches, but I believe that long-term wilderness living is most sustainable if it's truly in line with the way you prefer to live day in and day out, not just something you endure or experience every so often by "roughing it."

Interestingly, this tends to be lost on most folks. Compared to what many imagine when they think of wilderness survival, I don't look the part. I don't have burly boots laced up to my knees, talk about any of my big game kills, or take part in the discussions about which new high-tech steel can "really go the distance." I associate these things with "survivalists." I would never use this term to describe myself. I see survivalism as a fear based approach. Survival just means "not dying," after all, and I consider this setting the bar awfully low. I am more of a "wilder living enthusiast." For most days of boot camp I was wearing my buckskin skirt and a low pair of handmade deerskin boots, and had bobcat claws dangling from my ears.

We had days of meetings and tests, interviews and camera training. I never felt entirely comfortable, until finally, we loaded up into vans and left the hotel parking lot for the field.

Out in the woods, I felt more like myself and part of the group. Sharing a small camp night and day, the façades people wore to impress the producers fell away, and the multifaceted layers of the unique individuals who had been hand-picked for this trial were revealed.

We shared our life stories and motivations for being on *Alone* around the campfire at night. We worked on group projects and laughed and joked with one another. We talked about the tension of our shared drive to be selected for the adventure ahead and the hopes and fears that came with it.

By the time we finished the very important woods portion of the assessment—top secret, of course—it was clear I had the respect of the group. I also had two tanned rabbit furs, seven ticks I had to dig out of my belly and armpits, and a half-dried fish fillet. I still felt like the token weirdo, but also felt appreciated for it. Regardless, there were more than a few raised eyebrows as, unwilling to let perfectly good food go to waste, I spent the next two days moving that half-dried fillet around the manicured hotel lawn to get it dry enough to take home on my return flight.

On one of the final nights of boot camp, we had a watch party for the premiere episode of *Alone Season 5: The Redemption Season*, in which they brought back prior participants for a new challenge in Mongolia. We ate an absurd quantity of pizza, not sure whether our willingness to gorge ourselves to pack on weight for the show might be one of the "subtle tests" of boot camp. We collectively gasped in horror when Carleigh Fairchild, runner-up on *Season 3* and favored to win *Season 5*, got a fishhook lodged in her hand and was unable to remove it. Had she had a multitool, she could have used the wire cutters and pliers to remove it. Without them, try as she might, removing the hook wasn't happening.

Note to self: never go on Alone *without a multitool.*

There were clinking beers at the hotel bar and fond farewells all around on the last night, and hopes we'd see each other again in a few months, but there was no way to predict who would be on this adventure and who would sit on the sidelines. The importance of secrecy about our potential participation in the show had been drilled into us over the last week, and we'd all signed non-disclosure agreements. Technically, we weren't even supposed to be in touch until the moment the lucky ten of us were reunited for the week or two of basecamp that precedes the launch into the wilderness.

Still, I felt good, very good, about my chances. My return trip home from boot camp had nothing of the nervousness of the trip there. I settled back into the plush gray upholstery of the uncomfortably small airplane seat, ginger ale and tiny napkin in hand, and heaved a huge, satisfied sigh. I was pretty sure I had this thing, and the adventure was on.

It has happened more than once that just as I feel like things couldn't be better in my life, something shifts and sends it all into a tailspin. You'd think by this point I'd have learned to see it coming, but I was blessedly naive about the fact that I would have only a handful of days of relative calm before the storm hit.

7

HIGH GEAR

The second my feet hit my front steps back in California, I swung into gear. Plans, ideas, and questions for *Alone* were running on a constant reel in my head. It would be some time before I'd hear whether I was selected, but if I waited until I knew for sure, I'd have nowhere near enough time to prepare.

Gear selection would be crucial. Each participant would be issued camera equipment, a tarp to keep it protected, and some basic safety and first aid equipment. Beyond that, we could bring our own clothing, garments specified in a list we would be issued, and ten survival items—not a basic kit *plus* ten items of our choosing, *ten total*. Each basic necessity, like a sleeping bag or a pot to boil water, counted as one item.

And it wasn't just any ten; it was ten from a list of sixty or so items. Rifle and ammunition weren't an option, nor were a modern fishing rod and reel. The idea was to make survival out there possible, but very challenging. It wasn't the ten items you would bring if you were actually packing for a long-term wilderness stay—more like the ten things you might have time to grab before the explosion if your bush plane suddenly crashed. With only these limited items, I would have to be creative to get my needs met.

My clothing choices would be nearly as critical as my ten items. Living outside in harsh conditions, your clothing is your home, just as your calorie intake is your furnace. The problem was that I had no idea yet where I would be headed.

"Think something between the British Columbia season and the Mongolia season," we'd been told at boot camp.

There is a huge difference between those climates. BC is an extremely wet climate, and Mongolia an extremely dry one. Each dictates different wardrobe choices, and the right clothing could make the difference between a long and comfortable stay or a brief and miserable one. This left me with an enormous question. I would be living on my own in a harsh winter climate, likely underfed, where my life would depend on the quality of my gear. Should I do what doubtless everyone else would and buy the best modern gear I could afford? Or do what I've based my life and livelihood around and make handmade gear of natural materials?

The indecision was terrible—a constant hamster wheel of *what ifs* and worries whirred in my brain during the day and refused to release me at night. Early mornings found me tangled in my sheets, unrested, a notebook in hand, scribbling patterns and plans on paper I could barely see in the dim light, then scratching them out again.

There were several issues. Not knowing where I was headed, I didn't know if the gear I could make would be suited for the climate. Buckskin is fabulous in dry cold—it's quieter to move in and more comfortable than synthetics, and it breathes but also cuts the wind, unlike most wools. In wet cold, however, it's like wearing a sopping sponge—nearly as bad as cotton.

Time was also at a premium. Handmaking high-quality clothing takes a great many hours. Time was already short, and it wasn't just my clothing I needed to focus on; I also had my ten items to select and procure, and a variety of metabolic, physiological, physical, and skills training to do.

Amongst those furiously scribbled, early-morning notes was a whole regimen I developed for myself. I would do cold training, plunging myself into cold water regularly to build up my tolerance. I needed to build strength so I would be as fit as possible and still able to pull my bow, even under starvation-imposed weakness. Building my core muscles and flexibility meant I would be more agile and less injury prone, and with my history of joint issues and muscle pulls and tears, that would be essential.

I decided I'd let go of my intermittent fasting practice and instead go in and out of a strictly ketogenic diet a few times, to get my body used to the transition to ketosis—a metabolic state where the body burns fats instead of sugars for energy. Ketosis would be inevitable when I was living on a wild foods diet in an undisclosed northern locale.

Ketogenic diets are slimming though, so while I wanted to get used to living on one, I also needed to spend the summer packing on weight to bolster my calorie reserves, plus loading up on vital nutrients, to be flush with them before launch and thus better able to handle deprivation of key vitamins and minerals. The challenges of accomplishing all this, and doing it without causing any harm or injury, made my head swim. I knew I was going to need support for it, so I looked for both a personal trainer and a healing professional, to help me get fit while adding fat and to address my long-standing joint pain and shoulder issues.

I felt confident about most of my skills, but while I was capable and knowledgeable on the subject, I wasn't a very experienced hunter, and passive hunting strategies were a definite weak spot for me. I had some primitive trapping knowledge after so many years in the ancestral skills scene, but very little hands-on experience and no experience at all with modern snaring and snare wire. So here was my dilemma: if I made my own gear, I would have less time for all the rest of my preparations, and almost none for skills practice.

Should I scrap the idea of making my own clothing altogether?

Though I believe in the value of natural materials, trusting them and my skills as a seamstress enough to have my life depend on them was a risk. And that was if I had plenty of time to make the clothing, which I didn't. But this was an opportunity to truly put my skills to the test and to share them with the world. Was it worth it, even if it might shorten my stay?

One morning, many days into wrestling with this conundrum, I sat bolt upright in the dawn light and threw the covers off. The crux of it was this— what was the *Alone* experience actually about for me? Was it about "winning," or about being true to myself and having the most authentic experience possible?

Thus far, this whole journey had felt out of my hands and magically dictated. *Was this the time to compromise on what I believe?*

No, I decided. *Hell no, it wasn't!*

I would go as myself, representing what I love and living according to my values, or not at all. I would stop this endless questioning and commit to making as much of my clothing as possible.

After the epiphany and solid commitment to my truth, I took my first deep breath since I got home from boot camp. I felt settled down in my gut. This was right.

I scrambled in the bedside cabinet for a lighter and lit a beeswax taper. This time my notes were less chaotic, more grounded. I made sketches of a fur parka and hat, an oversized wool shirt with a hood, buckskin pants, and insulated buckskin overalls. I was just finishing a drawing of a handknit wool sweater when the pen started listing to one side and my posture sagged. I tossed the covers back over me, straightening out the twists and tangles, and let my fatigue overtake me. I lay down and got my first solid hours of deep, restful sleep in days.

When I woke up, I left a message for the personal trainer my former housemate had worked with, then called a chiropractor a friend of mine raved about and booked an appointment. *Perfect!*

8

A PUNCH IN THE GUT

itting in the chiropractor's office later that week, though, it didn't feel perfect. I was uncomfortable even before he started to give me the once over. The lighting was too dark for my taste, and the vinyl of the adjustment table was too cold.

Had he ever heard of electric light? Or cracking a window?

I shared my many concerns with him—chronic shoulder pain since my early twenties that occasionally became debilitating, a hip that got tweaked on a long trail run and bothered me for years after, a cramp in my calf that regularly threatened my morning jogs, and a persistent tightness in both Achilles tendons that made me hobble like an old woman for my first fifteen minutes out of bed in the morning.

"I've got some thoughts on all of this," he said, in a mysterious way that did anything but put me at ease.

He looked at how my feet fell to the side when I lay on my back on his table and made some notes.

"Just as I suspected," he said, more mysterious by the second. He grabbed my hand. "See how far I can extend your thumb here?"

"I'm pretty flexible all around," I answered. "I do a lot of yoga."

"Someone with your condition shouldn't be doing yoga," he said.

My condition?

He rubbed his dry palms over my arms. "You've got nice skin, too," he said. "Do people mention how soft it is?"

How could he know that? "They do, actually. Why?"

"None of these are isolated occurrences," he said. "They are part of a bigger pattern. It's nothing to do with your lifestyle; it's genetic."

"I'm sorry, I don't understand."

"It's called Ehlers-Danlos Syndrome, which means your body can't produce collagen protein. It makes you hyper-mobile and injury prone. Even small injuries result in scar tissue that lasts forever and creates bigger problems."

I felt like he had punched me in the stomach. What was this man talking about? Suddenly there wasn't enough air in the room—it was stuffy and hard to breathe.

"That can't be right," I said. "I'm healthier than most people I know, and very active and strong. Besides the shoulder, these injuries are just a recent phenomenon in the last couple of years."

Were they though? A block of ice settled into my stomach. I thought back to the groin pull fifteen years ago that had crippled me for weeks. The time my back went out at a skills gathering, when I'd had to depend on people coming by my wall tent several times a day to hoist me up so I could pee into a jar. The cold winter mornings when my ex-husband had helped me dress because my shoulders were so stiff and painful I couldn't lift my arms over my head.

"Yes," he said, "but you'll see, they're cumulative. They show up more as people age, and don't go away. Have you noticed anything else?"

"No," I said, refusing to own up to the snowball of incidents coming together in my mind. "And I've just had a very complete physical. They assessed everything about my health—blood work, EKGs, the full gamut. Everything looked great, except that my lung volume tested a little low. They said it was nothing to worry about."

"I'd bet that's related too. It also affects organs. Probably scar tissue in your lungs."

He looked down at my chart. "You're pretty active, huh? How do you exercise?"

"I run, ride my bike, do high intensity interval training, and practice yoga."

"You probably like yoga because it gives you a sense of satisfaction. It comes naturally to you because you're more flexible than most people, but you shouldn't do it. And stop running. Humans aren't meant to run."

This was totally counter to my understanding of physiology and human evolution. Plus, I love running—watching trail disappear beneath my feet feeds my soul.

"That doesn't make sense," I told him. "I thought humans evolved to run and be persistence hunters. I grew up around running culture. It's in my blood. My dad ran 100-mile races my whole childhood."

"And how did that go for him? Does he still run?"

Now condescension, too?

"Well, no, actually. He has foot, knee, and back problems. He can't run anymore."

"Exactly. It's genetic, remember? He's probably who you got it from. Stop doing yoga, and no running, high intensity, or high impact *anything* for you. Slow, gentle movements and strength training, that's it. Otherwise, you'll be crippled in a few years."

I sat numbly as he taped my ankle to keep it from bending "unnaturally far." I wanted to wince away from his touch, but I didn't. I vacillated between feeling grateful to him for illuminating mysteries about my body and feeling like he was the enemy.

I was so stunned by the news I could barely feel my body as I walked down the carpeted stairs. *Crippled?*

I thought I would get a few adjustments to help my shoulders and hip, and now I had a life changing diagnosis. It wasn't only the way I exercise that it affected, it was my entire life. I'm a hide-tanning instructor, a craftsperson, a farmer, and, and, and...Almost everything I do is physically demanding. Never run again? I would hate that, but I could manage it. But change everything about what I do and who I am? I couldn't begin to wrap my brain around what that would look like.

And what about *Alone?* I was supposed to live in the wilderness by myself, hopefully for many months. It would doubtless be enormously strenuous. Should a person in *my condition* even consider such a thing?

I drove straight from his office to the library. My internet research revealed he was right—people with Ehlers-Danlos Syndrome are fragile, injury prone, and at risk for organ failure. If too much scar tissue builds up in organs, they can suddenly burst with no warning.

Sitting in front of the glowing laptop in the hushed library, I had to remind myself my organs weren't actually collapsing at this moment, they just felt like they were. Only yesterday I had thought I was so healthy, but now I feared walking back to my car without a cane.

9

THE FALL

had plans to go surf fishing with friends the day after the appointment, and damn it, I was going to do it anyway! But on the beach fighting the pounding waves, I tweaked my thumb while pulling in the line. The next day it was worse—sharp pain when I made a fist—confirming all my darkest fears.

He was right! One fishing trip and I can't use my hand!

I wondered if I was becoming a hypochondriac. A day later my digestion was off. The "don't wander too far from the bathroom" kind of off. I didn't know if it was the stress, the adjustment to ketosis, or *my condition.*

Luckily the thumb improved quickly, and the boiling in my guts calmed down in a couple of days as well. I was still concerned, but I wasn't letting it own me. I would get a second opinion. I would carry on with my *Alone* preparation plans.

I was pulling a tote of homespun yarn off of my storage shelves, ready to dive into knitting the first of two sweaters I had planned, when my voicemail alert beeped at me. The call was from my hometown area code, but not a number I recognized.

I reached for the landline to check my message.

Cold seized my belly at the sound of my mother's voice, a hollow echo of her normal tones.

"Honey, I need you to give me a call right away. I did a stupid thing."

My fingers shook as I dialed the strange number. Something was definitely not right. If she wasn't calling from home, where was she calling from?

The nurse in her room answered. "Oh, you're her daughter? I'll put her right on."

She had left the message from her room. *Her room in the hospital*, where she had been admitted the night before, the nurse explained, when she'd fallen off a ladder and crushed her leg.

Time slowed and I watched as a dust mote floated past my face and caught a ray of sunlight. *No, no, no!* I took a sharp inhale, working to control my panic. When my mom came to the phone her voice was faint and slurred with painkillers.

My mother is an avid kayaker. On full moons, she and her friends load up their gear and head to the Sierras for a moonlit evening paddle. It had been late when she pulled her kayak out of the lake. Exhausted, she chose to leave the van where it was, rather than drive to level ground to set up the step ladder she used to load her kayak. She'd gotten the boat onto the roof rack, but when she leaned out to grab a strap to secure it, the ladder tipped on the slanted and uneven ground and threw her.

As she fell, her leg slipped through the rungs. The ladder, the angle of the fall, and her own body weight created so much torque as she went down that her own femur had pulverized the tops of her two lower leg bones. She'd had to drag herself around to the sliding door of the van and scream for her friends, parked farther away, to come help her. Thank god they hadn't finished loading up and were still there. Between several of them, they laid her out in the back of her van and drove her straight to the ER.

I couldn't believe her composure as she related the story.

"Well, I've had a good run of things so far," she said. "I knew something would slow me down someday. I guess now it's this." Her stoic resignation made something inside of me burst. I was the one sobbing out of control, gasping for breath, and she was perfectly calm, telling me it would all be okay. Of course, her veins were coursing with morphine, but still.

I'm an only child. Since my parents split when I was five, it was always just the two of us in our household. She had been my everything—the sole representative of my nuclear family unit. I'd lived with her and spent every other weekend with my dad.

Both parents were huge influences on me. Their love of the natural world and adventure made me who I am, but my mother was my rock. I was seven years old, and we'd been on our own for just two years, when she was diagnosed with cancer. Though she'd lived through it and been in remission for decades, that terrible time had seeded me with the knowledge that I would someday lose her. Having her taken from me prematurely has been one of my biggest fears ever since.

I was no longer that terrified child, and as I clung to the phone I tried to keep this accident in perspective. I mean, I knew she wasn't dying, but I couldn't shut off the tears or see it as anything other than apocalyptic.

The surgery wasn't scheduled until the next day. I knew it wasn't the nurse's fault, but I wanted to shake someone. *Another day?* My mother was lying there in agony with her bones crushed and they were going to let her go untreated for another twenty-four hours?

There was no arguing it—there was no solid bone left there. It wasn't a job for the surgeon on call. It needed a specialist, and he wouldn't be in until tomorrow.

The nurse nudged me off the phone. "She needs her rest. You can talk again later."

"Honey," she said before letting the phone go, "this is absolutely not going to interfere with you going on *Alone*. I'll talk to you soon."

I let the phone fall into my lap.

Right.

Competing desires dragged me this way and that. I wanted to rush to her. I wanted to lie down on the ground and pound it with my fists. I wanted to throw up. I wanted to get back to my damn sweater and a world where none of this had happened.

Questions raced through my mind: *Would she walk again? Would she be able to do the things she loved? To camp and snowshoe and kayak? She was seventy-six. Would she go from active and young for her years to senile overnight?*

I looked around at my piles of materials and thought of my ambitious preparation plans.

What did this accident mean for me? For my summer? For Alone? *Could I really go away, for who knows how long, with my mother in a wheelchair?*

Those questions would be answered later. All I could do right now was think about the next couple of days. As much as I wanted to hop in the car and drive to the hospital that minute, it didn't make sense. When I got to her place, I was probably going to be there for a while, getting a ramp put in and otherwise getting her house wheelchair accessible. This wasn't going to be resolved quickly, and I wouldn't let go of *Alone* until I knew for sure that I had to.

10

YOU WANT TO DO WHAT?

packed up all the supplies I thought I'd need for what would probably be a stay of several weeks at my mom's, or as many as I could fit in my station wagon: my bow and a quiver of arrows, yarn, buckskin, wool cloth, a bin full of dyes, and books on trapping and fishing.

Was I letting go of a single project in anticipation of this wrench in the plans? Nope, not a one.

This kind of drive to accomplish feats at the furthest edge of what was humanly possible was a longtime habit of mine. What I'd heaped onto my plate that summer before leaving for the adventure, though, went well beyond what could be considered simply "overly ambitious." Maybe it was desperation to disprove my diagnosis. Maybe it was just plain denial of the limits of time and space. Whatever it was, deciding that my priority on *Alone* was to go in the kind of homemade gear that really represents who I am and what I value, I clung to my plans with a tightfisted hold that bordered on maniacal.

Had someone proposed such projects to me earlier that spring, I would probably have told them it was a lineup that would take a skilled person a good year to complete. I had *two and a half months*, and I'd just become a full-time caretaker for my closest family member on top of it. What could possibly go wrong?

As luck would have it, my first session with the personal trainer was scheduled for the day I was heading out to my mother's, so before hitting the road, I shrugged into a sports bra and workout shorts and headed to the gym. I felt a little guilty for keeping the appointment during such an emergency, but I knew this emergency would be a long haul and that today might be my last chance to focus on my own needs for a while.

I worried I'd be doing exactly what the chiropractor suggested I avoid, but compared to my mother's concerns, mine seemed nominal. A genetic collagen disorder was rough, but hey, at least all my bones still existed, right?

The trainer wasn't what I expected. She was ripped, but not weightlifter-ripped. She had short, spiky, bleached blonde hair and was glamorous but in a punky, "don't look too hard at me or I'll slug you" kind of way. I wasn't sure if I admired her or was a little afraid of her.

I felt certain she was going to think I was crazy. Due to the contracts I'd signed, I could give her the relevant details but nothing about the actual television show. I scrunched up my toes in nervousness, glanced around the room to make sure no one was in earshot, and explained I was headed out on a solo wilderness adventure—maybe for weeks, maybe for months—and I would be taking, at most, two pounds of food with me. My goal was to be as strong as possible—strong enough to continue shooting a forty-five-pound bow, no small task for a person my size—even as I lost muscle mass due to starvation.

I also wanted to work on balance and strengthen my joints and ligaments to do all I could to make myself less injury prone. And I wanted to do all this while also putting on ten to twenty pounds of pure fat, so if she could advise me on that too, great.

Her black-lined eyes got a little wider with every statement. *You want to do what?* I could almost hear her thinking.

"Oh, and one more thing," I added nonchalantly. "There's also a good chance I might have a debilitating genetic disorder that makes small injuries or overworking potentially crippling for me."

I think it's a pretty safe bet that this was the most unusual training program that had ever been proposed to her, but she took it all in stride and didn't ask too many awkward questions.

She stared intently, one beautifully plucked eyebrow raised as I grunted my way through the "battle ropes," BOSU squats, and weight machines.

Afterward, my thighs quivered and my shoulders burned as I wiped my sweat off the equipment with a gym rag.

"No," she told me decisively, "you are not hypermobile. You would have already dislocated several joints in your lifetime if that was the case. You'd know it by now." A heaviness lifted from me, and I stood a little straighter.

"I see what he was talking about: you have a couple weak spots here and there we should address, but I don't think there's any way you have Ehlers-Danlos Syndrome."

Hot damn!

I knew she wasn't a qualified medical professional, so it wasn't a get-out-of-jail-free card, but with one vote for and one vote against, at least it evened the score. I hit the highway feeling far brighter and considerably more optimistic.

MY BIONIC MOTHER

The hospital staff assured me that the surgery had gone very well. I felt a little queasy looking at the X-rays of the substantial steel plate and countless long, evil looking screws. But hey, my mother was becoming bionic!

Visiting her in the rehab facility was worse. I tried to be courageous, but I couldn't hide the look of horror on my face when I saw her leg. The incision was long and deep, so rather than stitch it, they had used enormous staples. The force they exerted raised the flesh up, so now she had a big purple ridge running from well above her knee to halfway down her shin.

By the time they were ready to release her, I'd had a wheelchair ramp up to her front door installed, rearranged her furniture to make wide wheelchair aisles, added a toilet chair and handicap rails to her bathroom, and procured a bunch of other handicap-accessible accoutrements I hadn't previously known existed.

It was my job to keep Mom's wound clean, check for infection between the home nurse's visits, and refresh the ice in her water-circulating cast a couple of times a day.

We developed a routine. Mornings I helped my mom with her daily needs and did exercises to build my core strength, flexibility, and bow-pulling muscles. Nothing too strenuous—nothing that might risk pulling a joint out of place or, you know, spontaneous organ explosion.

Afternoons I shot my bow, researched potential gear for my ten items, and knit for an hour or two while studying books and YouTube videos about trapping. Now done with my ketogenic eating regimen, I switched to a steady regimen of stuffing my face before, after, and sometimes in the middle of my other activities.

My bow and the stacked hay bales out back were my solace—my only "me" time. You can't shoot and have your mind or heart elsewhere. You have to be fully present: the bow an extension of your body, the arrow an extension of your will. It's a meditation—literally—which is why Zen Buddhists are some of the world's best archers. Those moments of focus and the *thunk* of the arrow into the target kept me sane.

Days ticked by and still no word from the show. *Am I going to be selected? Is all this craziness in vain?* I had no choice but to keep my head down and keep plowing forward, regardless.

Over those first two weeks, sweater number one grew while my pants shrunk—or seemed to—as they struggled to contain my growing girth. While my hips and waist got bigger, my gear list narrowed. I had my sleeping bag picked out, an assortment of ferro rods to choose from, several cooking pots on order, a Leatherman tool I was happy with—the Surge model—and a friend who promised to help me customize it, a new recurve bow, and a high-quality saw and axe. The list of homemade clothing was trickier. I could dye wool and sew and knit at my mom's, but Mom didn't think the neighbors in her small trailer park would be thrilled about my hide tanning. Without more hides, my fur and buckskin projects would have to wait.

Forced to push many of my crucial projects off, I set to dreaming about sweater number two. The first one was already incredibly thick and warm. I'd spun the yarn out of sheep's wool and alpaca carded together. It was a luscious chocolate brown, cable knit with an intricate Celtic knot pattern to make it even thicker and warmer. I wanted sweater number two to be eye-catching—stripes of oranges, reds, and gray. The warm colors of flames and the sun to buoy my spirits and help me feel their warmth, the gray of bedrock and charcoal. The color choice was also strategic—unraveling the edges of the sleeves and hem would give me bright, highly visible colors useful for tying flies, making lures, and marking trails, as well as muted grays that would blend in with natural landscapes.

I did some quick calculations and ordered enough yarn for a warm, thick, oversized sweater. Boxes of yarn began showing up on the doorstep, creamy whites for the dye pot and deep heathered grays.

My mother had a lot of visitors in the weeks after her accident. Everything about the potential adventure was top secret, but many of them looked curious about my project choices. I was all sweet innocence. "Nothing to see here," I'd say, tucking the armloads of yarn out of sight. "I'm just whiling away the hot California summer by planning and working on a northern winter wardrobe." You know, the usual.

My mother did all she could to help me. I'd wheel her out into the living room, and she'd sit next to me, her broken leg out at an awkward angle, as she wound the yarn into large, looped skeins to prepare it for dyeing. We watched old *Alone* episodes and YouTube videos with the volume up high enough to drown out the sound of the circulating water that kept the swelling in her leg down.

"Did you make note of that, honey?" she'd ask, and I'd scribble some trapping tip down in my notebook and hand her another armload of wool.

Being marooned in my hometown also meant I was able to make an appointment with my primary care doctor. That visit was the brightest spot in those challenging weeks.

The paper on the exam table crinkled beneath me as I jiggled my leg in nervousness, waiting to be seen. If the chiropractor had been right, I'd have some serious reconsideration to do. But when he stepped into the room, the doctor was warm and welcoming and put me at ease. He listened to me and actually took my experience of my own body and health into consideration.

He gave me a thorough examination as I explained just what I was up to and what my concerns were. I breathed in and out under the cold stethoscope, kicked reflexively at the knee hammer, and read the eye chart on the wall.

My fingers gripped the cushion a little too hard and my chest seized slightly while he scribbled on his notepad, but when he looked up at me with a big smile, I felt the air rushing back into the exam room and I sighed.

"I see no evidence of hypermobility or any predispositions to injury or genetic disorders. As far as I can see you're healthier than average and just work your body harder than most."

I fairly skipped out to the parking lot. I had done it. I had trusted my own body and my intuition, and I'd been right to do so. How many times had I let others convince me they knew what I was capable of or what was going on inside me better than I did? I couldn't begin to count them all. I was done with that old pattern. My life was my own again, and I was damn well going to make the most of it.

Now if I would just hear back from the show about whether or not this adventure was actually happening, I'd be in business.

12

THE ARCTIC?

After two weeks, my aunt came to relieve me for a few days so I could make the four-hour trip back home, gather more supplies, and do some projects I couldn't manage at my mom's.

I was only half an hour down the road when my phone rang. I broke into a cold sweat the second I saw Quinn's name on my screen. *This is it! The call I've been waiting for!*

"Give me a minute," I texted back, and found a forested spot to pull off the highway. I needed my feet on the soil to stop my heart from racing and to gracefully accept whatever was coming.

I needn't have been quite so nervous about my acceptance—I'd been selected for the show, and it sounded like it hadn't even been a question. What I hadn't even thought to be nervous about, however, was the location.

My mouth went dry with her next sentence. "I'm sorry, where?" Had she just said *the Arctic*?

We'd been told it would be cold, but the region of Great Slave Lake was just below the Arctic Circle in Canada's Northwest Territories. It was infinitely colder than what I'd been preparing for and certainly not "something between the Vancouver Island seasons and the Mongolia season," as we'd been told to expect.

I had a few days to get back to Quinn about my acceptance of the challenge, and a lot of time on my drive to think about it. *Could I do this?* I was nervous, sure. I had exactly zero experience with arctic survival, but with the exception of Jordan Jonas, who had spent several winters living off his trapping in Siberia, I didn't think anyone else I had met at boot camp did either.

And after all my hemming and hawing about making my own versus bringing modern clothes, the Arctic had one major advantage—it was the perfect climate for furs and buckskin. While some parts of me cringed a little at the location, other parts celebrated. With renewed trust in my body, hadn't I felt I was ready for anything? Arctic survival for a girl from California was a pretty big helping of "anything."

After a couple hours of driving with my mind whirring, I was ready to process it all with someone else, so I called my friend Kristi.

"Hey, Honey Bun," she said as she picked up—*god I love Kristi.*

The tension drained out of my shoulders. She'd recently moved to the East Coast, so we hadn't spoken for a while. It was incredibly grounding to drop into the ease of relating with her. Sharing out loud all that was stirring in me helped me to better understand it myself.

"I can't say much, as I've signed a non-disclosure agreement," I told her, "but I'm gearing up for a very extreme wilderness trip. By myself." She may have had a pretty good guess, but she kept her cool and didn't let on.

"For starters, it's in an extreme northern location, which is definitely intimidating. I'm thrilled about the opportunity, though. It's the kind of thing I've dreamed about all my life. The part I really feel weird about is that it's a competition with a big cash prize. I feel like that taints it. I don't want it to be about the money or have it seem to others that it's that and not the experience itself that matters most."

She totally got it. She always does.

"Oh my goodness honey, I totally hear you. I've had all those same prejudices about money myself. And you know what, all it's ever done is kept me down and struggling financially. I mean, of course, right? Because that's what happens when you don't believe you're worthy of having something."

Her words were like a gong going off in my head.

I had almost always lived under the poverty line. I'm well educated and very capable, so could have pursued a well-paying career. But I'd always valued my freedom and wilderness time too much to be shackled to a regular, nine-to-five job. I'd also always had a healthy criticism of capitalism and its ugly history. I knew it wasn't entirely logical, but I'd never shaken an insidious inner conviction that money was somehow evil.

"I've actually decided to do something about it," Kristi said. "I joined a group focused on learning to shift long-held habits of rejecting abundance."

Oh my goodness, there are actually groups about this subject?

Kristi and I had so much in common in our passions, our life histories, and our way of approaching the world. Knowing that she had struggled with these questions too helped me see the deeper truths behind them—ones that had taken me decades of personal work and no small measure of counseling to unveil.

"Oh my god, Kristi, you don't know how important this is for me to hear right now."

I took a deep breath and steadied my shaky fingers on the wheel.

"You know what," I said. "You're totally right. If I'm really honest with myself, my whole history with scarcity isn't really about money; it's about not believing I'm worthy of having what I need—money, acceptance, love, all of it."

I was forty-two and just seeing it—and it took someone else's words to show me. Someone who believes they deserve happiness doesn't stay in relationships that actively do them harm. Someone who believes in their worth doesn't bend over backward to please others, nor put their own well-being on the back burner to make room for another's.

I hadn't fully grasped the degree to which I had done this all my life until I made a choice bad enough that I was *forced* to see it. In my late twenties, a year after my first divorce, I moved across the country to an unfinished cabin without electricity or running water, 1,500 miles from my friends and family, with an increasingly abusive partner. When I extracted myself from the situation, I spent a winter unraveling the mystery of how I'd let myself enter that situation, and then I found myself a very good therapist.

Now here it was again—more subtle but rooted in the same deep pattern. Sure, capitalism is destructive to people and the planet. Does it then follow that everything to do with earning money is always wrong and causes harm? Does having financial stress, and skimping on good food and self-care, make me a better person and more able to do good in the world? No, it handicaps me.

I wanted to do *Alone* for the experience. I also wanted to do it well, even win it. It felt important to me to represent a whole different approach to wilderness survival, because the images we usually see are of big strong men, most often with military training, with knives the size of their forearms strapped to their thighs and a pack full of fancy tactical gadgets. The implication, whether subtle or explicit, is that they are out to kick nature's butt. I wanted to show the world that living in the wild doesn't have to be about battling it. For me, it's all about knowing that I'm part of nature and am humbly willing to learn about and participate in it.

While winning *Alone* had never felt important to me personally, I also knew that Western society pays a lot of attention to such things. I believed someone like me winning would be good for the world. If I continued to subconsciously believe that money was wrong and that I didn't deserve abundance, though, I would be conflicted in my desire to be the last one in the wilderness on *Alone*.

"Kristi, I'm totally with you," I told her. "Starting now, I'm going to redefine my relationship to wealth and abundance as well."

For the first time in who knows how long, I began actually imagining what it would look like to not be operating under money scarcity.

As luck would have it, there was a lunar eclipse happening that night, and I was getting together with some friends to honor it. If the rocks and the universe had conspired to send me on my *Alone* journey, perhaps the moon and the universe could get together now to help me manifest this new prayer, a Woniya willing to usher abundance of all kinds into her life with open arms.

13

THE CREATIVE CYCLONE

After the eclipse get-together, I felt different. More dropped-in, more present and focused. I called Quinn and told her, "Heck yes, I'm in."

Now, for the first time since all this began, I was thinking seriously about what I needed to do, not just to get there, but to win it.

The location was as motivating as it was intimidating. In one of the most extreme environments on earth, I would need all the gear I'd been planning on, but beefed up to arctic proportions. Back home I pulled bins of furs and deer hides down from the shelves to tan, crates of wool to spin more yarn for the sweater already underway, and dye for the yarn of the one not yet begun.

Looking around at the piles of raw materials and not one finished garment, I wondered again if I was being crazy. This was *arctic winter* we were talking about. Should I give in and buy commercial clothing?

I tried to picture myself up there, working to survive in a harsh landscape while wearing modern garments I had no relationship with. Viewed by millions of people while representing synthetic clothing, instead of the work I've devoted my life to. Entering the Arctic looking like an invader wearing plastic clothes rather than part of it in wool and leather. I reminded myself that though I'd love to win, my priority was still demonstrating a beautiful, balanced, connected approach to survival rather than an extractive, dominating, modern one.

There was my answer, and for the final time, I threw compromise out the window.

For those four days back home, I was a creative cyclone. While deer hides and rabbit furs hydrated in buckets, I set up a folding table in the yard and dumped boxes of the white yarn my mom had helped me prepare onto it. Hand-painted yarns are an art; you can't just dump them in a pot and let them boil, as you would for simple, hand-dyed yarn. I mixed up dye powders with water and vinegar. I squirted squeeze bottles of every variant of flame orange and crimson red until each skein was saturated with brilliant color, then carefully steamed them to set the dye. I was making great progress until midday, when my housemate's four-year-old daughter, Emma, came out to help. It was a slower, but very sweet, household affair. By dusk, most of the yarn was dyed. So was the table, Emma's stool, the door handle, a good portion of the countertop, and god knows what else. By the time I fell exhausted into bed at midnight, having steamed nearly sixty skeins of freshly dyed yarn in small batches for hours, I no longer cared what else in the house was pink.

I tanned three deer hides, the bobcat, and a handful of rabbit furs in the days I had left, then packed it all back into the car for another caregiver stint.

14

THE WORLD'S BIGGEST SWEATER

The routine at Mom's was similar to the earlier visit, but in fast-forward. I threw myself back into the archery practice, strength and stability exercises, and weight gain regimen—but now not just with all the craft projects still to do, but arctic upgrades to add on.

Body fat was still coming on, but slowly. Finally, I had to shift from just more meals with larger portions to more serious measures—a lot more sweets and beer.

For a little while the routine worked, but before long my body rebelled. If I ate more than a small bowl of ice cream in one sitting, it would go right through me, taking whatever healthy food was in my bowels along with it. Making my way through an IPA had never felt like a chore before, but it got to where I didn't even want to look at one. My body was used to such a healthy lifestyle that forcing the issue was clearly counterproductive. While it meant less weight than I had hoped to put on, eventually I came to see this as a good thing rather than a handicap. A body so attached to healthy habits that it won't allow anything less? Yeah, I could live with that. It wouldn't be the last time on my *Alone* journey that I would surrender to my body's innate wisdom rather than forcing the issue. It was a habit that would serve me well in the months to come.

I didn't have much time left to dial in my ten items. I researched everything I could about Great Slave Lake—the terrain, the temperatures, the wildlife, and the plants. Learning it was a world class fishing destination, I added fishing gear to my "no questions about it" list.

That gave me:

1. Sleeping bag (waterproofed down and rated to minus forty degrees)
2. Cook pot (stainless steel with a locking lid that could also be used as a frying pan)
3. Ferrocerium rod and striker for fire making (six-by-half-inch rod with a carbide striker I could use to sharpen other tools)
4. Fishing gear (only barbless hooks and monofilament line allowed, but I put together a good assortment of both)

I could take six more items. I considered a food ration critical, and pemmican—a mixture of powdered dried meat and berries mixed with rendered fat—was the only one that had enough fat content to be worthwhile. Fat could be critical out there not just for its calories, but to keep my system functioning if all I was bringing in was lean meat and plant foods. At two pounds maximum it wouldn't be much, but it would help my body transition into reduced calories more gradually and give me a calorie and morale cushion I might need.

Five more items.

I knew it was a big gamble, but I didn't want to be out there without my bow. My long-term strategy depended on big game. No one had gotten any in the history of the show, and I certainly wasn't the most experienced hunter, but if I managed it, the win would be in my pocket. Plus, the security of knowing I could protect myself from hungry predators was no small thing. I added the bow and arrows to my "for sure" list.

Four more items.

I went back and forth about whether I needed both a fixed-blade knife and the folding knife on the Leatherman. I didn't trust that the locking mechanism on the Leatherman would hold up to the kind of abuse that I would be giving it out there, and without a knife, I would be in trouble. I decided to take a standard knife. That meant the Leatherman wasn't strictly necessary, but as one of my most essential tools, a backup blade wasn't a bad idea. It would provide that, plus the pliers could be critical for fishhook emergencies, the wire cutters would be very helpful for the snare wire I might bring, and a lot of its other tools could have important uses. My friend Rich was working on building me a modified Leatherman with a custom set of tools—some of his design and some of mine. It could be a game-changer. That was it, both the knife and Leatherman had to come.

Eight items accounted for and just two more to choose.

Did I need both a saw and an axe? I felt I did, but while axes are important for many crafting and woodworking projects, saws are more efficient for felling trees and better for many building tasks. They're also harder to accidentally sink into one's shin if working while woozy with hunger—an important consideration. At least one participant has been sent home by an axe accident. Trees that far north were reported to be only wrist thick or less—not the kind of wood that needs splitting. An axe would be important once the lake froze over, but who knew when that would happen and whether I would still be out there? Taking an axe would mean leaving behind something else that might be key to being able to stay that long in the first place. It was quite a conundrum.

I moved the axe to the "maybe" list and kept the saw in the "for sure" category. One item left.

It was down to parachute cord (a.k.a. paracord) versus snare wire. Paracord would be important for shelter building, net making, and a hundred other uses, but snaring is passive hunting, not calorie-burning hunting. If I didn't manage to bring in a moose, a steady supply of small game could see me through the winter.

Was there a way I could work around taking paracord? There are a lot of plant fibers that make good cordage, but I was too unfamiliar with the plant communities up north to count on them for my cordage needs. I didn't want to be up there without snare wire, though, and cordage material was a lot easier to come by in the wild than metal.

And then I had it. My first sweater was so warm and thick, the second one wasn't strictly necessary. Instead of using little bits of yarn from it here and there as needed, I could just use the whole sweater as cordage and be able to take the snare wire.

I wasn't allowed to knit it out of parachute cord, but yarn is string too, and if I unraveled the sweater I would have ten times more cordage than the eighty meters of paracord I could bring as a gear item. In fact, if I was strategic with my pattern, it could contain enough yarn to reknit into other garments too. I had already planned for the sweater to be very thick and extra-long. How could I improve on it to give me even more material to work with? *Holy crap. What if it was both ribbed and double knit?*

Ribbing draws in a knit garment, so even large sweaters wear as if they are smaller and more fitted. Double knitting is a technique that adds an additional layer to a garment, so it makes any knit item twice as thick. A double-knit, ribbed sweater of extra-large proportions was ambitious, but if it could be knit, I was confident I could knit it. I ordered several more boxes of yarn and dove in.

Whenever I wasn't out shooting my bow, feeding my face, or working on something else, I was knitting away at what I came to call—sometimes affectionately, sometimes in exasperation—"the world's biggest sweater."

I'm a fast knitter, but the monstrous sweater took an absurd amount of time. My fingers flew while I sweated under my piles of yarn, but I consoled myself with visions of all the things I could do with it up there. The sweater I had planned would be big enough for a giant. Even after using all I needed for cordage, I would still have a whole mobile yarn store on my hands. I could easily knit one or two smaller sweaters, leg warmers, mittens—whatever I needed.

But that wasn't all. Arctic winters are extraordinarily long and dark. Instead of countless hours twiddling my thumbs and counting the days, I could be tucked up next to a cozy fire, a pair of hand carved knitting needles and balls of yarn in my hands, letting my creative juices flow. The sweater wouldn't just be a great resource; it would also be a winter's worth of entertainment.

15

A GRAIN OF SALT

y mother became increasingly independent as my sweaters grew inch by painstaking inch. It was hard to imagine leaving her on her own, but we both knew I couldn't stay much longer without seriously jeopardizing my plans. We got the thumbs up from the doctor that her healing was progressing nicely and that she could be left on her own overnight. Between my aunt, Mom's friends and neighbors, and the visiting nurses, she was in good hands. And so, at the start of August, with roughly four weeks left before I boarded a plane north, I packed up my projects and headed back home. I arrived there with hundreds of decisions upon which my life could depend sitting heavily on my shoulders.

I had thought July was intense, with my catastrophic—and thankfully wrong—diagnosis, and my mother's accident. That had just been the warm-up. By the middle of August I was doing Google searches to see if it was possible for stress to stop one's heart. The near impossible task of carrying on with my gear-making mission committed me to a month of utter insanity. Not the best preface to a challenging survival feat in an extreme environment, but I had made my choice and was going to carry on until I managed it, or until my head exploded. I like to think it was foreshadowing—a lower profile survival experiment before the actual survival experiment. If I could survive that August, I could survive *anything*.

There were more hides to tan, winter worthy boots to create from scratch, a three-layer fur parka to make, and buckskin pants and insulated buckskin/ wool overalls to sew. And those were just the big projects. There were also a fur hat, mittens, wool scarf and two wool buffs, and the rest of my ten items to procure and modify.

I set up a crafting station in the yard, took over the spare room with my sewing machine and worktable, and moved my heavy, foot-treadled, 1915 leather sewing machine into the middle of the backroom.

Any time I wasn't feverishly working on something else, I worked on the world's biggest sweater. I knit as I did online gear research, knit as I designed my other clothing, knit as I was brushing my teeth...Okay, that last one isn't actually true, but you get the picture.

Going to the gym to work out with my trainer was the highlight of my week. No decision-making and no screwing up and having to redo seams—just me and the blonde masochist holding the stopwatch.

Dietary advice was part of her service, but she clearly didn't know what to do with me.

"Did you eat breakfast before coming in?" she'd ask.

"Kind of," I'd say. "I had a smoothie made of whole milk, nut butter, three kinds of seeds, coconut oil, bone broth protein, collagen, maca powder, and fruit."

Her eyes would bug out in horror.

"It's okay," I'd say. "I'll have a second breakfast when I get home."

One morning I came in excited. "It's working!" I told her. "I managed to put on another three pounds last week."

"For god's sake keep your voice down!" she said, looking around to make sure no one had heard me. "This is a *gym*! Are you trying to get yourself beat up?"

Still, those sessions gave me my greatest sense of success all summer. No longer holding back to protect my "fragile organs," I was getting stronger every week. I was confident that pulling my bow would be no issue, even with muscle loss.

By mid-August, the deadline to submit photos of my gear to the show's survival staff was looming over me. They'd never had anyone bring homemade gear like mine, so everything had to be documented and submitted for pre-approval. I understood why they needed to see it all—a homemade jacket made out of fishing line and beef jerky, for example, would be an unfair advantage. Submitting my photos would have been a lot easier, though, had a single item actually been finished. Trickier still was the fact that pre-approval was just the first step. I wouldn't actually be cleared to bring any of it until it was carefully examined in person upon my arrival in the Northwest Territories. Having poured every ounce of time and energy into these garments all summer, I could still be forced to replace them all with commercial clothing when I got there.

I carefully tucked and folded my clothing items, then photographed them from just the right angles, and passed the preliminary approvals. I guess they didn't look closely enough to see that neither sweater had both arms, nor that my parka had individual, unsewn furs laid against the inside rather than an actual liner. But why would they? Who would be crazy enough to have their gear half-finished less than two weeks before they left for the Arctic?

Soon, I couldn't remember the last time I'd gotten a full night's sleep. My hours in bed went from averaging six per night, to five, to somewhere around three or four, as the days ticked away. I tossed and turned all night and my body quivered with anxiety all day as I sewed. I no longer remembered what a normal heart rate felt like.

From the outside, I looked like a mad scientist, feverishly racing from my scribbled notes and sketches, to one of my many worktables, to my half-finished sweater, to my computer to place yet another order for a gear item that I would probably end up returning. Except that instead of the maniacal laughter of a mad scientist there was only panicked silence. Stray tufts of fur, bits of yarn, and scraps of buckskin dribbled from me like a trail of breadcrumbs as I sped between projects. "Woniya must have been here," I pictured my housemates saying. "The door handle is dyed green, there's a half-drunk smoothie on the shelf, and the door won't close because there's a piece of rubber boot sole and a scrap of bark-tanned deerskin wedged in it."

Little workstations for different projects began to spread, and then to merge throughout the house. The pile of gear on the table in the back office grew off the table and onto the floor.

As my weight gain efforts were suffering with the intensity of my focus on projects, my housemate Randall assumed the role of bacon fairy, minus the tutu. He showed up at my elbow regularly with countless plates piled high with crispy slices of farm style bacon and slabs of his homemade bread, dripping with butter.

When I heard that our pemmican must follow a traditional, low salt recipe, I was devastated. It meant my plan for bringing heavily salted pemmican to keep my electrolytes balanced was nixed. Hyponatremia—having too little sodium in the body—is a serious issue, leading to cramping, nausea, dizziness, and worse.

I was lamenting the issue with my friend Rich as we chatted about how the Leatherman he was modifying for me was coming along.

"What about a fastener for your coat made of salt?" he asked. "You know, a little barrel shaped toggle and loop system? Something like that."

I hadn't planned on using such a fastener, but it got me thinking. He had a point. Making something with salt that was a legitimate part of my clothing wasn't cheating, it was creative use of materials. I didn't need a toggle, but... *Wait a minute...I'd been planning to make silver buttons for my clothing so I could repurpose them as fishing lures, but what if I made them from something else?*

I ordered a three-pound bag of big chunks of Himalayan pink salt. My other projects took a back seat while I used a belt sander to work the chunks down into rough cylinders. The noise was deafening, and that belt sander never ran again due to the salt turning its insides to solid rust, but it was worth it. I used a hacksaw to slice beautiful rounds from the cylinders and a hand drill for the holes and, voilà, I had a handful of little pink discs that looked like high-priced rose quartz buttons. I still had the dilemma of figuring out how to keep them from melting in damp air, though. *Hmmm...*

In the morning I woke up inspired. I had a solution for keeping my buttons intact—cheese wax and food grade epoxy. Soon I was further behind than ever, but I had ten magical black buttons that could be the key to keeping my body healthy.

16

A BLESSING IN DISGUISE

The final week before my departure was an adrenaline soaked, sleep deprived blur. The one bright moment was a send-off ceremony with some of my close friends who were in on the secret. Everyone brought an item for my "*Alone* altar," and we went around in a circle for blessings and reflections. Friends spoke of my connection, resiliency, skills, big heart, and willingness to look at and deal with the hard things. One of the things that struck me the most was when a friend I'd known since we were both eighteen and living on the same floor in our college dormitories stepped forward.

"I've known you for a very long time," she said. "I'm so glad that you are doing this and happy to see that you aren't keeping yourself small anymore."

I had no idea back then that I was doing so and was shocked to hear it had been so obvious to my friend, yet here that theme was again, like in the earlier phone call with Kristi. Saying yes to this show and stepping forward to be seen by the world was a powerful adventure in more ways than one. It was a vote of confidence in myself, and it was long past time for me to cast my ballot.

As everyone spoke, I spun the final skein of yarn for the brown handspun sweater, spinning the prayers for my well-being right into the strands.

Then it was back to the slog for the last three excruciatingly stressful days.

It's still hard for me to think back on the drive to the airport without feeling nauseous. The flight left at 6:00 am, so I had to be there at 4:00 am. The long drive meant a 1:30 am departure from the house. Some of my clothing was finished; most still needed work. Luckily, we would have at least a week, likely more, between arriving in the Northwest Territories and being dropped in our wilderness locations. I was banking on that time being enough to complete everything. I ignored my piles of rejected gear items and focused on sorting my unfinished projects into piles—those that were done, those I could work on in planes and airports, and those that would have to be checked through to Yellowknife, the capital of Canada's Northwest Territories. They took up more space than I would have believed possible. Modern synthetics are usually lightweight and compressible—piles of wool and leather, not so much.

At midnight half of my bags were packed and the floor of the living room was scattered with arrowheads, fishing line, and deerskin. I knew I should be packing, but my parka lining was still just a pile of furs and my insulated buckskin overalls were in pieces. Hand sewing them on location before launch would take me countless hours—hours I was unlikely to have—and I still had the two sweaters and fur hat to finish, plus finishing touches on most everything else. It was too late to ditch the overalls for a backup plan. Instead of packing, I oiled up my antique sewing machine and got to work.

The *thunk-thunk-thunk* of the heavy iron foot pedal pounded in my ears, rivaling the panicked beating of my heart as I shoved the leather pieces under the needle. At 1:15 am, I threw them into a bag, three-quarters complete and far from pretty, but all in one piece. There was no time for the furs. I knew I ran the risk of customs seizing them at the border, as a coat is legal to cross the border with, but individual furs are questionable. What could I do though? If I didn't get on that plane, there would be no customs inspections for me anyway.

A friend met me in town and drove the car while I sat and stitched.

My mom was meeting us at the airport—she wasn't about to let me fly off to the Arctic without one last hug, and I didn't like the idea of leaving the country without seeing her out of her wheelchair with my own eyes. As we pulled up to the curb, there she was, leaning hard on her cane and smiling so big you'd think she had just finished her first marathon, instead of her first walk across a parking lot without her walker.

The inside lines were insanely long and my bags were incredibly heavy and awkward. Luckily there was an outside kiosk with a much shorter line.

"Can I check in here?" I panted at the man at the desk.

"Where are you headed?"

I scanned my ticket for the first connection. "Salt Lake," I told him.

"Sure thing."

I gave my mom a huge hug, told her I would be just fine and would call her from Yellowknife, then watched her limp away as I wrestled my bags into line.

When I got to the front, the man squinted at my itinerary. "Your final destination is Canada," he said. "International flights have to check in inside."

Aaaaagghh!

Though I hated asking for special treatment, my panic was at the wheel, so I pushed my way up to the counter inside the crowded terminal, passing disgruntled fellow travelers, to explain my situation. Explaining is a nice way of putting it. More honestly, I begged.

"I was in the wrong line outside, this is the most important flight of my life, and it's about to board," I told them, fighting to keep my voice at its normal pitch.

"Just get in line, ma'am. It's going to be okay," the woman at the desk said.

I didn't see how it could be. They were probably already boarding the first class passengers by now, but I shrugged the huge bags to the back of the line and leapfrogged them forward until I finally made it to the counter. *They know I'm here*, I assured myself. *They're holding the plane.*

"The flight to Salt Lake?" the same woman said when I finally got back to the counter. "That one is already in the air."

My stomach hit the tile floor. "You said it would be okay!"

"It will be. We'll get you there on the next flight."

She tapped at the keyboard as I struggled to hold back tears. I couldn't really point fingers, whatever I'd been told. I'd pushed leaving back to the last possible second. This was all my fault, and I knew it.

"Okay," I said meekly, absorbing the new reality, "as long as I can still make my final connection to Yellowknife."

More tapping. An eternity of tapping.

"I'm sorry ma'am, Yellowknife isn't exactly a common destination. There isn't a single connection available in all the US that will get you there today."

The keyboard noises faded away as it slowly sunk in, and I gave up on trying to stem the flood of tears.

I hauled myself and my bags out of line, dashed off a frantic text to the show staff explaining what had happened, and dropped down heavily onto a bulging duffle.

I had screwed up. Really screwed up. *Would they still even take me? Wasn't this the kind of thing they had alternates for?*

My mom picked up my call from the parking lot of a nearby gas station. Intuition had told her it might be a good idea to stick around for a while, just in case.

"How about a nice mother-daughter visit after all?" I asked her, trying to sound nonchalant while my insides were quivering with panic and humiliation.

As I repeated the ridiculous game of leapfrog to get my bags back out to the curb, my phone beeped with a text. It was the show's production office in New York.

GOTCHA, JUST GET THERE AS SOON AS YOU CAN. TOMORROW IS THE BEST DAY YOU COULD HAVE MISSED

I melted down into my boots, my insides turning to goo with wonder and relief. My mom was on her way back for me, and I wasn't kicked off the show. It was going to be okay.

I expected the adrenaline to keep me amped the whole drive, but I hadn't slept at all for over thirty-six hours, nor for a full night in weeks. I drifted off to the humming of the engine and woke up in her driveway.

It was like waking up in another world, the sun out and birds singing. With dawning awareness, I realized that, in fact, it wasn't a tragedy I had undergone, it was a reprieve. Twenty-four hours was an eon given the frenzied rate at which I'd been working. *And holy crap—my parka!* This meant I could work on my parka!

I set up Mom's sewing machine, dumped out my bags, and got to work. Hours passed as I stared at the five-inch space in front of my nose, pushing furs through the struggling machine. My mother, always more concerned with how hard I push myself than with what I need to accomplish, made me promise I would get some sleep that night. Good to my word, I collapsed into bed exactly half an hour before we had to load up to head back to the airport, and got *some* sleep. I'd like to say I woke up refreshed, but at least I woke up less than panicked. The sleeves weren't finished—I'd have to stitch the rabbit furs into them at base camp—but I had a parka I could wear that was actually going to make it past customs.

Getting in the wrong line had been a godsend and restored my trust in this crazy process. I was back on track, back in the magic, and after having felt like the stress would kill me, I now felt that the universe was still with me on this journey.

17

BETTER YOU THAN ME

Watching my bags float away from me along the conveyor belt, my tickets in my hand, was a beautiful thing. I had done it. I had survived the summer of absolute insanity, pushed myself further but accomplished more than I would have dreamed possible, and it was all coming together. I felt giddy as I made my way to the gate, lighter than air.

Several flights later, I was walking into a restaurant in Yellowknife to meet up with the rest of the group. After so many weeks of anticipation and the insane stress of the last forty-eight hours, it was surreal to arrive at all, much less make casual small talk over burgers and fries. Many of the faces I'd thought would be there were, but there were a few surprises. As much as I'd liked folks at boot camp and looked forward to reuniting with them, I was too embarrassed at missing my flight and stressed about my gear to be fully present. I was relieved when dinner was over and I could retreat to my own room, where it was back to my routine of frenzied sewing and knitting until my energy failed and I fell into restless sleep on top of the covers, the bedside lamp still on.

The next morning, I passed the gear inspection with flying colors—not only did they not take issue with my gear or the fact that one sweater still needed its second sleeve, they were also clearly impressed with the creativity and quality of my craftsmanship. *Hallelujah!*

The air outside was frigid and a brisk breeze blew icy flakes into my eyes when I opened the hotel door and hauled my bags out to where the group was waiting for me after my inspection. I hadn't really planned for freezing temps *before* launch, it being August in California when I'd packed. I'd expected it to be colder up here, but *holy crap—already snowing on the first of September?*

A few hours and another big, rich meal later, we were ushered onto the small plane that would take us out to the wilderness base camp, which would be our home until we launched. The timing of launch would depend on the weather and many complicated production logistics we weren't privy to. While everyone else hoped our prelaunch stay would be short, a week or less, I was crossing my fingers for as many days as possible to finish my sewing and knitting.

We loaded our gear and filed into our seats.

"Welcome to Yellowknife," the pilot said as he started his takeoff spiel. He gave us the run down on emergency exits and seat belts, then he stopped and looked at us for a while and sighed.

"I have lived here all my life," he said. "I run people out to the bush for a living."

Dramatic pause.

"But I have never met anyone who would head out where you're going, in this season, to do what you're about to do. Seriously, *no one* goes out there this time of year. It isn't done." He shook his head.

"Good luck you guys," he laughed, incredulous. "Better you than me."

Tense looks passed between the producers—they were clearly horrified. There were only two alternates to replace anyone who got cold feet, after all.

Yellowknife is on the shore of an enormous lake, but I hadn't even seen the water yet. I expected we'd be flying over it, but for the first twenty minutes of a forty-five-minute flight, all I saw was a vast landscape of low scattered trees, wide stretches of bare rock, and thousands of small lakes. What I didn't see was a single sign of any living creature—animals, game trails, human habitation—anything.

It was summer back home, but this landscape was mostly gray rock with scattered yellows. It was clearly already late fall here. My stomach sank. It looked neither inviting nor abundant. This craggy granite was where I was supposed to be making my winter home?

In another ten minutes, it wasn't a ton of little lakes we were flying over, but one massive one. Great Slave Lake is shaped roughly like an off-kilter slingshot. Yellowknife is on the west fork of the Y. It had taken all this time just to reach the eastern arm. At over 300 miles long, the body of water below us was unfathomably huge, and this was one of the skinnier parts of it.

As we descended half an hour later, the land went from a flat tapestry to starkly three dimensional—sheer rock faces, towering trees, and one glimpse of the first straight line we'd seen since Yellowknife: the gravel runway.

Base camp was a string of tents by the airstrip, our homebase from now until our launch into the wilderness.

Though the day was clear, the air here was every bit as biting as it had been in Yellowknife, with winds picking up more as the afternoon wound on. There were some small bushes along the edges of the runway, but farther into the forest diversity dropped drastically. The few existing shrubs were already red with fall colors or dying back completely. My initial impression had been right. This wasn't summer beginning to turn toward fall, it was late fall heading steadily into winter.

The forest was as intimidating up close as it had been from the air. Flat and boggy, it was dominated by black spruce, a northern conifer that doesn't mind wet feet. Thick sphagnum moss, shaggy green and velvety soft, covered everything. Besides the small, scattered bushes, very few other plants seemed able to grow up through the moss. A native of a dry, Mediterranean climate, with mountains and valleys and sweeping vistas, I felt suffocated by the closely clustered trunks and their nearly interwoven branches.

The first night a storm hit, and the tents shook and swayed like mad. They were all equipped with woodstoves, but the gusting winds blew the acrid conifer smoke right back down the chimneys. First one smoke alarm blared, then another. I ran out to help someone find the off button, and on my way back to the tent, looked up into the sky to see it pulsing with flickering columns of white light.

The northern lights!

These weren't the jaw dropping colors I had experienced in the few months I had lived in northern Ontario over a decade ago, but they were the first aurora borealis I had seen since then, and they felt like a tender welcome from an old friend. The forest might not be welcoming me just yet, but the sky certainly was. *You can do this thing*, it told me.

Though the guy lines of the tents were thick with frost and the cold bit right through my long underwear, I stood out under the brilliant, fluctuating sky until my teeth began chattering.

18

THE BEST SEND-OFF POSSIBLE

My cold tolerance grew day by day as my California blood remembered what it was to live in cold climates, like I had back in my twenties.

Base camp was a mixture of camera training, going over rules and procedures, interviews, and filming practice, with free time interspersed here and there. It was also an opportunity to continue stuffing our faces, as these meals would be the last dependable calories we might be seeing for a long time. There was camaraderie amongst the group, folks inventing throwing games played with tent pegs, but there was also a subtle undercurrent of competition and big talk, and a very different vibe than the bonding one back at boot camp. For the most part I kept to myself, neither capable of nor interested in that kind of posturing. I am a small woman—five feet four in shoes—from California, with obvious tree-hugging tendencies. As I was also clearly trying and failing to hide my massive anxiety, I didn't feel anyone was particularly intimidated by my survival prowess or looking at me as serious competition. That was fine by me. What they didn't know was that, while nervous about the environment, my anxiety was less about the coming adventure than the fact that *now we were in the wilderness*. That meant it was too late to buy backup wardrobe items. I was totally committed to my home-made clothing—much of which, despite having passed the cursory inspection, wasn't yet wearable.

I was content to be discounted as soft and underprepared, knowing that ego and false confidence are liabilities, while humility is an asset. My main concern was what I could accomplish in the next few days and how much sleep I would have to give up to manage it.

If I wasn't out at the archery range during free time, I was in my tent stitching madly. I could sometimes hear others talking to their loved ones from inside their own tents. The wi-fi on my outdated phone was long since broken, so that wasn't an option for me, and I wasn't sure who I'd be calling even if I could. While others were making the most of their last days of phone access, preparing to be incommunicado, I already was, and quite comfortable with it. A supportive spouse or family back home was a strength, certainly, but as I listened to the conversations happening around me day after day, I knew that my comfort and familiarity with being alone was one of mine.

As the weather grew increasingly bad—wet, driving snow and hail that were deafening against the tent walls—more of our orientation activities took place in the group mess tent. Eventually, the pressure to finish my projects became greater than the pressure to save face and appear prepared, so I began bringing my knitting into the group tent. While we were being briefed on bear safety and how to use a tourniquet, I worked on the final sleeve of my cable-knit sweater.

"Jeez, Woniya, cutting it a little close there, aren't you?" someone asked.

"Um, yeah, I guess so," I answered aloud. *Haha. You have* no *idea*, I thought. *This is just one of my many unfinished projects, but it's the only one I can easily bring to the mess tent.*

It was too crowded in there to bring the whole sweater in, so I brought in just the sleeve and knit the cables from memory. I managed to finish it just before our group photo shoot, sewed it hastily on, and then pulled the finished sweater and my buckskin pants on for the pictures. Apparently, the food cramming was working, as my pants were incredibly tight. I was giddy enough at having finally finished the sweater that I didn't care. The hardest part of the shoot, next to my belt digging into my belly, was working hard to look rugged and tough, when a beaming smile or goofy antics come more naturally to me in photos. When I got back to my tent and took the sweater off, I saw that while functional enough, the second sleeve was at least a third wider and several inches longer than the first. *Oops. I guess goofy took care of itself.* I didn't have time to reknit it; it would have to do.

In the last few days before launch, we had to finalize our ten items. I had brought twelve options, wanting to see the place before deciding for certain. Now I was wrestling with the last two choices. Hindsight, as they say, is twenty-twenty, and while it would end up having an enormous bearing on my adventure, there was no way for me to know in this moment what these choices would eventually mean to me.

I went with what made the most sense at the time. The trees, as I had suspected from my research back home, all appeared small enough not to need splitting. *Okay*, I thought. *I know I'll miss it, but I believe I can manage without the axe. Let's think this whole parachute cord thing through, though.* The weather was making me nervous, and the gusting winds had me seriously questioning going out without paracord. Would snare wire, fishing line, and sweater yarn be enough to lash together my shelter and secure my tarp against driving arctic winds and many feet of snow? The wind was already almost collapsing the tents here in base camp, and this was just September.

I pictured a tarp whipping in the wind, secured by a thin strand of brass. Wire doesn't have the tensile strength of cordage—bend it back and forth a few times and *snap!* Friends from up north had told me it would be crazy to attempt northern survival without trapping wire, but they said the same thing about doing it without paracord, and I couldn't bring both. Besides, most trappers use cable, not wire, and whatever the material, I was no trapper.

I talked over my thoughts with another participant. "Well," they asked, "how much experience do you have trapping?"

"Actual hands-on experience? None," I answered.

"And how many people have been successful trapping on *Alone* before now," they followed.

"To the best of my knowledge, none."

"Right. So how likely do you think you are to be the first one?"

It was a good point. Trapping was uncertain, but shelter building and driving winds were both givens. At the last possible moment, second guessing my sweater plan, I switched out my snare wire for parachute cord and left the wire behind.

The memory of a lot of orientation camp was a blur to me after launch, but the moment of that choice remained crystal clear, as I thought back on it soberly over the next weeks and months.

My pile of "good enough" clothing projects grew, but the pile of ones I wasn't sure I could trust my survival to hadn't yet disappeared. When the announcement came that a window of clear weather was coming and we would be launched in two or three days, I kicked into even higher gear. Keeping the woodstove in my wall tent stoked so my fingers would be warm enough to work, I stitched into the wee hours by headlamp.

The last day before launch was chilly and gray, but thankfully without pre-cipitation. It was a big day. The local native people in that region are the Dene, and though it was a plane ride away, the show staff were bringing the chief of Lutselk'e, the closest village, out to meet with us. We all stood out near the runway to greet him.

I hadn't been comfortable with the idea of entering native land without the blessing of its people and had hoped to contact them somehow, but it hadn't been possible. I was utterly thrilled to hear that the show was bringing the local chief out to us.

When the stairs from the small plane were lowered onto the gravel run-way, it wasn't just the chief but almost twenty tribal members of Lutselk'e Dene, from elders to teenagers, who climbed out. After the group had been offered snacks and coffee, I poured myself a scalding cup and looked around to see a beautiful elder grandmother sitting on a straw bale by herself. The deep lines on her face spoke of a long relationship with the land and a lot of wisdom.

"May I join you?" I asked her. She gave me a big welcoming smile and beck-oned me over. I don't drink coffee, but it seemed right to share the sacrament with her, so I took a swig and asked her the question I'd been holding for all these months, since learning where the show would be taking place. As is so often the case with place names, my understanding was that the name Great Slave Lake was an unfortunate legacy of colonization and antipathy between neighboring peoples. The last thing I wanted to do was participate in that legacy. "How do I best address the lake in your language?" I asked.

"I don't know how you'd spell it in English," she told me. "But I think it would appreciate being called 'Tu Nedhe' or 'Ku Nedhe.'"

Appropriately, the translation is "big water."

After coffee and snacks, it was announced that a ceremonial fire had been started for us to make offerings and ask the blessings of the ancestors for our journey.

As I knelt down by the fire to the sound of rawhide drums, tears rolled down my cheeks. The warm reception we received, the blessings of these people, and the opportunity for sacred ceremony before departure was all I had hoped for. I felt profoundly welcomed and encouraged by the people of this place and the ancestors. It was the best send-off possible.

Before I was ready to see them go, the group packed onto the plane and headed back to Lutselk'e.

Later, I sat in my tent waiting for the staff to come and watch me do my final packing for launch. I could still taste the coffee on my tongue as my eyes played, yet again, over my pile of gear. It was absurdly large and bulky. I hadn't finished the second buckskin mukluk; it was still just some scraps of leather wrapped around my felt liner. There were other incomplete pieces as well, but everything was more or less serviceable. It was hard to fathom all I had accomplished in these few frenetic, adrenaline-saturated weeks.

Along with the other gear and clothing, I had my uniquely modified Leatherman and saw; a beautiful quiver of home-tanned leather and fur; my homespun, handknit mittens and hat; my homemade fur hat; the insulated buckskin winter overalls; a homemade parka of fur and buckskin; the handmade leather boots with knee-high felt liners; and two monumental handknit sweaters.

They weren't my best work, but they finally existed in the flesh and not only in my delirious, over-ambitious dreams.

I had achieved the near impossible and made it through an incredible emotional, mental, and physical trial to be standing here now, bags packed, goals achieved, and neither my health nor my mother's health in peril. I had done it and was still on my feet and ready for adventure.

It was incredible to think that in the eyes of the world, my *Alone* journey was only starting tomorrow. They'd never know what an enormous success just making it to launch was for me. There might be hardship to come, but it would be of a wholly different nature. As far as I was concerned, the survival adventure that started in the morning was my reward for the tremendous effort of having made it through the summer.

Our bags packed and trundled off to the staff tent where we wouldn't have access to them until the moment of launch, I felt a relaxation I hadn't experienced in months. I was so unused to the spaciousness and lack of pressure that the rest of that evening felt utterly surreal. While my own anxiety was substantially diminished, the rest of the group's was still building. To lighten the mood and send us off well, we had a steak dinner and entertainment, in the form of the casting staff sharing their "most likely" list. So *this* is what they'd been giggling over until late the night before...

Ray: "Most likely to find psychoactive substances out there and eat them."

Donny: "Most likely to find a cave and sleep in it for the whole adventure."

And of course, Woniya: "Most likely to make amazing things...*Most* of them are *almost* done..."

I laughed along with the rest, the truth undeniable. As usual, I'd been far more transparent than I realized. For all I knew, a tent wall silhouette of me sewing and knitting furiously had been the evening entertainment for the late nighters in the camp this whole time.

Merriment over, we were ushered off to bed to get all the sleep we could before our predawn breakfast and launch preparations.

As we settled in for our last night of relative comfort, Ray walked up and down the aisle between the tents and read us poetry about bravely meeting the adventures to come. Nothing left to knit or sew, I drifted off for my first and last full night of sleep at orientation base camp.

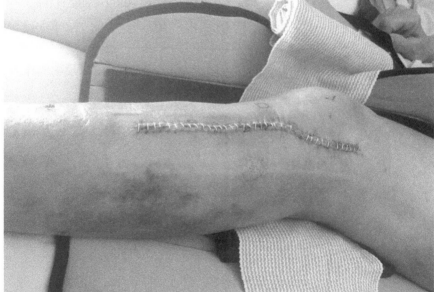

TOP: Me nose-to-nose with the second bobcat, shortly before skinning and eating her. BOTTOM: My mother's crushed leg, two days after her surgery, complete with Frankenstein staples.

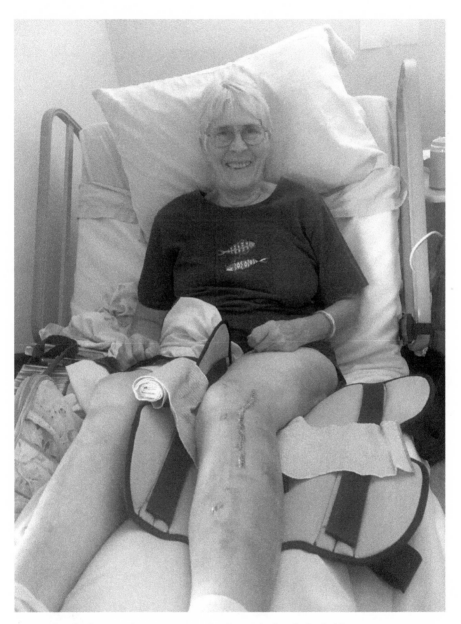

My mother, looking as chipper as ever after her ordeal with the ladder.

Sweater number one in the photo I submitted for *Alone* approval, August 2018. Cable knit with homespun yarn of wool and alpaca fibers, folded to make it less obvious it has only one sleeve.

My housemate's daughter, Emma, helping me dye the yarn for "the world's biggest sweater."

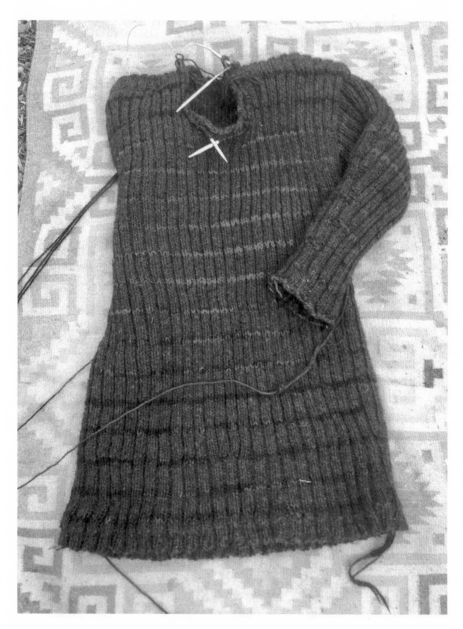

The "world's biggest sweater" still in progress, as it was for countless weeks of my *Alone* preparations.

My handmade leather boots with felted wool and buffalo fur liners.

PART TWO

LIVING ON
BEAUTY

19

LAUNCH!

I wake to the sound of scuffling in the tents all around me and dash from the warm sleeping bag to my clothes. It's still hours before sunrise and the icy air bites right through my woolen long johns as I fumble around in the dark tent.

Breakfast is festive, everyone jovial as we help ourselves to our last real meal in who knows how long. The occasional sideways glances and forced laughs reveal the tension and nervousness behind the chipper façades. Breakfast sticks in my throat, which is dry with a combination of nerves and excitement. I take a big swig of tea and work it down.

After as many pancakes and sausage links as I can stomach, I take my place in line for our official prelaunch weigh in. I tip the scales at just under 150 pounds—pretty substantial for me and my small frame. I've managed to put on 22 pounds since spring, probably a handful of them here at base camp.

The producers and survival staff come out to shake our hands and see us off, and we load up our gear and head out to the far end of the runway.

We'll be launched one at a time via helicopter. After that, we are on our own. Entirely. After over a week in our tight-packed little tent village, listening to one another snore, it's hard to imagine.

Cameramen dot the runway. The name of the first to launch is called. We line up to wish her well, our hugs awkward in our puffy parkas, all of which are tighter than when we arrived.

Forty minutes later, we're all relaxing against our stuffed backpacks, taking every opportunity to savor comfort and conserve calories, when I hear the thrumming of the returning helicopter and look up. The producer is walking toward me.

"Okay, Woniya," he says. "This time it's you."

It's actually here!

The rotors are deafening, and the wind they kick up stings my cheeks as I heave my bags into the weathered side basket of the helicopter, but I'm buzzing with so much adrenaline I hardly notice. I refused to be launched wearing anything else, but my buckskin pants are now so tight that I can barely get my leg raised for the big step into the cockpit. I take the ladder with a knee, stuck until I get a push from behind and a hand up from the pilot. I feel like a whale sewn into a leather corset, but the embarrassment is lost in the hilarity of it—I just hope no one is filming this.

In less than a minute I'm strapped in with a headset over my ears, heading off to my new home, over a thousand miles north of anywhere I've ever been.

I don't remember when I've ever felt so alive. I'm like a child in my big headset, unsure how to use it. We soar into the air, banking away from the runway. The straps of the safety belt cut into my chest as I strain against them for a wider view.

The vastness of the lake and the emptiness of the wilderness are staggering. Not just enormous, but impossibly complex. Dotted with islands, large and small, and cut into tiny bays by innumerable fingers of rocky cliffs, they make me think of the fjords of Norway. The lake's surface is every shade of blue, gray, and green—incredibly shallow here, deep and black there. Over and over I wonder if I'm actually seeing the far shore, then we rise higher and I realize it's only another large inlet.

There's a cameraman sitting next to me, and I know I'm supposed to engage the camera somehow—say something or look dynamic and daring for the viewers—but I'm transfixed and don't want to miss a second by looking anywhere but out the window. It isn't just that it's beautiful—these moments are vital. They're my one chance to get a larger perspective on this place before I'm dropped into it to fend for myself.

Where are the game trails? How does the water move across the land? Are there fishable lakes? Rivers? How much forest is there and how much bare earth?

Underpinning my wonder and excitement is somber wariness. It looks seriously inhospitable—largely barren, with big expanses of open rock sandwiched by low sphagnum bogs. What forest there is seems to be small stands of thick spruce—hard travel, but good moose habitat.

I try to keep my bearings, but we are zooming around in every direction—over ridges, back out over the water, then over rocky land again. It isn't long before I can't point to the place we took off from just moments ago. I feel like a kid in a pin-the-tail-on-the-donkey game, getting spun around before being released, pin in hand. It's just as well because this landscape is far too vast to wrap my mind around. The only thing that matters is the donkey itself—the home zone I am about to be dropped into. My job is to find the best place within it to build my new life, and pin the tail there.

And then, in what feels simultaneously like a brief second and an eternity, we bank and start to descend. My stomach jolts and the giddiness evaporates. All my awareness focuses on the land in front of us. It's a gentle slope of gray, open rock growing larger every second. On top is one small stretch of level granite, an open arena studded with sparse vegetation. I can see the trees and shrubs bending sideways with the force of the wind from the blades. Before I have taken it all in, I feel the scrape of the helicopter skids on the rock. We're here.

20

TRUSTING MYSELF TO THE WATERS

unbuckle and step to the edge of the helicopter. I can't tell if it's the noise of the rotors or my heart pounding in my ears. It's all the same anyway—the rush of the wind, the roaring noise, the *thump-thump-thumping* within me. A cacophony of sound, sensation, and emotion. The stifling heat of being over-dressed in the small, climate-controlled cockpit, the musky scent of my body odor—punctuated by that sharp sourness that comes with too much adrena-line—and the cold wind off the water. Then I'm down the steps and it's all over in a moment—no time for extended goodbyes with the crew, as there are eight people back on that gravel runway still waiting for their own launches.

I rush to set up the camera and tripod. This is the one moment of our jour-ney that has been dictated: "Get a shot of that helicopter flying away and leav-ing you alone in the wilderness." Everything beyond this moment is up to me.

I catch my breath as the rotors hum to life again, and a blast of air hits me right in the face. I'm overcome by the thrill and power of it and struggle to hold the tripod steady against the wind of the blades.

"It's happening!" I scream over the sound of the engine, my voice so high-pitched with excitement that it sounds strange in my ears. I can hardly con-tain myself, but I can't jump up and down and still hold the camera steady, so I simply laugh and let the wind draw hot tears from my eyes.

The helicopter goes quickly from enormous and earth-shaking to nothing but a far-off noise. My breathing eases as the thrumming fades away into nothing. I have been picked up, like a seed by the wind, taken away from my self-inflicted chaos, and plunked down in a world that feels infinitely far from all of it.

The adrenaline fades slowly, and I'm surprised by my own stillness. I didn't realize I was shaking until I notice that it's stopped.

I breathe in deeply, inhaling the clear air off the lake. The gray water reflects the pale morning light and a patchwork of fall colors paints the trees along the shore.

I've really made it. I exhale out the soul crushing stress. I inhale again, drawing my spirit back into my body from where it's been hovering just outside it for these last gut-wrenching weeks. I can almost hear it asking, *Dear god, is it safe to come back home?* And yes, poor neglected inner self, it finally is. I feel like Woniya again, for the first time in months.

I turn in a circle. It's wide open, barren, and rocky where I stand, with low stands of dwarf birch trees squeezing up through cracks in the bedrock. Around their bases are smaller shrubs, brilliant red against the golden brown of the birch leaves. These give way to a carpet of gray-green reindeer moss, which gives way to bare rock.

The dark spruce forests around base camp, unbroken by vistas or bright hues, felt oppressive and intimidating. This is entirely different—expansive and colorful. I can see for hundreds of yards and feel so drawn to every direction I can hardly decide what to see first. *Holy crap—three minutes on the ground and I already love it!*

Scouting for a home site and getting my bearings are the primary goals for the day, but I don't want to do anything until I greet the lake. From this moment on, it's going to be my lifeline, and it would be rude to start out by turning my back to it.

I strap the communications bag on. The awkward weight on my hip is a visceral reminder that this thing has really begun. It contains a big, blocky GPS device we refer to as "the yellow brick," because that's exactly what it looks like. It sends a signal of my location to the production team every few minutes, and at the bottom is a big red button—the emergency tap out button, which I've already decided to treat as if it doesn't exist. While I'm out here, this bag will be attached to me every waking moment, as will as many cameras as I can carry. I'd better get used to it. I scuffle around in my backpack for my cook pot and then, with a GoPro strapped to my chest and a big camera on a tripod beside me, I head down the rocks to the shore.

The stone is smooth underfoot, polished by glaciers. This is some of the oldest rock on earth, I learned from Dan Bree, one of the producers, during base camp. In certain places, one can even find stromatolites, fossilized remnants of bacterial mats that were one of the first life forms on the planet. I feel transported in time, like I'm the first and only human ever to have stood in this place. It's easy to picture myself surrounded by ancient seas oozing with primordial life.

As I've been trained to, I repeat the walk to the shore several times to get different camera angles and perspectives. The blocky granite shelves act as steps and make the hike easier. Finally, I'm standing at the water's edge where the shelf of granite drops off to the lake's surface, with three running cameras beside me. The water is calm here, but choppy and flecked with foam farther out.

I scoop up a handful. It's crystal clear and icy cold in my hand. I wince a little as I pour some over the back of my neck, where I'll feel it most, letting it greet me as I greet it—one of my regular routines for meeting wild water.

"I'm so excited to finally meet you, Tu Nedhe. Thank you for having me." I feel awkward speaking it aloud, conscious of the cameras rolling in what should be a private moment.

I thought I'd begin by asking permission of the lake to be here, but somehow that doesn't feel appropriate. I can already feel a welcome from it, feel that I'm wanted here. I'm surprised at how clear that message is. I want to start well hydrated, so I bend down with the cook pot to fill it with water to purify, but I freeze before it touches the water. *This isn't right*, something inside me says.

I've been committed to avoiding anything that could mean an early tap out, and diarrhea from giardia or another water-borne disease is a sure recipe for it. My plan has been to boil the water, but crouching here with the pot in my hand, I know I can't do that. Practically speaking, boiling it every time would be a major handicap. I don't have a water bottle and it's a hike to get down to the lake. It'll be hard to stay hydrated if I have to stop to build a fire every time I need a drink, but what actually stops me isn't that—it's a feeling. It's the difference between what I felt holding this water in my hand and the one I get pushing the pot toward it.

The local Dene told me they drink right from the lake, and I'm more remote here than their village is. Can I, too, safely drink right from it? I'm not born to this place, but I came here to live for the long haul. That means surrendering myself to it. If my first act here tells the lake that I don't trust my body's well-being to it, what kind of relationship am I building? How can I earn the trust of this place if I don't offer it mine?

Screw it! Before I can reason myself out of it, I set the pot aside, reach down with both hands and lift them up, brimful of lake water. I drink it all down, slurping the icy cold right into my core and dribbling it down the front of my wool shirt.

Whatever the consequences, I'm all in.

This isn't the first time I've gotten a strong message to surrender myself to the wild and trust in what it offers me, nor that I've chosen the less comfortable path when a wisdom that feels deeper than my own bubbles up in me.

The first hiccup in devoting my life to ancestral skills came a few years after college graduation. Before then, it had been easy to dream of running off into the woods with only the knife on my belt as soon as I was finally free to do so. Then the reality of how hard that would be settled in, as did my need to support myself. I worked seasonal jobs in environmental education for my first years out of university. Eventually, at an outdoor school in northern New York state, I met Chris, a man I would later marry. At first he seemed interested in ancestral skills, but over the years, it became clear that the skills that were my passion were only a passing interest to him. We lived a fairly rugged life, cutting our own firewood for our cabin in Vermont, gardening and tapping maple trees, but it felt too domestic for me, and I didn't know how to integrate the life I dreamed of with the one that worked for him. I felt increasingly far from the lifestyle and skills community I loved. I was losing my sense of self.

Influenced by him, I figured it was time for me to grow up, get a real job and cultivate stability. The harder I tried, the more lost and miserable I felt.

Truly miserable. Frighteningly miserable. Wouldn't-it-just-be-easier-to-run-my-car-into-oncoming-traffic miserable.

I thought perhaps returning to academia, and a career outside doing field research, would help me find the wildness I craved, so I began a master's program in environmental science. It was no good—I wanted to be a part of the wilder world, not do studies on it. In the hope that committing to the relationship might help me feel happier in it, Chris and I married. Our marriage only left me feeling more trapped and desperate. Finally, I had to look at my life and admit that I couldn't go on. I wasn't happy in my marriage, I wasn't happy in school—I wasn't happy period.

I left my husband, and while the loss, grief, and guilt wracked me, I also had the sensation of taking my first deep breath in years.

I was nearly done with graduate school and decided I could stomach one more season of research to finish my degree. I spent the summer driving the back roads and national forests of Oregon, documenting populations of an invasive weed and releasing beetles to help control it. The long hours in the field by myself gave me much-needed time to process, grieve, and heal.

One particularly hard afternoon, feeling sad, confused, and lonely, I was walking a seldom-used logging road in the mountains and looked up to see a strange creature—small and brown and apparently carrying something—running toward me. I froze stock still, dumbfounded. I had studied mammalogy and was fairly certain that I was seeing a rare and little-known mammal called an *Aplodontia*. Its mouth was jam-packed with greenery, and as it got closer, I could see colorful wildflowers bobbing at the ends of the stems it held in its teeth.

Aplodontia have no close relatives, but they look a bit like pikas, mammals related to rabbits that clip flowers and grasses throughout the summer and store them in "hay piles" to eat all winter. Perhaps *Aplodontia* do the same?

Whatever its reason, it trotted along toward me, oblivious of my presence until it was less than ten feet away. Then it looked up, startled, dropped its mouthful, and ran back the way it had come.

I laughed aloud, and then burst into tears, so grateful to this strange little animal for shaking me out of my dark cloud of tangled emotions.

That moment, when a rarely seen wild critter came toward me in my grief and dropped a bouquet of wildflowers at my feet, was profound. It marked a turning point in my life. I felt held; I felt spoken to. The land and the wild had reached out, offered me comfort, and told me that though it might feel hard now, everything was going to be alright.

That night I set up camp and cooked my dinner by a swiftly running stream. I sipped my tea with the flowers in a mason jar beside me, watching the light reflect off the moving water. *I am like a trout in this stream*, I thought to myself. I had been living in a shallow pond these last years with Chris. The water was warm, resources were abundant, and it was safe and predictable. But it felt stagnant to me, and I was slowly suffocating. Leaving the pond for something unknown was terrifying, but just as the trout only thrives in cold, rushing water, the pond life was not for me. Divorcing Chris was the first step in leaving behind the comfortable waters I knew and jumping into the cold, turbulent water of the mountain stream. I didn't know where it was flowing, but it was moving and dynamic and engaged all my senses and my skills to navigate. I felt alive again.

When I returned from my fieldwork, I took apart my buckskin wedding dress and turned it into a backpack.

Three months later, I was living in northern Ontario in a rustic cabin deep in the wilderness and learning about the northern forests and how to live in them from a local Anishinaabe family who took me and two friends under their wings.

On the day of the wild bouquet and my epiphany about the mountain stream, I made a commitment. I would trust my inner truth, even when I found that truth sad or scary. When the wild world spoke to me, I would open my ears to it, and trust what it had to say.

If I hadn't been true to that commitment, I wouldn't be here now. Trusting myself to these wild waters is part of what this place is asking of me, and I want it to know that I'm listening.

21

MY TRUFFULA TREE

head back up to the landing pad, my one point of orientation, and pack up for my scouting mission.

About fifty yards to the southeast is an island of low rock just above the water, not very large, but big enough to harbor a few small stands of forest. I'd love to start by exploring it, but it's just close enough to trigger my curiosity and just far enough through icy water to guarantee hypothermia. Instead, I head north, directly away from shore, with my bow strung and an arrow nocked. Within a few days the game in the area is likely to know of my presence, so though it isn't my main goal, today could be the best hunting I'll have.

My skin prickles—a new landscape, a new mystery around every big boulder and every stand of trees. Even now, chock full of calories, I know I should walk with measured steps and conserve what I've got. I'm so eager to see everything that my spirit urges me to race ahead and take it all in, but I resist.

I work my way past a field of big, blocky boulders that's going to be a serious ankle breaker when covered in ice and snow, but a great source of building material. I can already see some nice-sized rocks for deadfalls, a primitive style of trap for small game that works by dropping a rock onto an animal that trips the trigger mechanism.

Beyond the boulders the land slopes downhill. I'm in a low forest of stunted black spruce trees and thick sphagnum moss bordered by granite cliffs on one side. Even so, it's nowhere near as thick and oppressive as the forests around base camp. Every step makes a deep depression in the soft surface—it's the kind of terrain that feels fun at first, never knowing how deep each boot will get swallowed—but becomes exhausting quickly.

I've gone maybe 100 yards when I'm surprised by the glint of sunlight off of water through the trees below me. *Please let it be a beautiful little fishing lake like all the ones I saw from the helicopter!* But after a few more steps it's clear this is big water I'm looking at, not a small lake or pond. Apparently it isn't a stretch of south-facing shoreline I've been dropped onto, it's a peninsula, and a narrow one at that.

The branches of the alders that line the shore tangle in my bowstring as I elbow my way through them, and I have to keep stopping to untangle it. That frustration leads to greater disappointment as I pass through them to the shore. *Damn!* I'm looking at shallow, reedy water, the kind that looks only inches deep but will suck you in, knee-deep in muck, within a few steps. Definitely not my fishing spot.

Across the wide, shallow bay is another narrow stretch of land—Island? Peninsula? It's impossible to say. Far to the north, where the horizon is shimmery with distance, I can see a distant shore where land and water come together again. There's a low sound in this direction, the rushing of wind through countless branches, I'm guessing. The mainland looks like the kind of choked forest I'd expected to find here. I pull my wool shirt around me a little tighter and turn back the way I came. Okay then, for now anyway, this peninsula is my home turf. The mainland can wait until I've finished scouting here.

I retrace my steps and head east until I'm on top of the cliffs I saw from below. From here I can see the landing pad and my pile of gear and in the other direction, the far end of the peninsula.

It's easy to travel the open rock and to keep my bearings as I can always see the lake on one side or another, and often on both. The landscape is similar overall, a patchwork of small stands of trees and open stretches of rock covered in spongy reindeer moss. Unlike the sphagnum moss that carpets the ground under the trees, reindeer moss grows on bare rock. As its gray-green color and unique, springy texture indicate, it isn't a true moss at all, but a lichen.

Though the land is similar everywhere, little variations in terrain make each place feel unique. There are mats of cranberries and crowberries, covered in red and black globes, in every crack and crevice of the rock. My stomach, currently conditioned to three huge meals a day with countless snacks in between, gurgles a little at the site of the berries, reminding me how long it's been since my predawn breakfast, but I push on.

The ledges feel human scale—like stairways from one level to another, built for my ease and convenience. I'm standing on one such ledge when I hear a cacophony of honking and catch my breath as a flock of enormous white birds flies past and settles onto the water of the north bay. Swans! I throw my arms into the air and give a holler. *Really? I get all this?* This whole landscape of intermittent forest and granite with no sign of anything human except me? This peninsula of rock that looks carved by an artist's chisel, rippling with gold and orange and cherry red under a blue sky—and now the world's most majestic waterfowl too? It's in every way the polar opposite of the environment that had me cringing at base camp. My cheeks hurt with smiling as I climb down from the rock steps onto the next expanse of open granite.

I must have been dropped at a narrow part, as the peninsula widens dramatically as I head east. Here there are dazzling white birch trunks shining amidst the dark green of the spruces, and then up ahead a familiar looking low bush with smooth round leaves, already turning crimson. *Yes!* Closer up I see small dark balls against the glowing red. *Blueberries!* They're on their way out, shriveled and sour with fermentation after freeze/thaw cycles, but worth stopping for. Their tartness bursting over my tongue brings my senses alive.

If this is drop shock, I'll have a double serving. The show's staff have seen it time and again on *Alone*—even the toughest, most prepared outdoors people can crumble during the first few days of finding themselves truly alone in the deep wilderness. They call it "drop shock." We were warned about it, and I didn't know what to expect today, but at the moment, the only drop shock I'm experiencing is the dropping of all the apprehensions I had leading into the experience.

The sun is passing its zenith, and it's warmer than it was any day of base camp. As delicious as it feels right now, I know night will be coming sooner than I want it to, so I need to stay focused. I pick up the pace and walk the perimeter of the peninsula out to its tip, then cut back through the middle of its width to the narrow spot where I started.

The rest of the afternoon I scout the west half of the peninsula—wider than the east half, and with deeper forests punctuated by higher cliffs. Before

I head into the thicker trees, I tie a small piece of hot pink paracord to a low branch to help me find my way back to my gear, my own version of a trail of breadcrumbs. Here the forest is transitioning to the kind I saw on the mainland—dense and dark and not particularly welcoming. Heaps of building material, but my stomach drops at the thought of living here. Sheltered, but claustrophobic. The water access is treacherous at best and offers only muddy, rank water for the boot-sucking effort of getting to it.

Trudging back to my gear along the southern shore, completing a circumnavigation of the peninsula, I see a huge birch with a dark blob on its side. *Chaga!* This fungus grows in wounds on paper birch trees and makes a wonderful tea that is earthy, delicious, and highly medicinal. *Hooray!* I may not have anything for dinner, but I've got the makings of quite a few nice pots of tea.

Scouting conclusions: this place is magical and beautiful and I'm already in love with it. It's also barren and exposed, and what limited resources it has are already drying up. There is a ton of bare rock and a lot of thick moss, but very little actual soil, and I've seen none of the edible and medicinal plants I had hoped to harvest, just one medicinal fungus. Nowhere did I find the deep water I need for fishing—not even off the very point, the spot I'd deemed most likely. Survival here is going to be no picnic.

It's late afternoon and my head is beginning to pound. I haven't drunk water since this morning and I've been hiking for hours. I head back toward where I left my gear, and this time, I recognize some of the terrain—here is that low, densely forested place where I can see the water through the trees, there is that stretch of uneven rock where I have to watch my footing. Scanning the tree line ahead I see a strange profile, unlike any of the other trees. It looks like a lollipop. It's a spruce, but a little taller than the surrounding ones, and has a bare trunk that ends in a dense tuft of branches at the very top. It's a hell of a landmark, so I head right for it. There, on the branch of a birch tree growing next to it, is the piece of pink parachute cord I'd tied on earlier. I hadn't looked up to notice I was marking the spot with the most distinctive tree on the peninsula. *No, not a lollipop*, I decide, looking up at it from below. *It's a truffula tree.* Yep, it looks just like a truffula tree from Dr. Seuss's *The Lorax.*

Just beyond it is a wide rock avenue that leads right toward my gear. The small cluster of trees between here and there is just enough to break the wind, but I can see through them in all directions. The grove is close to the drop spot but not right at it, which also means good access to the water. It isn't a south slope exactly, which would be my preference in terms of getting the most light and warmth from the sun. It's at least on the south side of the peninsula, though, which is as close to a south slope as I'm likely to get from what I've seen. Plus, it's bordered by an amazing landmark I can see from a long way off. My gut sense and the landscape agree, this grove of trees is home.

22

THE OTHER SURVIVAL SKILLS

The sun is descending quickly now, and I want a temporary shelter set up before it goes down completely. I cut a small spruce tree to use as a ridge pole and carefully limb and peel it so it's smooth enough not to damage my tarp. By dusk I've got a low, lean-to style shelter, with a fold of tarp beneath me to keep my bedding off the damp ground.

I haul myself and the camera down to the lake to gather water for an evening "meal" of tea. My head pounds harder with every step, but the beauty of the sunset reflecting off the lake soothes the ache. I'm finally here. I would take this hunger and pain with this incredible beauty over the chaos and stress of the last three months any day, no question.

I guzzle as much as I can hold then stand looking at the dark water stretching out before me. As the distant glow fades into the horizon, I sing my friend Ida's sunset song to praise the sun and thank it for the day.

Sun's going down. Beauty is unbound. Day to night, night to day. Blessings on you on your way. Oh-way-oh. Praise be to the sun.

Back at camp the cold is already pressing down on my shoulders as I draw the ferro rod and multitool from my belt to make my first fire on the land. A spark catches the fine wisps of birch bark I've laid out, and the smoke curls around my face as I blow the flame into a nest of spruce twigs. I heave a deep sigh as the fire's light and warmth reflect back onto me from the lean-to wall. Nothing says home like a fire in the hearth. I make spruce tip tea, easier to prepare than chaga. Green and tangy, it doesn't exactly scream "dinner," but it's full of vitamin C and I need the liquid. I stare at the flickering light for another hour then drag myself out for a final pee before bed.

It's already well below freezing outside the small circle of my fire. I peel my bra off under my clothing and toss it to the back of the shelter. My head is still pounding and my belly rumbles in confusion at the shift from absurd abundance to near total lack as I settle into my sleeping bag for my first night.

Not quite enough hours later, the rays of the rising sun catch me in the face. The cold air stings my nostrils and the last thing I want to do is emerge from the cozy womb of my sleeping bag. Instead, I reach one arm out and fumble with the camera and tripod to document my morning and my plans for the day, a routine I'll repeat every morning from here on out.

That done, I savor one last moment of warmth, letting the sun paint its kaleidoscope of colors on the insides of my eyelids, then shiver into my clothes. I'm buttoning up my pants but not done dressing when a rising pressure in my guts prompts me to find a place to make a quick hole, so I toss on a sweater and boots and head out. With so little soil to dig in, I pick a spot of deep sphagnum moss well away from the shelter for my latrine. The moss seems to choke out all plants but cranberries and Labrador tea, both iconic plants of the northern boreal region. As the name implies, you can drink an infusion of Labrador tea leaves. They're everywhere out here, so I don't bother harvesting any in my urgency to do my business, but I don't want to waste these cranberries. I pick a beautiful red handful before digging my hole and squatting in the undergrowth, then mark the spot with two crossed sticks so I know not to dig in this place again.

The movement down below has woken up my stomach, which growls and gnaws at me. I'd love to hunt, but since I arrived in Yellowknife, yesterday was the only clear and mild day we've had. Sleety snow like we had at base camp, and worse, could be here any day. Caught unprepared in an arctic storm, I could die of exposure in hours. It takes weeks to starve to death, though, so I ignore the hunger and head back to camp.

I need to disassemble last night's shelter and decide what the heck I'm building today, but I want to dress properly first. The last thing I did yesterday was toss my bra aside, but I can't find it anywhere. I'm sure I'll get less self-conscious as time goes on, but it's going to be a big filming day. It's still warm enough that I'm wearing only a few, snug layers, so I'm not doing it braless. I walk a circle around camp and then go through everything I've got. Nothing.

Stumped, I let the bra go for now and launch into the work of the day. I take down the temporary shelter and get a sense of the space I've got to work with.

"What's your favorite type of shelter?" Quinn had asked me back in our first casting interview.

I could tell the answer mattered, that I was expected to rattle off different styles and my experience with them. But I couldn't—it was a silly question.

"Having favorites doesn't serve in a survival situation," I answered. "Preconceived ideas and attachment to them aren't survival skills, they're handicaps. Flexibility, observation, and the ability to adapt to what the environment calls for; those are the real survival skills."

Here is a case in point. I'd had some ideas about what I might build out here—of course I did—a low, yurt-like structure perhaps? A bent willow wickiup? But nothing I had pictured is going to work in this space or with the materials I've got. Instead, I need to listen to the land, take stock of my resources, and go with what they dictate.

An idea takes shape, and I move my things out of the way to make room to work.

I've got the space all clear, but seriously now, *where the heck is my bra?* Did something drag it off? Then it hits me like a slap to the forehead—*Wait a minute. I've already been here for a full day. I've harvested trees, chaga, and berries, but I haven't given anything back.*

I sometimes go through phases where I lose things all the time. I know I put my keys in my backpack, for example, and then I go through every pocket but there is no jingling metal to be found. I do the same thing three times to no avail, then sometime later I look again and there they are. I used to find it maddening, but these days, I've got a theory about it.

I'm basically an animist—I believe in the sentience of the world around me, and not just the things with central nervous systems. I fumble it sometimes—I'm a flawed human after all, raised in a modern culture that constantly takes without thinking twice—but I try to remember to always ask permission before I gather anything from a wild place. If I get a yes, I strive to harvest respectfully and to give back in some way, whether it's thinning around the plant, leaving it some food or water, singing an impromptu song, anything. When I'm caught up in my own needs and not making offerings, things of mine occasionally go missing. If I'm not remembering to do it myself, it seems, the world takes its own offering. When I realize my mistake and make an appropriate gift, I find what I'm looking for in a place I've already checked. Darn forest fairies!

What have I got to offer this grove? I came with such limited gear that there isn't much to spare. Then I remember the pendant. It was a charm a fellow instructor at an ancestral skills event had given me, a copper disk embossed with a stylized deer's head. It was originally a necklace, but before the salt buttons idea, when I thought I'd be making my own silver buttons, I tied it onto my wool shirt as an additional button to help cinch the neck closed. With my bulky sweater I can't cinch the shirt's neck down tight anyway, so it's still there but no longer useful.

This image of the deer head has always held special significance for me, and now it's as if I planned it. We're far north of deer range up here, but I've come dressed in buckskin, and in my life back home, venison is a staple. What better gift is there to offer the land I'm asking to feed me than something that means clothing and food back where I come from?

I choose a lovely, twisted willow snag on the south side of my shelter site, aim the camera at it, then approach it, aware of the soft duff under my feet and the spicy scent of spruce needles in my nose as I drop deeper into the present moment.

"My name is Woniya," I say, feeling awkward yet again about speaking my prayers on camera, and wedge the narrow disk into the split trunk of the willow snag.

"I want to be here in a good way. I humbly ask your permission and your blessings to build my life in this place from what you have to give and to make the substance of my body from your substance. If you're with me, I intend to stay as long as I can and to share the story of my time here with the world, to inspire people to live in a more connected and respectful way."

It feels well received, so I turn back to the clearing and start over.

Without a shovel, I need a digging stick to level the ground, so I cut a nice length of a birch trunk to make it from. The axe I left behind would have come in handy for working the end down into a wedge shape for digging, but I'll have to make do with my saw and knife.

When I go to grab the saw from my pack, my bra, which had apparently been wedged between my backpack and my sleeping bag stuff sack, falls to the ground. I stare, stunned, at the black shape against green moss. *What the heck? That's impossible.*

I'd just moved those bags—paying attention—and never saw it. The part of me that believes in magic wrestles with my rational brain. *The bra is here, impossible or not.* Magic wins. I pull my shirt off and shrug into the bra, not willing to let it out of my reach, and get back to work.

The digging stick I make isn't as useful as a shovel, but it does the job, and doubles as a pry bar for lifting up mats of moss to use as insulation and bedding.

As I work, I go over my shelter criteria for building in this environment:

1. Orientation—I want my thickest, sturdiest walls in the direction the blustery weather and storms roll in from, and the door sheltered from prevailing winds.
2. Sealed Walls—I want to keep the warm air in and the cold air out. This means tight walls and plenty of insulation.
3. Size—I don't want it any bigger than necessary. Additional square footage is more space to heat, and I'll be warming it with either body heat or firewood, both of which cost me a lot of calories. I want the roof as low as possible for the same reason.
4. Roof Pitch—I'm building for snow, and plenty of it. Triangles are incredibly strong and stable, and steep pitches shed snow, while flatter roofs bend and buckle.

5. Best Use of Materials—Efficiency saves me time and effort, which means saving calories.
6. Hearth—This climate calls for an indoor fire for warmth, light, and cooking. I need to make sure the shelter is built with a hearth in mind.

I settle on a slanted A-frame—tall enough to stand up in at the entrance, but with a ridge pole that slopes down so there's less dead space to heat at the foot of my bed. That gives me both a steep pitch and a triangular cross section, so a polar bear could do jumping jacks on the roof and it wouldn't collapse. I'll keep my fire toward the front of the shelter, where there will be more room to cook and store firewood.

Cutting my materials right here where I'm building would save calories—which matters—but so does spreading out my impact to minimize the damage I do to the forest, so I shoulder my saw and look for spots that would benefit from selective thinning. When I find an area where the trees are crowded, I lay my hand on a white spruce and ask, "Are you willing?"

It's hard to describe how I get an answer—not in words certainly, but a feeling. A "no" feels like resistance, a "yes" like a yielding. I feel a "yes." Whenever I kill an animal, I do my best to use as many parts as possible. I make the same promise to these trees. I limb them where they stand, then haul the trunk and the armfuls of spruce boughs back home.

All afternoon I cut, haul, and film, until the rock ledge behind the shelter, my "back porch," is piled with limbed logs and branches and it's time to start building. As I walk through one particularly thick stand of trees, I see another impossible thing—a mushroom growing out of the end of a tree limb. Not actually growing, I see, stepping closer. The stem is broken off and the skin is wrinkled and desiccated.

A squirrel yells at me from a neighboring tree. *Oh wow—a squirrel must have carried it here to dry for winter food!* Once I've registered it, I notice more mushrooms in every stage, from perfectly fresh to totally dry, in other branches as I pass back and forth hauling poles. I tuck some of the driest ones into my pocket. They are too dry to identify and I'm not going to take risks with wild mushrooms, squirrel endorsed or not, but you never know when squirrel bait might come in handy.

Back at the shelter site, I start my building project by peeling some parachute cord. Having almost left it behind, I'm not taking an inch of it for granted. It might look like a lot now, but these eighty meters could get used up quickly if I'm not careful. Luckily, every strand of 550 parachute cord is made of a strong outer sheath surrounding seven thin inner strands. Separate them, and that's eight feet of string for every foot of paracord.

To peel it, I cut a piece to expose the inner strands, then tie them to a tree trunk and inch the casing away from the innards. It's kind of like skinning the world's longest earthworm. Now I can use the tough outer sheath for serious lashing and the inner strands where I can get away with less strength.

To make my cordage go even further, I do some careful saw and knife work to notch my support poles so they fit snugly together and need only a light lashing of inner strands to make sure they can't come apart when under tension.

Now I've got a sturdy ridge pole up, incorporating living trunks to support it, for a shelter that is extra strong and literally rooted to the earth below. I grab the ridge pole with both hands and draw my knees up off the ground. I dangle there like a monkey and the pole doesn't budge. I'm in business.

It's time to attach the tarp, but growing right through what will be the back of the shelter is a small birch tree. When I ask if I can cut it, I get resistance—a sense that if I reached for my saw right now my hand would feel like it was moving through thick pudding. It's as clear a "no" as if it had spoken to me.

Shit. This tree is truly in the way of the building, but there's no point in asking for permission to cut it if I'm going to ignore the answer. This isn't just a futile exercise—the land is paying attention. If I ignore a no, I'm demonstrating a lack of integrity, and why would anything be willing to die to feed or house me if my word is no good? This is the Arctic—I can't force it into submission, I need it to *want* to work with me. It will be enormously inconvenient, but I leave the tree standing and re-strategize the back wall. *Being true to your word, now that's a survival skill.*

We've each been issued one thin, woven poly tarp, to make sure we can keep our camera equipment dry. Any slack in the tarp and the wind will catch it and tear it to shreds, so to get it nice and tight I lash a horizontal pole midway between the ground and the ridge pole on each side.

I pass a loop of cord through the first grommet and put a short, thick piece of wood into the loop so the tarp is held in place by the wooden toggle, not the cord itself. This distributes the pressure and puts less stress on each grommet—the same tactic I employ back home when I lace a deer hide into a rack to frame-soften it.

I'm working my way around the back side of the tarp when a glint of light catches my eye. *What is that?* I peer up at the flash and there, sticking straight out of the green plastic, is a long, narrow shard of metal. My shoulders sag and my head drops. *Damn it, I've got a hole in my tarp!*

Then my head whips up again. *Wait a minute, I think I have a needle!*

I grab the small piece of metal. It's got some spots of rust on it, but it is mostly smooth, shiny steel and the perfect size and shape for a needle. I poke it into the fabric of my pants. There's a second of resistance, then it slides right through. *Yes!* With a little sharpening and polishing by the file on my Leatherman and an eye pierced on one end, it'll be an ideal needle.

This is an incredible gift, far outweighing the tiny hole in my tarp it made, *but where in the world did it come from?*

I haven't seen any indication of other people having used this place, and anything this small would have rusted away within a year or two. It must have either arrived when I did or been dropped by the crew that scouted our locations who knows how many weeks ago. I am pretty sure it wasn't in the tarp yesterday—even if I hadn't noticed it while making my temporary shelter, I would have dislodged it while taking down and folding the tarp. Maybe it is some piece of the wire mesh of the gear box on the outside of the helicopter that fell into my things? Metal from some piece of safety gear or camera equipment that has lain here for weeks until my tarp scraped over and snagged it? Either way, it's an amazing find, and what are the chances of my even having seen it? A thousand to one at least. Had it been lodged in my clothing, it would have been an injury hazard. Had it fallen out at any other place in this whole landscape, it would have disappeared into the sphagnum moss or duff, and I would never have known it was there. But it didn't. It landed here, perfectly poised to greet me at eye level.

No one who hasn't spent months scrambling to make their clothing and then been launched into the Arctic with less-than-finished gear could possibly fathom the significance that this one tiny piece of metal holds for me. It makes everything possible. It negates the worry of having hurriedly made clothing that could eventually fall apart on me.

I look around at the grove of trees around me—feeling seen, feeling recognized. I started the morning with an offering, and my bra came back to me. I didn't cut the birch tree when not doing so was a serious handicap, and now here is an almost perfect needle, one of the things I need most out here. I don't know whether to laugh or to cry, but I'm struck with wonder and, let's be honest, also a little creeped out by the strangeness of it.

I wrap my precious gift in a piece of buckskin from the unfinished mukluk and tuck it into a secure pocket of my backpack.

Lengthening shadows have almost swallowed the forest, so I work my way swiftly around the rest of the tarp, securing it to the frame, and stand back. It's a solid structure with a nice taut roof, and I've got more building materials piled up here and on the back porch. A heck of a day's work.

I'm eager to get the walls filled in with bushy spruce tops, but I've been hard at it for probably six hours now—it's amazing how much you can do in a day when you aren't stopping to prepare and eat meals. Instead, I head down to the lake to haul water and sing the sun down. I'm committed to seeing each day closed with intention, rather than pushing myself every second. Balance, too, is a survival skill. So is gratitude.

Standing on the shore, the last of the day's light on my cheeks, I think about what the sun means to me here. "Thank you for shining on me today," I say. "Your light not only allowed me to work on my shelter for many long hours, but nourished the trees I built it with. I appreciate it."

I sing the sunset song, in what will become my nightly ritual. Singing the sun, the water, the day, to sleep. Always three times, as three feels most magical, and what a magical day it's been.

The wind picks up and the waves start to pound the shore as I head back home. Even under the tarp my hair whips against my cheeks with stinging tickles. Survival pressure whips up my heartbeat. *Is this the end of the window of calm? Another storm pushing in?*

I take some time to brush in the windward wall by the light of my headlamp, then build a cozy sleeping nest, using my clothing as padding and insulation from the cold ground, while I heat water for my first pot of chaga tea. *Mmmm, dinner.*

A hundred swirling thoughts fill my head as I stare into the embers at the close of my first full day here—plans for building, strategies for fishing spots and moose hunting, ideas for berry-harvesting containers. And overlaying it all, the dawning realization of what a truly enormous impact not just filming, but filming well, has on my time, energy, and calories, all of which my long-term survival depends upon.

23

SELF-CARE MONDAY

omething is wrong. It's pitch black and the air is full of smoke. Not wood-smoke but a muskier, heavier scent. I pry the hood of my sleeping bag open half an inch to look out but can see no firelight or burning embers. *Damn it, what is going on?* I ease the zipper down until I can poke one arm out, grab my headlamp and, by its light, feel around the fire pit. Nope, nothing hot there. In fact, my arm is already tingling with cold—*how many degrees has it dropped tonight?* With no obvious danger detected, I let the mystery go and fall back asleep.

When I open my eyes again, the morning light is blinding, and my eyes are so dazzled I see nothing but white. No, wait. I'm not just *seeing* white, it *is* white. I sit up and a layer of snow sloughs off me, revealing the bright red sleeping bag beneath.

Wow. I started my shelter the morning of day two, and I'm already behind. Winter doesn't mess around up here.

I catch another whiff of smoke. Now in the light, I can see a wisp of it, its color off-white against the bright snow. It's coming from the ground right next to the head of my bed. No wonder it woke me up. I had dug down to mineral soil for the fire pit, but a small root caught and burned underground, setting the duff eight inches away smoldering. I'm lucky it didn't melt my bag.

Today's first task is going to be making a real, rock lined fire pit and hearth.

It's probably twenty degrees colder this morning than yesterday. I squirm around in my bag to warm up. The back of my right leg is hot and itchy, probably irritated from where it touched my wet socks and boot liners, which I pulled into the sleeping bag last night so my body heat could dry them.

At least the back end of my digestive system is still working, even though the front end is starting to get out of practice. On my way back from the latrine, I scope out some hearth rocks. I haul a huge flat rock back with me and set it upright as a sturdy backdrop to the fire. It will serve as a reflector—bouncing the warmth and light of the fire back to me. I widen the pit and line it with smaller rocks, then add more reflector rocks. I'll eventually want a chimney too, but until I've got actual walls there isn't much point.

I spend the morning cutting and hauling more poles and organizing them by species and function. White spruces are tall and straight with branches spreading out in a flat plane. They're great for structure but don't offer much insulation. Black spruces are small and dense, and the tops and branches are like bottle brushes. They're perfect for walls that break the wind and keep out the bitter cold.

I've got two heavy trunks on my shoulder when another flock of swans passes, followed by a pair lagging behind, flapping wildly and calling out in awkward voices as they struggle to catch up. The sound of my own laughter, such a human noise in this vast unpeopled landscape, shocks me. I can't imagine how different my time out here would be if I wasn't a naturalist—endlessly thrilled and entertained by the world around me, comforted by the company of the trees and birds. It isn't food, but it does manage to feed me.

By midday, the snow has melted off everywhere except the deepest shadows and I've got a good pile of material to work with. My belly gnaws and moans, but I remind myself that the calories I'm burning now will be paid back later in calories I don't have to spend shivering because of a shoddy shelter.

It's late afternoon when I realize today is Monday, and that makes it Self-Care day.

Once, years ago, a potential sweetheart visited me in my one room cabin, looked around, and asked, "So where is your couch, or cushions, or you know, a comfortable place to sit down and relax?"

"Hmmm..." I cocked my head to one side and thought about it. I had been living there for two years at that point and the question had never occurred to me, much less an answer to it.

I've spent a lot of my adult life living without many of the basic com-
forts most take for granted—central heating, refrigeration, indoor plumbing, etc. When I moved to an off-grid homestead in Oregon my goal was
to grow, hunt, and gather as much of my own food as possible. The
problem was that there's no quitting time on your own farm, and there's
always a longer list of tasks than time to do them. Plus I wasn't just homesteading. I was also building onto my home, working part time to pay the
necessary bills and spending time driving around the country at my own
expense to teach ancestral skills for free. I ran myself into the ground. I
could often be found in the garden at 11:00 pm planting by headlamp.
I would go and go until an injury or illness forced me to rest. It wasn't
healthy or sustainable, and over time—and through the dissolution of
my second marriage, for which these habits were partly responsible—I
began to see that. I also saw the deeper patterns—the feeling that my
worth was in what I accomplished, not in who I was, and the place in me
that didn't feel valid enough to have wants or needs. It was only in recent
years and after leaving the farm that the patterns had started to shift.

The past summer had been a throwback to those behaviors. The desire to
bring my whole self—buckskin and craftiness and all—to *Alone* and its viewers may have been honorable, but it had also been a wild ride of intense drive
and self-denial.

Self-care isn't generally touted as high on the list of survival skills, but I
know well where a lack of it can lead, and I now consider it critical. It helps
keep us healthy, relaxed, and content, and these things absolutely matter in
long-term wilderness living. Pushing too hard with a system hopped up on
adrenaline burns through calories faster, impedes digestion, and gives one
tunnel vision—not just metaphorically, it literally narrows the range of vision.
It also lowers brain function, leading to poor decision-making and a higher
likelihood of silly accidents.

Before leaving for the north, I had decided to remind myself of the importance of self-care and enjoying myself, by designating two days of the week for

certain activities. Thursdays would be Dance Party days—because if I'm not loving my life out here enough to be able to dance about it, then I shouldn't be here—and Mondays would be my Self-Care days.

Making a decent shelter is an important self-care task of course, but by that definition everything I do here is, and nothing will ever feel special about Mondays. Shelter is for future Woniya—Mondays need to include something for the here and now Woniya.

Today, I decide that instead of pushing through the gnawing hunger and continuing to build, I'm going scouting for food.

I take my bow and quiver and head out, scratching again at the itchy spot on the back of my leg.

First for some food that doesn't run away. I lie down on the cold granite and stuff my face with crowberries. I'd never heard of crowberries before coming here, but they're an abundant ground cover that seem to cover nearly a third of the rocky ground up north. Only an inch or two tall, each tiny branchlet is topped with one or two jet black berries. They're mild in flavor and slightly sweet, but more watery than juicy. I squish the berries between my teeth and guzzle the liquid, but the seeds and skins accumulate into a gritty wad I can hardly choke down. Eating them feels more like work than pleasure, but I manage a pint or two, then move on to a cranberry patch.

Cranberries are the opposite of crowberries. Anything but watery and bland, they're so sour my face squinches up when they touch my tongue, but I continue to pick handful after handful. Finally, my tongue and cheeks feel raw, my teeth are starting to ache, and my stomach feels tight and acidic.

As I heave myself to my feet, a squirrel chatters at me from a high branch. It doesn't flinch as I bring up my bow, inhale, hold, and release the string. My arrow passes millimeters from its torso and the squirrel disappears down the trunk in the same instant. It takes a while to find the arrow—I wish I'd specified hot pink for all the feathers of the fletching, not just one per arrow.

I spend another hour hunting, taking a few shots and finally heading home empty-handed except for an old Pepsi can I found bobbing at the water's edge. My legs wobble on the uphills—the hunger is finally getting to them. What has felt like a minor slope the past couple of days now feels daunting. My mind wanders to thoughts of the bag of pemmican in the top of my pack, its sides beautifully smeared with white lard. If you've never gone three days without eating while working your butt off in the bitter cold, you probably don't think of lard smeared on plastic as tantalizing. It's a first for me too.

"The problem with rationing your food too hard," Dave Holder, the lead survival consultant for the show had told us at base camp, "is that going without food doesn't just sap your calories, it shuts down your whole digestive system. Once that happens, you might still bring in food, but most of it will pass right through you, doing you very little good."

Alright Dave, I hear you.

Of all the show's staff, Dave is the one I felt an instant bond with, and it grew with every day of our prelaunch base camp. Small in stature but enormous in knowledge, competence, and heart, his genuine care for the well-being of every participant is palpable. He is not only a skilled survival expert, but also shares my interests in botany and plant medicine and is devoted to honoring the land and its people in ways that resonate with my own approach. I trust his advice implicitly and decide it's time to put it into action.

Back at the shelter I pull out the pemmican and spend a moment just looking at the bag. I make a ceremony of every part of the process—cracking the plastic zipper and taking a big sniff of the rich, meaty smell. It's quite firm at this temperature, so I unwrap the solid block, then turn the bag inside out and lick the fat off of every corner and crevice before turning my attention to the pemmican itself. The fat sings on my tongue, and I let the sensation roll over me for a minute and then take my first nibble from the block.

I sigh deep down in my core and relief washes over me, my knees almost buckling at the delicious taste. I sit down on the camera case to be sure I don't topple over. The combination of the oily fat melting over my tongue, the salty richness of the meat, and the slight sweetness of the berries is overwhelming. I've never eaten anything so amazing. The taste kicks the hunger up so fiercely that I wolf another bite before I can stop myself or slow down. I'd love to demolish half of it, which would still be smaller than the volume of an average meal in my other life. Instead, I muster my will and carefully wrap it back up.

That evening, between two brushed-in walls and the new hearth and reflector rocks, I feel far warmer and cozier than I did last night. I use my Leatherman to cut the top off my Pepsi can and then fold down the edge for a smooth rim, and soon I'm relaxing in the glow of the fire with a new teacup in my hand, hungry but pleased with myself.

The light dancing over the smooth flat surface of the large reflector rock strikes a chord—*Wait a minute*...I dig a coal out and let it cool, then use it as a piece of chalk and write "M 3" on the largest hearth rock, standing for Monday of day three. Now I've got a way to mark time and a weekly calendar.

Again, as I lie back in bed, the spinning hamster wheel of strategies starts—deadfall traps, fishing poles, moose calls, etc.

Can I dry crowberries? How do I make cranberries more palatable?

24

BETTER THAN A TATTOO

A cold wind is blowing across my face when I wake up. Snow has drifted in again—from the east this time, my only wall that's still open—but at least my sleeping bag is still red, not white with snow. I'm anxious to start fishing, aware that I can't keep working like this forever without more food, but I have to continue building until I know my shelter isn't going to keep filling up with snow.

If I needed a reminder of how long it's been since my last true meal, I've got it. For the first morning since my arrival, there's no sensation in my gut besides the empty ache of hunger. No nudge to take my "morning stroll." There's only so long I can expect to have something coming out when so little is coming in, and I really want to keep my digestion working for when I get those fish and that moose, so I grab the cook pot to get serious about a real breakfast with vitamins and fiber. The raw cranberries were hard on my belly, but they are the best food source I've got right now, so I'm determined to find a way to make them appealing. I head out to the rocks and harvest them until I've got three cups, a true bellyful, and decide to make cranberry sauce, cooking them down with water so they'll be tastier and more hydrating.

They simmer and pop over the fire, turning the lake water a gorgeous hot pink. I scrape some of the congealed fat off the pemmican bag and add it to the pot. It will add calories and hopefully help my body absorb the vitamins better too. *Rich, fatty Cranberry Surprise for breakfast! I feel like a queen.*

When every berry has released its ruby contents into the water, I take it off the fire to cool. An iridescent oily sheen swirls around each berry. It looks delicious, but at the first sip, I gag, my tongue crinkling up into a puckered little ball. *Oh my god, it's disgusting.* Cranberry Surprise indeed. The "surprise" is that they are less palatable cooked than raw. How did diluting them with water actually make them *more sour?*

I chug as much as I can, managing about half the pot, then put it down and belch loudly. I clench my abdomen and stare into the camera, rolling as always, and hope the burps don't turn into something more solid.

Defeated, I heave a deep sigh and pull myself to my feet to carry on with construction. Acid belly aside, harvesting materials is so satisfying I can't stay downcast for long. The peninsula feels more familiar every day. The forests and ledges are becoming extensions of my living area, not unknown wilderness, and I find myself using names for them as I choose where to head—the back porch, the north woodlot, the avenue, the southern squirrel hollow. I feel most capable and most like myself out here working in the woods, taking my signals from the land and the trees themselves.

Walking back home with another spruce pole on my shoulder, though, I feel the hot, itchy prickling on the back of my right thigh again. *Okay, seriously, what is up back there?* I drop the pole on the back porch, lower my pants and gasp. It's not just my imagination. There's an angry red welt on the back of my leg. It's raised a good quarter inch and is almost two inches across. It sings with heat as my fingertips brush it and throbs in the cold air. There's another smaller bump rising up beside it. *What is going on?* I'm not exactly a delicate flower and not prone to rashes or welts. I'm swathed in clothing twenty-four hours a day, and it's too cold for much insect activity, so I can't imagine anything has been biting me.

I search my sleeping bag and clothes anyway, but find nothing, as expected.

I carry on working, but now that I know they're there, I'm constantly aware of the welts and their impact on my already overtaxed and undernourished body. *It's okay,* I tell myself. *I can handle this. Just please don't let it get any worse.*

Before lighting my evening fire, I sit and stare into my pot of Cranberry Surprise. The cold fat is congealed around the berries. There's no part of me that wants to eat them, but I need to empty the pot to haul water, and the fat, unappealing as it looks right now, is too precious to waste. My stomach cramps a little just from the smell, but I choke it all down in one go. My throat is still tender from the first round, and this time the berries burn the whole way down and my belly seizes up around them. I can feel my pulse throbbing in my temples as I crouch over my midsection, trying not to vomit. *Well, that didn't work.*

My frustration with myself is almost as painful as the burning in my stomach. *I should have known better.* I was getting a clear "no way" message from my body, but I ate them anyway.

I don't throw up, but it's hours until the burning fades. First my thighs and now my stomach? It's only day four and my body is already breaking down.

Alright body, I sigh. *I hear you. From now on, you're in charge. I'm not going to think I know better than you, and I'm not going to make you eat what you tell me you don't want.*

I'm still moving slowly the next morning—functional, but definitely not quite normal. I don't ever want to see a cranberry again, much less eat one, but at least the acid burps have let up.

My belly isn't up for fishing, but I can still do something to prepare for it. I'm roughing out a trout on the handle of my newly carved "fish-flipping spatula" when I hear a flutter in the trees outside. There's a flash of black and white and a scolding, *chick a dee-dee-dee, chick a dee-dee-dee.*

Hey, I know that call! I rush outside in my socks with my heart racing, the cold ground and icky belly forgotten, and stare up into the spruce branches. It's different from the ones back home, but there's no mistaking it. Sitting on a low branch right outside the shelter is the very ball of fluff I've been hoping to see out here, a chickadee, and now I can see other branches shaking with the rustlings of other members of its small flock.

"Hi, Little," I say to this one, in what I hope is a welcoming, soothing voice. "Little" or "weensy" are my favorite terms of endearment for anything less than a quarter of my size—babies, puppies, songbirds, tree seedlings—you name it.

Chickadees are rarely still for more than two seconds together. This one cocks its little striped head at me for a couple of heartbeats, flutters to the ground for a few hops, then flies up into another small spruce, inspecting the undersides of its needles for snacks.

You could hold a chickadee in a cupped hand and hardly know it was there. They are minuscule and almost comically round, but their striking black and white heads are their most distinctive feature. Boisterous and acrobatic, as likely to be dangling upside down as perching, they are cute and utterly hilarious as they go about their gymnastics routines. It would be easy to discount them as just that, but these little suckers are also tough as hell. This is the Arctic, with winter rolling in stronger every day. Most other birds have already flown south, but this little furball is here to stay. Actually, tough doesn't really sum it up—lots of things in the Arctic are tough. Chickadees are also *feisty*. Not content just to show me up, catching food all around the treetops while I've been starving for days and laid up by a pot of cranberries, these ones are also yelling at me while doing it.

And I'm so happy about it I could cry. I love these little creatures with a fierceness that makes my chest ache. Everything about them. The way their scolding yell is pitched somewhere between obnoxious and endearing, their diminutive size, and their cheerful playfulness in the harshest of conditions and places. They are tiny, but huge in presence. Somewhere between my favorite bird and my spirit animal, there are few other creatures whose presence right now could mean more to me.

I wanted to bring chickadees out here with me so badly that I considered getting a tattoo of one—a first for me—last summer. Really though, I didn't just want to bring them along; I wanted to *be* one out here. And maybe I am. I too am small and curvy. I'm also energetic, capable, and tough, though like them you might not know it from my generally silly and bubbly demeanor. While I wasn't thrilled about starting to go gray at twenty-five, I love that I managed to do it in stripes. Now, just like a chickadee, I've got one dark stripe down the middle of my head and two solid lines of white on either side. I look more like a chickadee with every passing year.

The summer had been such a hot mess that the tattoo never had a chance. Still, I'd known that if this was to be a significant journey, chickadees would somehow be part of it. Now here they are before me—*so much better than a tattoo!*

Food or no, cranberry belly or no, I now know this is exactly where I'm supposed to be.

This life is blessed. Uncomfortable and challenging, but every day there's some new wonder—flocks of majestic swans or stashes of mushrooms in the treetops. Every day there are more tasks than I can possibly get to, but I'm also adding to the ease and comfort of my home here with each one—a Pepsi can teacup, a spatula for cooking, a calendar on the hearthstone.

My bellyache gone, joy bubbles up in me like a call note from a chickadee. I get suited up for fishing and pack my tackle.

Crouching on the wet rocks, I use a piece of thread and a snip of hot pink paracord to make a passable fly, attach it to a leader, and wind off a good length of line. I manage to cast it out about ten feet, where it promptly sinks to the bottom, which is ten inches deep. I'm fairly certain no good-sized, self-respecting lake trout would be caught dead in ten inches of water. Adding pebbles for weight gives me better casting, but a line that sinks even faster and gets hopelessly tangled in the blocky rocks that line the bottom. *Damn!* How am I ever going to use that spatula for trout if I'm fishing in less than a foot of water?

I cut some dead, lightweight willow branches that will float on water and try different combinations of rock weights and carved wooden floats. After well over an hour of trying like mad, I succeed in getting my line only twenty feet farther out—gaining maybe three more inches of depth—and losing two of my twenty-five hooks. *Damn, damn, damn!*

The wind is picking up, sucking the warmth out of my cold, wet hands. Damp, exposed, and kneeling on wet rocks, every minute I'm less able to tie knots with my stiffening fingers. Finally, I relent and tuck my hands into my armpits until they work well enough to turn the cameras off and pack up.

This is seriously concerning. I've been assuming that fish will be one of my major calorie sources out here, but if the rest of the peninsula's waters are this shallow, I might be in trouble. I remember the joy I felt seeing the chickadee earlier and the bouncy, resilient spirit in me that resonated with it. *Perhaps it's too early to feel this disappointed—it's my first actual attempt at fishing.* Even as I tell myself this though, I remember only too well all the scouting I did and the fact that I found no shoreline more promising than this anywhere. *It's not all or nothing. I'll keep honing my fishing game. There's got to be a way.*

But there are bigger fish to fry out here, so to speak—of the antlered variety. It's time to move on to an even more important food mission.

25

MOOSE MISSION

On my way home I shoot at a squirrel and watch my arrow pass right between its legs, then disappear into the forest behind it.

It's gone, utterly. I look everywhere, spiraling out in wider and wider circles, then finally give up. At least I didn't lose one of my precious moose broadheads. Those are reserved for something a lot more filling than a squirrel—but first, I need to find an appropriate birch tree to peel so I can make a moose call.

I drop off my fishing gear at home and head out to where I remember seeing a good-sized birch. I can see its white trunk shining out between the darker grays of the spruce trees, almost glowing in the late light.

The first hard freeze happened before we left Yellowknife, and that means the moose rut should be on. A male moose will travel miles in response to the sounds of a female's call, which isn't hard to imitate, so what I need is the proper megaphone to amplify my voice. Birch bark is the perfect material, but not just any birch will do. It needs to be large, straight, and without any lower branches. Peeling birches doesn't kill them as long as you cut only the outer bark, but it has a big impact, so I also want one healthy enough to easily afford the sacrifice.

This one looks perfect, so I lay my hand on it and ask if it's willing. Feeling a "yes," I do the most natural thing in the world—I pull down my pants and pee on its roots.

There are a lot of schools of thought about appropriate offerings, but I've got my own philosophy about it. I don't generally have a perfect copper charm to offer like I did my second day here, so in my regular life I often leave something beautiful from the natural word that doesn't exist where I'm harvesting, like rocks from the coast while in the desert, or vice versa. Even better is offering something that the tree or plant actually needs. Water and nitrogen are their two biggest needs, and human urine is full of both. In my opinion, it's the offering that nature intended.

Pulling my pants back up, I graze my tender thigh and wince. The smaller welt has caught up with the first and together they cover a good five square inches of the most sensitive part of my leg. *Come on body, what is going on?*

It's delicate work peeling bark in cold weather, especially with no sap running, but I cut carefully and use my fingers to gently ease it off, until I'm holding a beautiful piece of smooth bark with only a few minor splits.

Birch bark is a traditional material for watertight containers, ladles, canteens, and more. I'll eventually want some of those too, but right now nothing is more important to me than a moose call.

I warm the bark over the fire to make it pliable, then roll it into a cone shape and lash it tightly with a narrow strip of buckskin that I trim off the bottom edge of my parka.

The next morning my eyelids flutter open earlier than usual. My body already knows it's moose-hunting day.

There's a little fresh snow on the ground, but the sky is utterly clear and the tea dregs in the bottom of the cook pot are frozen solid. *Yes!* Sound carries farther in clear, cold weather.

But oh, my lord, it's freezing. I pull on every piece of long underwear I've got and dig out the pair of socks I've been waiting for a special moment to put on—a thigh-high gray wool-cashmere blend. I pull on my buckskin pants and do a couple of experimental squats. They were so absurdly tight on launch day I haven't worn them since, but now they are perfectly comfortable. There's nothing better for hunting than buckskin pants. They smell more like smoke than human, are infinitely quieter than synthetic pants, or even wool or cotton ones, and when faded and stained like these, they blend into the woods seamlessly. More important is the message they send to the wild things—*I may be out here with the aim of killing you, but I love and respect you enough to use every part of you.*

I draw the diamond file of my Leatherman over the edges of my broadheads—ones I brought because they are heavy and sturdy enough to take a moose—until I can see just the barest glint of the rising sunlight along their edges. I tuck the arrows with their sharpened broadheads into my quiver, stroking the soft bobcat fur of its ruff and asking her to be with me today, then push my wool scarf down amongst the shafts to keep them from clattering as I walk.

I don't want to take time for a fire, so I put the frozen chunks of tea in my pockets and suck on them as I glide through the trees toward my hunting spot. I've chosen one where the prevailing wind should take my scent out over the lake.

The silence breaks in a honking cacophony and I jump, more nervous than I'd realized. It's another flight of swans heading south. I use their noise as cover to dart across an open area with lots of crackling twigs.

Finally, I'm at my spot, cameras in place and broadheads at the ready, and I raise the call to my lips, using my fingers to pinch my nostrils closed to better emulate the nasal voice of a female moose in heat.

Here goes. Low and guttural at first, then rising up in range as I raise the call high, "Mwaaaah," and then drop again to a deep "uungh." I wait ten or fifteen seconds, then repeat the call with more power.

I wait, picturing the shaggy beast out there somewhere, knee-deep in a boggy lake, raising its head in my direction. But I have no idea where in this vast wilderness a moose may be. If there is even one in calling range, it could take it hours to reach me. Calling again too soon could tip it off just as easily as making human sounds, so instead of calling again I shift my weight back and forth in an effort to keep warm as the long minutes tick by.

After half an hour I'm freezing, but visions of thick moose steaks and crispy fat keep me in place, my belly twisting inside me.

After a full hour I raise the call again, pouring all my hunger and all of my prayers into the birch bark and echoing out over the hills. It's a good effort, but my hope is fading. Soon, I know, I'll be too chilled to aim well, if I'm not already. I want a moose so bad I can taste it, but here's the thing: I've never called a moose before. I've been told it's no great feat—in the mating season, bull moose can be so hormone crazed they'll come to the sound of a chainsaw—but still. I've cooked and eaten moose meat, but thus far I've only practiced my calls in the back of my mom's trailer park in California after watching YouTube tutorials. If determination and will are enough, I've got this, but am I kidding myself that they *are* enough?

The wind picks up and stirs the leaves around me. It's blowing the wrong direction, spreading my scent across the mainland instead of across the lake. In two and a half hours I've heard nothing but the swans and am starting to shake with cold. I'm done. I pack up and point myself toward the truffula tree and home.

Another blowout, but like the fishing, it's just my first try. Somehow, somewhere, the food will come—won't it?

26

DANCING WITH MYSELF

On the way back home, I notice my lips feel raw and irritated. I shouldn't have left this morning without melting ice for drinking water. Chapped lips are always my first sign of serious dehydration. Sometimes I'm so resilient and good at dealing with discomfort that I forget it's often a sign I need to do something different. I run my fingers over my tingling lips. I need to build water-drinking routines into my other daily routines. Thinking of routines reminds me—*today is Thursday!*

It's Dance Party day! I selected my two weekly routines to divide the week up nicely—Self-Care Mondays for practicality, Dance Party Thursdays for pure enjoyment.

Agreeing to film my wilderness survival adventure and share it with the world was a big step for me, but being bold enough to film myself dancing is next-level. I've made it this far, so while I'm a little nervous, I'm all in. *Look out world!*

Watching prior *Alone* seasons, it was clear that most of them have come down to suffering contests. That isn't what I signed up for. I'm here because I *want* this experience, not to force myself to *endure* it. Dancing is one of my biggest expressions of joy. While I was preparing for *Alone* back home, I knew I would likely be cold, hungry, and uncomfortable out here, and that joy might be rather limited in supply. I made myself a promise that at least once a week, I would make time to call it forth and let it run through me in the form of dance.

The shelter still needs work, and I want to scope out more fishing spots, but experiencing joy and fostering a positive mental attitude are important survival needs too. After making a warm pot of tea and spending a few hours on the shelter, I head out to look for my dance floor.

I push through the back woodlot to where a series of ascending blocky rocks rise up to the highest cliffs on the peninsula. From here I've got an awesome view out over the water to the north.

This routine isn't just for show, it's about reminding myself why I'm here and expressing my zest for life. I want to feel free in my body and really dance, not just go through the motions. I can never dance in shoes, much less clunky boots, so even though the sun is on its way down, and it wasn't exactly warm even when it was shining, I strip down to my long underwear and pull off my boots. The cold air feels good on the hot welts, but the frigid rock beneath my bare feet steals my breath away. No matter, it'll help distract me from how sheepish I feel in front of the camera right now. I check myself out in the camera's view screen. My lips are definitely looking a little red and puffy. *Drink more water, Woniya!*

I'll be more spontaneous for future dance parties, but I've had the music for this first one picked out for weeks. A dance party all alone in the wilderness—this obviously calls for Billy Idol's "Dancing with Myself."

The dancing is awkward. Turns out it's a lot harder to feel the music when it's just in my head. I close my eyes, picture myself obscured by the darkened lighting and streamers of the junior high dances in my old school gym and let the beat roll through me. Soon I'm jumping around the rocks with my arms up over my head. By the time I click the cameras off, my armpits are sweaty and there are little tufts of reindeer moss kicked up all around the "dance floor." That's one mission well accomplished!

The sky is beginning to redden as I pull my pants back on and thaw my feet with my warm hands before slipping on my socks and my boots. The rocks slope northeast, away from the setting sun, but the north bay catches and reflects its light so now the whole northern mainland is taking on the rosy glow. I'll call these the "Sunset Rocks," I decide.

The temperature is dropping fast, so I work on my shelter until there's almost no light left to see by and realize that while I danced in the sunset, I didn't sing my evening song. It's late and dark enough now that instead of going out to the water, I step out to the open ledge of the back porch and sing my heart out there, my face pointed west and my eyes closed. When I open them again, the light has shifted. No, it isn't just that it's shifted—it *is* shifting, growing brighter and brighter in front of me like a sunrise in time-lapse. It fades again and begins glowing somewhere else. *It's the northern lights!*

I run for the camera, hoping I won't be too late, but as the darkness descends further they only intensify, shifting from throbbing light to dancing ribbons of color. I gasp, sucking in the cold air so fast it burns my lungs and sets me coughing. Unlike the pale northern lights I saw before launch, these are vivid blues and greens, colors I'd have sworn were made up just for neon signs, but here they are in front of me, just beyond my reach. *So beautiful!*

I lose track of time, mesmerized, until I realize the camera battery is dead and I'm nearly too stiff to move.

As I drag myself to the shelter, the air sparkles like glass, and cuts just as sharply. I make a fire and sit as close to it as I can, straddling the whole hearth until I'm warm enough for the laborious process of laying out my sleeping nest.

I want to hold those dancing lights in my mind forever, let them lull me to sleep with their magic. Instead, as soon as I lie down my mind starts to buzz with the familiar reel of thoughts. *Should I make a gill net? Would it work better to make one out of fishing line or paracord innards? Is there a way I can build a small raft to get a line out into deeper water? Is there a better spot for moose on the mainland?*

I don't notice the whirring slowing down, but at some point I wake up in the pitch dark to the sound of a *kathump-kathump-kathump* not far from my head. Some animal has just run past the shelter. A galloping noise, but not heavy enough or clattering enough to be a hooved animal.

I strain my ears in the darkness of the shelter, but it doesn't come again. *Is my hunger conjuring up dream beasts to satisfy my prayers? Am I missing a hunting opportunity, or am I starting to lose my mind?* I don't know the answer, so eventually I burrow deeper into the sleeping bag and nod back off.

27

GIVING IS RECEIVING

I n the morning, the light is diffused and gray and I can barely keep my eyes open. Dark clouds have rolled back in, swollen with snow and looking as heavy as I feel. My puffy lips ache and burn. Not just burning around the edges, like chapped lips, but a deeper, tingling ache that's reminiscent of...*Oh no!*

I turn on the camera, find myself in the view screen, and zoom in on my lower lip. *Crap!* Three huge cold sores are bubbling up just beneath the skin. That's three times more than I've ever had at once. No wonder it looked so swollen yesterday; the entire surface is nearly covered in erupting sores. First my thigh and now this? *Body, what is happening?*

But I already know the answer. Two and a half months of the most intense stress I've ever endured, pushing myself halfway through the night, every night, right up until the day before I stepped into the helicopter—*yup, that would do it.*

You know how sometimes when you're in a hard situation you handle things okay when the pressure is on and there's no other choice, then collapse as soon as you get a breather? I know that being dropped off in the arctic wilderness to survive on my own might not seem like a breather to most people. Compared to the multiple hells of my mom's accident and wondering if she would ever walk again, being told I had a crippling condition that could make my organs explode, and the absurd stresses of my ambitious preparations for this adventure, however, that's one hundred percent the case.

What's actually shocking isn't the current state of my lips, but the fact that I've made it this far without a collapse. My body isn't conspiring against me out here; it has stoically held it all together even as I piled unsustainable burdens onto it for days, then weeks, then months. It knew that any major calamity before launch might have resulted in an alternate coming in my place, so my body allowed the stress to accumulate until things felt less like life or death—which ironically happened only once I was dropped by myself to survive in a challenging, unknown environment. Now the stress is popping out in one big wallop that feels like it's trying to tear my face off. As a matter of fact, looking closer—*holy crap*, the upper lip is also swelling up with smaller blisters. And I thought dancing was the most vulnerable thing I'd be doing on camera out here—turns out it's just being willing to share this face with the viewing public.

Part of me wants to sink in despair, utterly defeated, but instead, I reframe the catastrophe.

Okay, let's take stock. I feel terrible and I'm going to be on national television with my face looking like a B-movie monster, but as painful and mortifying as that is, it's also a sign that my body is working with me. It finally considers itself safe enough to express what the madness of the past few months did to it and to find its way into balance. Whether I see it as a curse or a blessing is up to me. Lips heal—it could have been a bleeding ulcer or a hernia instead.

Nice work body, I tell it. *You've totally got this.* And now, understanding why I feel like I've been drugged, I roll over in bed and go back to sleep.

When I wake again hours later, the bottom blisters have merged into one big blister, but I feel more like myself. I could just stay in bed, I know. Doing so is a decent survival strategy under extreme calorie deprivation—but I don't want to just extend my stay while slowly wasting away, counting the ticking seconds—I want to *live* here. Lying around isn't in my nature—actively doing all I can to make life here better is, and a person my size doesn't have enough stored calories to play the waiting game.

As I stand up and dress, I get that familiar tug in my midsection that hastens me out of the shelter and toward my latrine area. *Hooray!* At least something in my body is working again!

When I'm done doing my business, I'm a little woozy. Not a great sign, and my lips won't heal without protein, so I decide to eat more pemmican.

I take the long way home to gather some dry firewood, so my route brings me right past the birch that I peeled yesterday. There's a cluster of smaller birches next to it, mostly dead and well into rot, but there's one with decent bark that I might as well harvest. Not canteen quality, but good enough for a container of some kind.

My knife goes through the pulpy wood like butter and the bark comes off in whole rounds. As I peel one off I see a little pit in the rotten wood, and a ribbed white shape in the pit. *It's a grub!* It's tiny—about a sixteenth of an inch wide and a quarter inch long—but hey, it's still a grub! And grubs are made of meat! Well, not exactly, but they're animal protein.

I look closer. There are a few other occupied holes. I painstakingly peel each little larva out of the wood and place it on a piece of the bark. I go over the whole tree, and in the end I have seven wee beetle grubs. They probably amount to less than a quarter teaspoon. Not enough to bother with in normal circumstances, but right now just the thought is enough to make my mouth water and my belly grumble.

I carry the bark out in front of me with two hands, walking like I'm carrying a sleeping baby that just stopped howling.

I build a small fire under the lid of my pot. The grubs sizzle and dance on the lid in less than a minute. Then—*pop!* One bursts with the heat and jumps right out of the lid! *Nooo!*

I use my sweater sleeve as a pot holder and grab the lid, but another pops out as I'm moving it. *Aaarghh!*

The remaining five stay in the pan. Well cooked, they're stretched out and rigid, looking like miniscule crinkle cut fries. One at a time, I savor each tiny larva. The flavor is delicate and nutty. My whole body sighs, and I rock back on my heels in bliss. I went to graduate school for entomology—bug science. Insect biology professors love serving up larvae to capture the student's attention on the first day of class. I've eaten my share of mealworms and crickets, but none of them ever tasted like this. Hunger is the best seasoning, they say, but this isn't just the flavor, it's that my body feels the food in a whole different way now. It knows on a deep cellular level what every morsel of it means. But five grubs, amazing as they are, aren't going to rebuild the skin on my lips, so I unpack the pemmican bag.

I'm about to take a bite when I realize that last time, I forgot to feed the ancestors first. It's hard to give any of it up, but somehow the fact that I have so little makes it even more important to feed the sacred that, in turn, feeds me. I roll up a waxy little ball of pemmican and spy a large boulder with a divot on top in front of the shelter. A perfect offering spot. I exhale onto the tiny ball, adding my breath and warmth to it.

Thank you, ancient ones, I say in my mind as I place it on the boulder. *I remember and honor you and ask that you be here with me. Watch over me and help me stay well and fed.*

When I eat my own small ball of pemmican, it feels bigger somehow. Richer. The sweet is sweeter, the meat meatier. The hunger is still there, but I'm more aware of my feet on the ground instead of woozily floating slightly above it.

I make ancestor plates regularly at home, but it's generally more ceremonial than visceral. Out here I can *feel* it. Somehow, the less I have to give, the greater the positive impact of giving some away. The more I feed the greater world, the more I feel nourished by it.

What started off this morning as a calamitous day ends feeling like a blessed one. When I feel the thumping gallops of the dream beasts echoing through the rock in my sleep in the night, I don't bother wondering whether they are real or imagined, I'm just glad that they seem well fed and are still showing up.

28

LOVING THE WORLD IS A SURVIVAL SKILL

Over the course of the next few days, my lips open up into raw, crusty sores and more welts appear, popping up on my left thigh now, as well as my right.

The gray light of each dawn finds my cold fingers packing up a spruce bark tackle box with the endless variations of gear I made by firelight the night before: shiny Pepsi can lures, endless variations of hand-tied flies, willow floats, and stone sinkers. I carve a wooden hand reel and two long fishing poles of willow, one for each shore, for better casting. I try my luck at fishing spot after fishing spot—north bay, south bay, and the peninsula's tip. I try reedy shores, clear water, and everything in between. Nowhere do I see so much as a ripple, nor does my line ever touch water over two feet deep. Every morning as I walk back home—chilled, damp, and empty-handed—I'm aware of the pulsing heat on the backs of my legs and the rub of my wool clothing on the raw welts.

Continuing to pour myself into fishing, less hopeful every day that my luck will change, is grueling physically and emotionally, but it's what staying long term requires, so I don't give up. I alternate fishing trips with more moose missions, and while I find a pile of very rusty tin cans one day, all full of holes but still worthwhile containers, I don't bring home any food. I lose several more arrows shooting unsuccessfully at squirrels chattering at me from the treetops and finally promise myself I'll only shoot at the ones in lower branches backed by rocks instead of open air, so the arrows can't disappear into the moss.

I'm very aware of the fact that with every failed food mission, I'm further drawing down my calorie reserves. Unable to give my body the protein it needs to heal, I devote myself to doing at least something right—drinking a full pot of tea every morning and night, and as often as I can manage throughout the day.

I persist. I strategize. I lie awake at night pouring my heart out to this place and asking for its guidance.

It's looking more and more like neither fish nor moose are likely to be on the menu. Squirrels appear to be the only abundant game I've got, so it's time to give them more attention.

Strategy 1: Squirrel pole. A squirrel pole is a wooden pole—usually a branch or narrow trunk—with small snare loops along the length of it. They can be put up angled, as a ramp up into a tree from the ground, or placed horizontally between trees. They are effective when built well with the right supplies—supplies I don't have. I do my best to make a decent squirrel pole, but all I have to work with is fishing line, which isn't self-supporting like snare wire. I try to use branches to support my fishing line snare loops, but it's nearly impossible to keep them round and open. When I'm done, I wedge the finished pole into place with little confidence.

Strategy 2: A baited arm-hold trap. I weave willow branches into a makeshift, open work basket. I tie little fishing line nooses all over the top, pile dried mushrooms under it, and weigh it down with rocks. If a squirrel reaches through for a mushroom and gets its paw caught in a noose while I'm nearby, I should be able to get to it and dispatch it before it can escape.

Strategy 3: Deadfall traps. I haul medium-sized flat rocks back to camp. I harvest dry willow and carve it into several figure-four mechanisms that can balance a rock and then drop it quickly when pressure is put on a trigger stick baited with a dried mushroom.

Conclusions: Squirrels could care less about dried mushroom bait when there are dried mushrooms in nearly every spruce tree between here and the mainland, and awkward squirrel poles are useless.

Next, I try making new arrows so I can be more cavalier with my hunting and take riskier shots without worrying about losing arrows. I make a wedge out of hard birch wood and I cut a nice straight spruce, but when I go to split out arrow shafts using a carved wooden wedge, I find that the growth rings are so close and the wood so hard, that my attempts to split the log just chews my wedge to pieces. Arctic trees are some of the toughest on earth. Nothing short of a good axe or a steel wedge and sledgehammer are going to dent it. I'm out of luck.

I'm giving it everything I've got, and still my clothes are noticeably looser every day. The sores on my lips have crusted over now, but I'm not getting enough food for the skin to regrow. And yet, every sunset as I make my way out to the open rocks for my nightly ritual of singing down the sun, I forget the empty ache of my belly and the burning in my lips as I watch the dance of the last light across the waves. I truly mean it as I give thanks, once again, for another day. Finding something to be grateful for every day is an anchoring point amongst my other routines, and I can hear the quaver of it in my voice as I let the last notes of my song ring out over the rocks. In a few months, the hours of daylight I had today might feel like a distant memory, so I might as well treasure every one I've got.

Each day I work from first light until it's time for the sunset song. The wobbliness in my thighs comes and goes, but though the hunger never leaves me, my legs continue to carry me and do what I ask of them. There are still a lot of cranberries around, but just thinking about them still makes my stomach clench and my mouth water with nausea.

One day I decide to wander down to the blueberry zone.

The bushes are getting harder to see as more of their brilliant red leaves lie faded on the ground. Every time I come the berries are more shriveled and increasingly apt to squish before I can get them to my mouth. I lick all I can off my fingers, where the sour juice mixes with the bitter spruce pitch and gets significantly less delicious. But still, they're blueberries, and even bitter blueberries are amazing compared to none at all.

I'm probably not gaining many more calories than I'm spending, but I carry on, crawling into the thickets on hands and knees, until the front of my buckskin pants are stained a deep purple.

When I'm cold enough that I have to stop or risk hypothermia, I pry my eyes from the low bushes in front of me and see that the sky is already glowing with color. There's just enough cloud cover to bounce the dusky golden light back down onto the rocks, where the pale granite diffuses it over everything. It's that magical time of day when you feel like you've suddenly stepped into another world.

I'm out on the end of the peninsula, where the rocks are wide open and I'm more aware of the wind and the waves and the vast scope of this place. Everything feels magnified—the sky above me immense, the cliffs on the distant shore even more rugged and mysterious than usual, the water in front of them impossibly wide. The exhilaration warms something inside me even as the wind sucks the heat from my hands and face. I want more. I want all of it, so I climb a little higher until I'm as far up the rocks to the north as I can get. From here I can look out across the lake in three directions. It's been more days than I can remember since I've had a real meal. I have been working to the edge of my capacity, and still not bringing in any food but these meager berries every few days, but I can't remember the last time I felt so incredibly happy, so blessed. There's no other place in the world I want to be. I can't believe my luck. I could have been dropped anywhere, but they put me here— here on this jaw droppingly beautiful peninsula, the most incredible place on earth—where the chickadees flit and the aurora dances before my eyes and I can hear the voices of the ancestors whispering through the trees.

My heart aches trying to hold it all. A gust of wind sets the brilliant yellow birch leaves fluttering in the golden light. Emotion wells up behind my eyes and I let it flow. I turn in slow arcs, overwhelmed by it all, salty tears stinging my crusty lips. I don't even know why I'm crying, it's just all so wild, so impossibly wild and rugged and untamed that I can't hold myself back. I love it so much there are no words for it, there are only tears, and laughter, and then more tears. I weep with awe at this place, and with joy and wonder and gratitude. I adjust the tripod, hating to film this moment, but knowing this is the most important footage I can give the world. More real and true than anything I can share about traps or shelter.

"This right here," I tell the camera. "This is what it's all about. Loving the world so much that you can't help but weep about it. *This*, everyone...This is the real survival skill."

And I feel warm all the way back to the shelter.

29

MAKING OUT WITH A BIRCH TREE

Though getting extra hours of sleep is a great way to conserve calories, ironically, most people have a hard time resting well while calorie deprived. I'm getting used to the routine of lying awake for an hour or more before falling asleep and then for another hour or two at some point in the middle of the night. I keep my ears strained, but the dream beasts never gallop through during these wakeful times, only in the dead of night when I'm somewhere between dreaming and consciousness.

Each morning I grab a handful of spruce tips from the wall and toss them into a pot of hot water. It's lovely to have tea fixings within arm's reach, but I need to do something about these walls. Spruce needles are resinous—once they dry out, this whole place will be a tinder bundle. My plan has been to build solid log walls around the hearth to prevent accidental fires. With the wind that whipped through my walls last night though, it feels clear that no amount of packed boughs are going to stand up against arctic storms. If they are coming right through in September, I don't want to see what they can do in January. I'm going to need solid walls everywhere, not just around the fire, and soon.

I look into the camera and wince. My lips are so stiff with dried pus that I can't drink without them cracking open. Before I can enjoy my tea, I soak the toe of a clean sock in it. It stings against the raw flesh of my lips, but it's warm and comforting, and spruce has mild antimicrobial properties. As the tea drips down my chin, the hard crust softens and sloughs off. When I can move my lips with less pain, I guzzle the rest of the pot, sour with the vitamin C of the needles. The warm liquid hitting my gut starts another sensation there, and I cross my fingers I'll be able to poop today. *How long has it been? Am I even keeping track anymore? Are berries alone enough to keep my digestive system moving?*

I heat a second pot of tea and peel the long johns off of my oozing thighs—losing a little of the tattered skin stuck to the cloth in the process—to give the same treatment to my welts. They are still weeping a bit, but starting to scab over, thank goodness.

My plan for today was another moose hunt, but after a sponge bath to reduce my scent and touching up my broadheads, I pause and just stare into the fire.

Nothing is as simple as it appears in a situation like this. Every expenditure of energy must be carefully weighed. Calories spent versus potential for calories earned. Resources gained versus daylight lost. I've had no luck anywhere near the peninsula with my moose calls and have seen no sign except nibbled twigs from months earlier in the season. The farther I range from home, the farther I have to haul back whatever food I gain. And I don't have free range to wander—each participant has an assigned area that they aren't allowed to leave, but there are no visible boundaries and no maps. The only way I'll know if I'm out of my home zone is if I wander past the invisible "geofence" and get a beep on the GPS device that sends and receives signals. That means if I get close to the edge of my home zone and wound a moose, it could wander beyond my boundaries where I can't follow it without being disqualified.

The whirring hamster wheel in my head is incessant, thoughts tumbling over each other in every waking moment. Food, shelter, firewood, containers. When we get heavy winds and fresh snow, shelter pops to the top of the list. When I'm dealing with cold sores, welts, and constipation, self-care leapfrogs back up. There are never enough daylight hours for everything.

I laugh at my concerns of last summer, thinking that one of the challenges would be avoiding boredom in all my spare time. *Oh, the irony!*

I head out to call for moose in a new location anyway and am returning home, disappointed, when I pass a grove of birch trees and one tree jumps out at me and grabs my attention.

"Hey," I can almost hear it whisper. "Over here."

I'm generally on the lookout for good birch bark, but I wasn't even thinking about it just now. It's uncanny how the longer I'm out here, the more the landscape answers my questions before I even form them.

I'm about to ask if it's willing to be peeled, but of course it is—that's why it reached out to me.

I've never gone so long without human contact, but the word "lonely" has never crossed my mind. The bigger the gap in companionship, the more communication I receive from the land around me, like this tree that basically waved at me to get me to notice it.

My thanks flow through my fingertips as I lay my knife against the trunk and give it a good whack with a fallen branch. I've released the bark at the top of the section I want to peel and am working on the bottom cut when I notice a shiny line running down the birch bark. *Water?* I wipe it with my finger and lick it. *It isn't water, it's sap! Oh my god, it's birch sap—but sweet!*

I have tapped a lot of maple trees, and the unboiled sap has been refreshing, with just the slightest hint of sweetness. It takes forty gallons of maple sap to make one of maple syrup, and at least twice that much for birch syrup, by all accounts. It's cold enough by now that there shouldn't be any sap running; it should all be safely stored away in the roots for the duration of winter, as it's been in every other tree I've cut thus far. Even when it's truly flowing, there's no way it should be this sweet. And yet, here is this delicious nectar flowing out of a tree I would have walked right by if it hadn't flagged me down.

I'm just about to lean in for more when I freeze, remembering the scabs on my lips and suddenly terrified I've contaminated this generous tree. *Is it too late? Have I already transferred the sores?* Then I catch myself and laugh out loud. *Oh my god—it's a tree, Woniya! It doesn't even have lips. It's not going to catch your cold sores.*

Clearly the line between human and non-human is already fuzzier for me than I'd realized. Still giggling and lit up with delight at the flavor, I give myself over to the sweet stickiness, lapping at the cut marks and chasing the drips running down the smooth trunk. I hold the GoPro out at arm's length, imagining how the scene will look to viewers back home. "There's Woniya out in the woods by herself," I narrate, "making out with birch trees."

Eventually, the sap stops running, and I don't want to harm the tree by cutting it more than I need to. The flavor lingers on my tongue long after the encounter. It tastes like a promise. Other creatures are surviving in this place. There's food here, and this land seems to want to feed me. It's just a puzzle I haven't yet solved.

Another flight of honking swans whips my head up. It's becoming an almost daily phenomenon, but today the energy is different. They are flying high and fast without stopping. I understand their urgency, but flying south isn't an option for me, so it's time to get my walls shored up.

30
A PLACE TO CALL HOME

've got a dilemma. I want solid walls outside of my spruce boughs to stop the wind from packing ice and snow into them, but that leaves dry branches around my fire, so it doesn't solve the whole "every wall of my shelter is a dry, resinous tinder bundle" issue.

Double walls with insulation in between would solve both problems, but would be a tremendous amount of work. If I don't bring in more food than just birch sap, the effort might use up enough of my reserves that I won't need to be worried about the harsh winter weather anyway; they might have me packed onto a plane home before it arrives in earnest. *What to do?* Should I build for the long term, trusting that things will work out for me, even though in a week and a half I have managed to gather only a few handfuls of berries, seven grubs, and a few tablespoons of birch sap? Or do I conserve calories and do just what's necessary to get by, knowing it won't see me through the winter but might grant me another couple of weeks out here before I burn through all my body fat?

I know the logical answer—that it's foolish to waste the calories I have left in a big building effort. But logic is just one way of knowing, and not necessarily the most trustworthy. Instead, I breathe deep into my belly and hold each option in my mind, sensing my body's reaction to it.

The answer is clear. The logical, but fear-based route—conserving calories rather than building substantial walls—goes against my instincts and makes my body contract into itself. It's a deep body "no." Choosing to trust—building for winter and believing that the puzzle pieces of how to remain that long will fall into place—feels like a sigh. A relaxation throughout my core. My body says yes to it. *Double walls it is!*

I lay my biggest trunk on the ground for a sturdy sill log and begin stacking the smaller-limbed poles of rough-barked black spruce up into an angled wall against the outside of the boughs. I lash them occasionally as I go, to make sure the walls are structurally sound enough not just to withstand arctic blasts, but errant bears out looking for a final snack before holing up for the winter.

Lashing with paracord innards, thinner than spaghetti and a good deal floppier, is an exercise in frustration. I look around and see a jagged triangle of wood in my firewood stack—the piece that results from sawing my firewood partway through and then breaking it the rest of the way. I carve it down into a long, smooth hourglass shape, tapered to a rounded point on one end. I wrap a length of cord around it, then tie another one onto the end of the first with a surgeon's knot, and repeat. Soon I've got a long wooden spool of thin cordage that I can easily pass back and forth through my wall like a netting needle. I've invented a new building tool—the paraspool.

Chinking the wall with fluffy sphagnum moss as I go, I've got a waist-high, totally solid wall by the time the sun is getting low.

It feels ten degrees warmer tonight as I huddle around the hearth for my evening tea. It's wonderful knowing I have at least one wall that even arctic winds can't blow snow through, but the outer wall has pushed the boughs in tighter, closer to my fire. It's oppressively dark and cramped inside now, and even more flammable than when I started.

The next morning I stare at the interior wall considering this new dilemma. I'd figured on making my interior wall just like the outer wall, but fall equinox isn't far away and when the daylight goes, it's going to go fast. I imagine sitting huddled around the fire between dark gray walls for countless hours of pitch-black winter nights. I contrast that with living in light-colored walls of peeled poles—walls that would reflect the light and heat of the fire back at me and into every corner of the shelter. They'd also dry quickly, adding insulation instead of staying wet and heavy all winter. No brainer. At the same time, peeling every pole will easily take four or five times longer and cost me a lot more calories.

I've been limbing with the sharpened back of the folded saw, using it like a machete, but I have yet to try using it as a drawknife. *Let's try it out before deciding whether or not to peel my poles.* There's a little birch tree with a funky side branch not far from the doorway. I wedge a pole between this branch and the trunk and, with one end there and the other on top of my wall, I've got a perfect sawhorse.

I lay the back of the saw against the pole and pull it toward me. Curls of bark peel off like butter and the clean, spicy scent of spruce pitch wafts up with every stroke. My whole body tingles—this is exactly what I was picturing when I was designing this tool back home. The peeling is so easy and satisfying, particularly after striking out on hunting and fishing day after day, that I find myself singing before I've done half of the pole. My body hums, tuning to the work. It's as if the sawhorse tree grew this way, with this unusual side branch, in anticipation of my needing a woodshop space right here. I don't even stop to ask myself if I should build the inside walls with peeled poles; I just begin on another after the first one is peeled and smile gleefully as bark piles up around my ankles.

I wedge each peeled pole in behind the angled uprights of the shelter's frame and they are held in place by the tension of the spruce boughs pressing in. At three logs tall, it already looks like a wall instead of a particularly thick patch of forest. I can finally see the home I've dreamt of emerging from this humble shelter.

I'd love to just keep peeling, but though I've got trunks lined up along my front walk, they all need to be limbed first.

Now I use the sharpened back edge of the saw like a machete again, standing the pole on its butt end and whacking off one branch at a time. I alternate limbing and peeling and am going along at a good clip. Soon I've got just a few more poles to limb. The second to last one has some particularly thick side branches, and as I give one a good whack, searing pain stabs through my right thumb. I drop the saw in shock. *What did I do? Hit the branch with my thumb?* I look down at my glove.

*No, no, no...*I can see a ragged slice in the thumb of the glove, and through the deep ache in my thumb I feel a slimy, wet texture against the grain of the leather—blood. *Oh god!*

My chest tightens and my breath is shallow and fast. I'm terrified to pull my hand out of the glove, but I have to. *What if the tip of my thumb doesn't come with it?* I ease the glove off and look down. My thumb is flowing with thick crimson droplets. I shake the glove, wincing in anticipation. A spray of blood dots the ground, but no thumb tip, thank god.

The camera is rolling, of course. I film everything out here besides my increasingly rare latrine trips. I tip the lens down to get a good angle on it as I assess the damage.

Don't let it need stitches, don't let it need stitches, is my mantra as I grab the first aid kit and start to clean it. *Of course, I do have that homemade needle...*

It's bad, but not as bad as I'd feared. There are three deep holes in the pad of my thumb, as if someone drove a knife into it several times. At first I can't understand what happened, but then I figure it out. The locking mechanism that keeps the saw folded got loose from the whacking during limbing. On the other hits I had been grabbing the blade and the handle together, thus holding the saw closed. Apparently on the last strike, my grip had been just on the handle and the saw had opened a bit. When I raised it, my thumb slipped between the blade and the handle, and when I hit the branch, all that force had driven the tines—the half inch, double row, razor sharp tines—straight into my flesh. If they had gone much deeper, they would have neatly sliced off the pad of my thumb. As dumb as I feel for this stupid mistake, I know I'm actually incredibly lucky.

I hold it over my head and apply pressure. It takes a while, but eventually the blood slows enough that I can tell it's going to be alright, not anything I need to mention to the production crew. Needing medical assistance is an automatic tap out, and there's no way I'm leaving here for something like this. I cut some medical tape into little strips and tape each hole closed like a doctor would do with butterfly bandages.

After giving my nervous system a while to come back to normal, I assess.

I'm not going to be doing any more limbing or peeling today, and wedging the long poles into the wall requires more force than my hand can take, but I can start on the framing of the front entrance.

I place two uprights on either side of my new doorway, sinking them a few inches into the ground, then measure out a horizontal pole for the top and notch the corners for a snug fit.

My door uprights go to the top of the roof peak, and I stack short lengths of poles into the slot between them and the front of the structure. It works perfectly. *Look at that! A wall!*

It's decided. From here on out, it's no longer a "shelter." A shelter is something temporary that you hole up in for a little while. What I'm looking at here is not just a work of art, it's a cabin, and a cabin is a place you call home.

I face the camera, standing in front of my gorgeous new doorframe. In my delighted exuberance, I completely forget my thumb, raise my arms, and do a big self-high-five.

"Aaaargh! Ow!"

31

THE DIFFERENT HUNGERS

very time I move my hand in the night, the throbbing wakes me up, but by morning it's less tender and the throbbing is dull and distant. Which is a blessing, because in the night, my lips cracked and bled—now the cracks are deeper than the original sores, and I can only take so many calamities at once.

I'm concerned that my lips are getting worse rather than better. If they don't start healing soon, they could get infected, and I want to avoid that at all costs.

At one time, the idea of a lip infection might not concern me. Now I know better.

Years ago on the Oregon homestead, I had been working under incredible stress trying to finish a cabin before fall rains hit. My husband, Bryon, and I were working fifteen-hour days, seven days a week. My body was holding up okay, until my lips started to feel funny. First they were sensitive, then they hurt, then they started to puff up. About four days in, I woke up with my face stuck to my pillow. There was orange fluid oozing from my outrageously distended lips. I looked like a super model after a bad silicone injection. I had a staph infection in my lips, the result of pushing myself so hard that I depleted my system and an opportunistic infection took hold. It took a long time and an intense course of antibiotics to get it under control, and the fear of ever dealing with that again has never left me.

What I have now are clearly just cold sores, but my body is under as much stress now as it was then, and I don't want to take any chances. Between the cold sores, the welts, and now my thumb, it's time I made myself some medicine. What can I use, though, having none of the medicinal herbs I hoped to find here?

Aha! I've got it! There's a plant I know from Ontario, sweet gale, growing on the southwest shore. The Anishinaabe friends who hosted me in Ontario told me it's highly medicinal, a cure-all of sorts.

The medicine of sweet gale is mostly in the seed heads. They are pungent, spicy, and sticky with resin. Closing your eyes and taking a deep whiff, you can imagine yourself entering an old apothecary shop, with rows of dusty jars lining the walls and envelopes of bitter, fragrant herbs on the counter. I don't need much for my salve, and it's so potent that even on the short walk back home it stains my pockets yellow.

I pour the sweet gale into my pot lid and scrape a fingerful of my precious pemmican fat in as well. I heat it gently, stirring it constantly as the oil takes on the vivid yellow and medicinal qualities of the plant. I've been collecting hard balls of spruce pitch for fire making and glue, but it's also antibiotic and good for wounds, so I powder some under the flat of my knife and crumble it in as well.

Now I need a container for my medicine. I spy one of my pieces of birch bark—*that will do nicely*. I warm the bark to soften it and fold it into a small rectangular box. I cut some short lengths of small, green spruce branches, split one end of each and use them as clips to hold the folds in place. Presto—*birch bark origami!*

I pour my warm salve into the little box and my wilderness apothecary is in business.

I swipe up a fingerful, touch it lightly to my lips, and sigh with relief as the crusty sores begin to soften. Knowing I can make my own medicine from the land gives me peace of mind almost more valuable than the salve itself. I coat my lips and dab it onto my thighs and thumb with satisfaction—*no more anxiety about infection!*

That taken care of, hunger is now my most pressing concern. My head swims as I stand up. Days keep passing, and I'm barely eating, but I'm reluctant to dig back into my pemmican. Every day I go hungry, the little bag of it feels more and more like gold. It isn't just physical; it's psychological. Knowing I have it means everything. It's my little bag of happiness and well-being; why would I give that up for a couple of minuscule meals? But my pants have more space in them every day and soon I'll need more holes in my belt to keep them up. My body is shifting faster than I would have thought possible. I should be more methodical with my pemmican consumption. The block has dwindled and is now roughly four by four by eight inches. I carefully cut off a one-by-one-inch cube and scrape off fine shavings with my teeth, savoring every bit and making it last a full, heavenly, five minutes.

Every moment out here I'm exponentially hungrier than I've ever been, and yet the hunger is entirely different than I imagined it would be. I'd thought of it as one thing with many levels of intensity, but now I know there are many kinds of hunger. There's habitual hunger—based not on caloric demands, but on entrenched behavioral patterns. When you're used to eating at noon, for example, you typically start feeling hungry ten minutes before, whether you had a big breakfast that day or not. Then there's physical hunger, based more on need. This one is present for me these days as a constant ache in my core. Sometimes it's just background noise that I barely notice, but occasionally it rears up in sharper, more urgent waves, and I find myself dropping what I'm doing and wandering out to the berry patches or roaming the woods with my bow. Then there's a different kind of hunger, one that's less physical but takes over my mind and fills it with images of dark red beaver meat sizzling over coals and bear cracklings crumbled over fillets of lake trout. The physical hunger, though ever-present, is much less uncomfortable than I imagined it would be. It's the psychological hunger that takes over my brain with constant visions and cravings that is most challenging. What amazes me though, is that, while this hunger takes over my thoughts, it has yet to control my actions (with the exception of the one time I took a second bite of pemmican before I realized what I was doing). Every day I have intensely powerful food cravings, yet I spend hours within an arm span of the pemmican and manage to resist reaching for it except for those days I choose as "pemmican days." Somehow, under extreme calorie duress, I'm showing more restraint than I've ever had in my normal, calorie-saturated life. I'm stunned by the difference, and frankly, incredibly impressed with myself.

Right now, the hunger is pressing, and one bite of pemmican isn't quieting it. I pick and eat as many crowberries as I can manage—which is only a couple of handfuls—then remember the delicious grubs. *If there was one tree with grubs there should be others, right?*

I head back to the spot and knock over two more rotten birches. I go over every inch of wood under the bark, but there's nothing. I've never been somewhere so devoid of insect life. Apparently, there were only seven grubs on the whole peninsula, and I went and ate them all at once.

I return to my building project with only the watery berries in my belly. It's slow going, as my thumb can't take the impact of whacking the branches off of my poles, and sawing them takes much longer.

The evening hours are when the hunger hangs heaviest. I feel warmest and most content when working on the cabin, and most tortured by long hours by the fire contemplating my empty belly. I shift my activity patterns accordingly, working on the cabin well into the dark hours by the light of my headlamp.

Tonight when I finally settle in, I've got a high wall of blond wood bouncing the fire light back at me. Against its bright backdrop, I see a caddisfly—similar to a moth—flap past me. My hand darts out and grabs it before I even realize I'm reaching for it. I've never considered eating a caddisfly before, but trout do it. If I'm not eating trout, I might as well go right to the source and eat trout food.

I put the pot lid onto the rocks above the coals, wait a minute, then toss the small insect into my hot pan. The scent of burning wings hits me at once. *Damn, it's already too hot!* I wrap the edge of my thick sweater sleeve around my hand as a hot pad and grab the lid, but now there's another burning protein smell filling my nose.

I drop the lid before I feel the pain, expecting to see a scorch mark on the sweater, but it has already burned right through the sweater and into my hand. My thumb and fingertip each have a hardened yellow line where the rim of the lid touched them. The finger burn is mostly superficial, but on my thumb, the burn has gone through the calloused surface of the pad, and I can see the raw tissue beneath glistening red. *Holy hell, that's both thumbs down!*

It hurts like anything, but the heat cauterized the wound. I'm far more concerned about the hole in my sweater, which is already starting to unravel.

Burned and stabbed, oozing lips and throbbing thighs, empty belly and shaky legs, and now the sweater I worked so hard for starting to come apart. I'm quite a sight, but through it all, I'm still happy just to be here, and hey—at least it was the overly long sleeve that burned! How lucky is that?

The caddisfly is scorched, but I eat what's left of it, laughing at myself. There are more calories in the burned portions of my finger and thumb—maybe I should have just nibbled on those and saved myself the effort.

32

SURVIVAL FOODS

The next morning I'm on my way back from another failed fishing mission when I see a great rock for a chimney stone. As I'm awkwardly scuffling home with it, I notice the swath of reindeer moss I have kicked up in the process. *Okay, okay, I hear you reindeer moss.* "I surrender," I sigh, and shove the moss, almost resentfully, into my pockets.

I had hoped it wouldn't come to this, but it's reached that time.

"Survival foods" are called that not because they're great to have in a pinch, but because you would never want to eat them unless you had no other choice. True moss isn't edible, but as reindeer moss is actually a lichen, and some lichens have food value, it's considered a survival food. I have eaten some decent lichens in my day—rock tripe in the Midwest and *Bryoria sp.* in the Rocky Mountains. Not delicious, but doable. Reindeer moss, on the other hand, not only has low food value but also has toxins you need to eliminate before even thinking about eating it. It produces acids capable of breaking down granite over time, which will do a number on your digestive tract unless you boil it in several changes of water first. Hungry as I am, there's nothing in my body that looks at it and thinks, *Oh yeah, that's definitely food...*

But I can do the math. The hard physical labor and freezing temperatures are burning through my reserves at an alarming rate. There's no sign that my moose calls are working or that I'm ever going to catch a fish in these marginal waters. It's time to start thinking seriously about survival foods.

A lot of people talk about the inner bark of trees as a survival food, but that's when the sap is actually flowing in it. Besides the fluke of that one amazing birch tree, every ounce of sugar is stored deep in the roots this time of year.

Even so, I've tried. I've tasted the inner bark of the spruces I've peeled and tried other birch trees too. Not happening. No other birches have had flowing sap, and the spruce bark is disgustingly bitter and tastes like turpentine, which it basically is. Maybe getting some lichen in my belly will steady the wobbling in my legs.

Speaking of legs—I haven't checked my thighs for a while. I drop my pants and see that, while the lumps are still raised and red, there are no new ones, and the existing ones look less inflamed and more scabbed over than they did yesterday. Progress! *Thank you, wilderness salve!*

I gather up about a gallon of reindeer moss, shaking the gravel from the bottom.

Even after soaking in water, the "moss" is remarkably springy and tough. Boiling it in four changes of water will be an all-day commitment and a lot of trips down to the lake. The first boil turns the water a yellow-brown color that I'm hoping shows the toxins leaching out, but does little to change the texture.

I get to work building as the second round heats up.

So I can keep more wood dry, I decide to add a firewood alcove to the front of the cabin. I begin by sorting through my materials. I've been selective with the branches, using only the bushiest ones for insulation and piling the scraggly ones I've deemed the "wimpy branches" to the side. I need to stay close to feed the fire and keep the boil going, so I can't head out and harvest more trees and branches. *Wait a minute*, I think. *These scraggly ones won't shed snow, but they're great for structure. Why have I been considering these boughs less worthy?*

Screw that judgment. They might not be bushy, but that doesn't mean they aren't important resources. After all, I was what most people, myself included, considered a wimpy kid, and look where I am now.

Public school isn't kind to small, brainy, socially awkward children. I always chose my seat carefully on the bus, well within view of the bus driver, so the two bullies, girls a year ahead of me in school with something to prove, couldn't corner me as easily. In first grade, some boys in my class literally picked me up and stuck me headfirst into a trash can. It was utterly humiliating. When I cleaned myself up and got back to class, I whispered to the teacher why I was late coming back from recess. She shamed the boys in front of the class, and I was even more mortified. A real boost to my popularity ensued, I assure you.

Our early experiences are powerful conditioning. Even when, in college, I finally started believing in my physical capacity, it was tentative, as I'd had a lifetime of training reinforcing my self-deprecating beliefs. No one who knew me back then would have imagined the woman I've matured into, yet here I am, surviving on my own in the Arctic, building my own cabin from what I can find in the woods around me.

There is no such thing as a wimpy branch, I decide, *only a branch that has yet to find its true calling*. I launch into altering the cabin. I add poles to reform the space to accommodate my wood storage and use the redesignated "fully functional, sparsely needled branches" to shore up the gap between the alcove and the rest of the wall.

By the time the alcove is complete, and I've gotten my north wall a few poles higher, it's near dark and I'm on the fourth boil. While the water is paler every time, the lichen hasn't changed perceptibly since the first boil. I've blown through most of my firewood cooking it for so long, so before eating, I spend an hour cutting more—probably using more calories than I'll get from the lichen.

Ice crystals are sparkling in the black air around me as I cut and stack the last of my firewood. Finally, it's time for my reward. *Dinner!*

I rewarm the pot, grab a handful of reindeer moss and begin to chew. And chew. And chew.

There is no flavor, but that's okay, I hadn't really expected any. What I did expect was that chewing the stuff would be the first step in actually swallowing it. That doesn't seem to be the case. Sure, the pieces are getting smaller and smaller, but apparently none of them have any intention of going down my throat. It feels just like chewing on a green scrubby pad. They say you can eat this lichen, but is there some critical piece of information missing, like there is about when you can and can't eat inner bark?

I force the wad down, little by little. You could swallow a green scrubby too, if you were determined to—does that make it food?

I take another wad of lichen and try again to chew and swallow it. Like the crowberry seeds, it triggers my gag reflex. My body is very clear that it doesn't want this. I think of Jesse on *Season 5* of *Alone*, eating almost a whole spruce tree worth of bark just to have something to fill his belly with, and then ending up with a medical evacuation for obstructed bowels. I've had zero urge to poop for days. Do I want to take a system that's already under stress and cram it full of something it doesn't want and likely can't process?

I give up, dump the rest of the pot onto the rocks by the fire and heat water for my standard dinner—chaga tea.

In the morning the lichen is dry, so I toast it over the fire until it's crunchy and golden and try it that way. The texture is different but no more palatable, and my body is no more enthusiastic about it. Cross another survival food off the list.

There's still uva-ursi, also known as kinnikinic. It's a low-growing manzanita that thrives at high altitudes and in northern regions like this one. There's a lot of it around the peninsula, and though its clusters of bright red berries look appealing, I've never considered them food. The fact that they seem totally unmolested by wildlife in a resource-limited landscape is not a good sign. Still, I harvest a couple of handfuls and give them a try. The biting astringency sucks my mouth up into a pucker. Astringent foods are constipating—*no freaking way I'm adding that to the mix.*

I try every possible way to prepare the uva-ursi berries. Cooked, they're no different than raw, so I try peeling the skin off and eating only the mealy flesh, with the same results. Boiled, baked, powdered, or pulverized, they are no different. Prepared every way, they shrivel my mouth, and my body is clear about its feelings.

That's it, the last of the survival foods I have. At least I can say I tried everything.

33
LIVING ON BEAUTY

Having established that no food is coming in unless I change my strategies, I rally my energy for a scout farther afield. If I can't fish the big lake, maybe I can find a smaller one. There's a small depression in the bluffs, what looks to be a mile or so inland. I won't know my boundary line unless I cross it and get a beep on my GPS device, but I'm guessing the spot I'm looking at is within my allotted land base. It's a haul, but if it is a lake and I can put up a supply of smoked fish with a few days' effort, it will be worth the hike.

I take a double bite of pemmican to fortify myself and head up the rocky ledges between the cabin and the mainland. My legs feel good today. I love walking the open rocks—the land and water spreading out in every direction and the wind slapping my loose hair against my cheeks. I spend a while combing my fingers through it every couple of days, but hair ties were off-limits and keeping it from becoming a tangled rat's nest is a constant struggle. I set up the camera again for one of those "windswept and rugged" shots of me negotiating the bluffs, bow in hand. I note some landmarks from the top to help me navigate.

Once I'm confident I've memorized the lay of the land, I hike back for the camera, then out again. Every step of forward progress is three steps when filming—out with the camera rolling, back to gather it up, then out again to where I'd gotten before I turned around. Three times the effort, three times the calories.

The plants are different on the mainland, and I can see some sparse vegetation upslope whose scraggly shape looks familiar. I get closer and—*yes! Wild roses!* They've already lost most of their leaves, but beautiful red rose hips, the fruit of the rose plant, are still clinging to the branches. There isn't a lot to them, but the flesh, made softer by the hard freezes, is chock full of vitamin C. They do, at least, have considerably more food value than air, which is my current alternative. I eat what I can and fill my pockets.

My destination is straight uphill, and I snack on them as I climb. In my regular life I also snack on rose hips, but first I usually carefully scrape out the seeds and the little hairs that cling to them. The seeds are hard, and the hairs are like fiberglass, itchy in the mouth and throat. Back at our prelaunch base camp, Dave told us the native people where he lives call them "itchy bum fruit." Apparently, the hairs make it through the digestive system unscathed and come out every bit as irritating as they went in. I'm unconcerned. Judging by the last week, I might never poop again. If I do, I might just relish the itch as a reminder of a job well done.

It's amazing to be so far inland and up this high. The open ledges give good views in all directions and are bounded on either side by what seem to be solid stands of white birch. I spy a dark lump on one of them and shimmy up the trunk to carve off a nice piece of chaga.

Before I want them to, the open rocks level off into soil, and in no time I'm elbowing my way through thick forest. Raspy branches grab at my hair and pack, making my progress frustratingly slow. Every ten feet or so I realize my hat is missing and turn around to find it clinging to a branch behind me.

I come to the edge of the stand and swing wide to avoid the thick trees—a less direct route, but much less infuriating. By midday the pemmican has long since worn off, but amazingly, my legs continue to feel strong.

I'm getting close. I'm headed into a bowl of land, with ridges all along the skyline. *Please be a lake, please be a lake.*

The trees give way to low shrubs and the moss thickens. I crane forward—I can't see the middle of the bowl yet, but I can see where the trees stop. I set up the big camera again and hike holding the small one, the moment of truth palpably close.

But—no. My belly sinks. It's a low spot, yes. There's water, yes. It's about six feet across, less than a foot deep, and frozen solid. It isn't a lake; it's a tiny, frozen mudhole.

Double damn! This was my best hope for a lake in all the land I can see from the peninsula. But then, I'm up here now, over ten times higher than the tallest rocks back there. *Can I get even higher? High enough to see other possibilities?* The surrounding peaks are too sheer to climb, but I remember noting a more manageable one on my way up.

The big camera set to watch my ascent, I hike with a handheld camera and a GoPro. This is the most exposed I've been in my time here. The wind whips my hair around and steals the breath from my lungs, but the land spreading out below me sends a thrill through my body that's better than warmth.

The difference between what I can see here versus from the rocks back on the peninsula is like the difference between a movie theater and IMAX. I'm nearly as high as I was in the helicopter, but here the view is 360 degrees, and there's no glass between me and the land. I turn around and gasp—the distant cliffs that make my eastern backdrop from the peninsula aren't the mainland at all; they're yet another long narrow spit of land. Beyond it is more water than I have seen all at once. I can also see the finger of low, forested land I always stare at from my own north shore, wondering if it's an island or a peninsula. Now I can see the water wrapping around the far side of it. It's an island. The immensity of the world spread out beneath me floors me. I know the other participants are out there somewhere, but as far as my eyes can see there's no sign of anything but rock and trees and endless water.

I feel more than ever like the only person on earth—and it isn't lonely; it's exhilarating. When I've climbed high peaks elsewhere the landscape looks foggy and surreal from the top, but here it's up close and technicolor, as if I could reach out and touch it. I throw my arms wide and scream with exhilaration. I suck in the cold air, breathing in the wildness, the wind and rock, the orange and red colors dancing in the branches and the foamy white caps along the infinite shoreline. And I'm fed. I don't feel the emptiness in my belly; I feel the fullness of what it is to be so in love with a place that there's no room for anything else.

When I get back to the camera there are tears streaming down my cheeks, but I don't care—I want the world to see this. I want everyone out there to know this unbelievable feeling of joy and freedom.

I didn't see any food prospects from up there, but I saw the world—the whole world. That is enough, and more than I could have asked for.

The wonder lingers the whole way back down and onto the peninsula. My legs don't fail me for a second—not a wobble, not a quiver. When I get there, I drop my pack and head right out to the rock arena for my weekly dance party.

I'm juiced up with the hike and the emotion, fully in my body, and channeling the moment on those rocks into the sway of my hips and stomps of my feet. I dance until I'm breathless, then, sweating and laughing, I thank the sun for its light and sing it down into the lake before heading back home.

In the days that follow, something shifts in me. Time passes. I work on the cabin. I work on other projects. I call for moose. I try to fish. I haul stones for a chimney and carve trap sets for deadfalls, with no more success than before. But I no longer spend my days thinking about how hungry I am. I haul water, poles, and firewood. I eat my scant ball of pemmican every other day. I build the walls of the cabin, at every opportunity making the choices that will help me be here long term, rather than the ones that save energy now but sacrifice comfort and sustainability in the winter months.

But I no longer feel weak or light-headed. The welts begin to heal, and no new ones rise up to take their place. My belly feels different—not full, certainly, but not twisting and achy. I haven't had even the slightest urge to poop for a while, but as I'm barely eating, I decide to stop worrying about it.

I know logically that I can't go on like this forever, but there's something inside me that clings to the idea that maybe I can. I've got loved ones back home eating a little extra on my behalf and doing their best to "beam me the calories." Maybe those calories are reaching me. Maybe the energy is getting here though the substance isn't. Maybe I've learned to shift my metabolism, to feed myself on what is here instead of focusing on what I lack.

That's it! I realize, and it resonates deep in my core. *I'm learning to live on something different. I'm learning to live on beauty.*

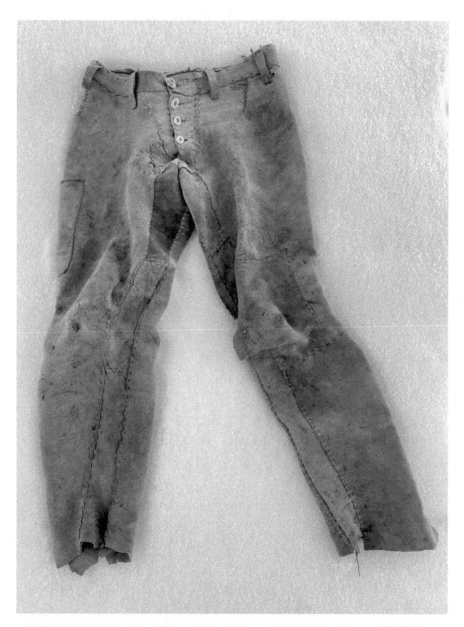

The fifteen-year-old, home-tanned and handsewn buckskin pants I wore on Season 6.

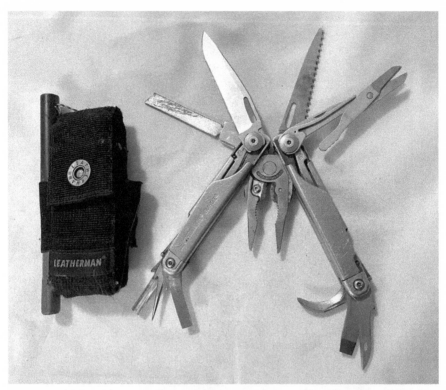

TOP: The Leatherman Surge, with a variety of special modifications, which I depended on in the Arctic. BOTTOM: My paraspool, with lengths of paracord innards tied together into one long strand of cordage.

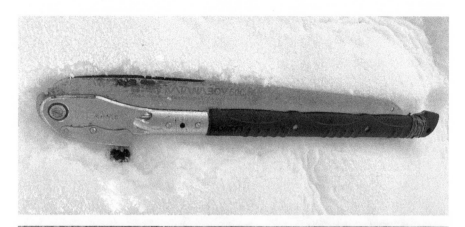

TOP: My Silky Katanaboy folding saw, shown still sticky with spruce pitch. The dark line on the lower left is where it is sharpened for use as a drawknife and cutting edge. BOTTOM: Me with a mountain chickadee in 2021. Years after my *Alone* Season 6 adventure, chickadees are still one of my favorite animals on the planet. *Photo by Taylor Donovan, January 2021. Used with permission.*

Detail of the homemade, wool-lined, buckskin overalls that were part of why I missed my original flight to Yellowknife. The button is one of my salt buttons, dunked in black wax.

PART THREE

EMBODYING ARTEMIS

34
SURVIVING AS A WOMAN

'm more settled in my mind and body after my epiphany about living on beauty, but I don't let it keep me from my hunting and gathering efforts. I'm hiking up the mainland to pick more rose hips the next morning, when I see ducks in the reeds near shore. The water looks shin-deep at most, so I drop my gear and shrug off my bulky sweater as quietly as I can, and creep out toward the water with my bow.

The reeds are so thick I can't get a clear shot from shore, but I've got my tall rubber boots on, so I take a chance and step into the lake. *Nice*—the ducks are feeding so intently, heads down in the muck, that they don't notice me. Fifteen feet out, the water is only up to my ankles. I'm getting so excited that it's hard to move as slowly as I should. *This might really happen!*

Their low quacking and splashing masks the sound of the mud sucking at my boots, but by the time I'm close enough for a good shot, they start to drift farther out toward open water. *Damn it.* I'm about to miss my chance, so I take one more step to steady myself before drawing my bow. My foot sinks in past where the bottom should be and suddenly my right leg plunges down into the water. Before I even grasp what's happening, it's thigh deep. Cold water rushes into my boot and swirls around my leg. The shock of it takes my breath away as I wrestle to free my leg without tipping face forward into the lake. My hands sink into the muck, giving me nothing to push off of, but the outstretched bow in my hand gives me better purchase. I use it to heave myself back upright, but now the lake is exploding with frantic flapping. Crap, there goes my duck dinner. Everywhere else around me the water still looks shallow. Apparently I managed to find the one deep sinkhole.

I'm too concerned with what I need to do to keep myself safe to feel the disappointment. It all happened so fast that I hardly feel the cold yet, but I need to get warm and dry before the adrenaline wears off and the shivering starts. I wade awkwardly back to solid ground, wrench my boot off, and pour out the thick brown water, very grateful I was smart enough to leave my sweater on shore.

Back at camp, I peel off my dripping clothes. Even wrung out, they are brown and stained. *Looks like it's laundry day.* I've still got one dry pair of long johns, but my buckskin pants are soaked and my welty thighs, though healing, are far too sensitive for my scratchy wool pants. *Wait a minute*—I rifle through my pack and find the oversized wool buff I made from a sweater and pull it down over my long underwear. *Heck yeah! Why didn't I think of this before? A skirt! Perfect!*

Being excited to wear a skirt on television is a dramatic turnaround for me. I went a good portion of my early adulthood adamantly avoiding skirts and dresses.

It's less true now than it was thirty years ago, but there's still a serious gender bias in the fields of bushcraft, survival, and wilderness skills, not to mention carpentry and other things I like to do. Tired of being talked down to and having to deal with inappropriate comments, in my early twenties I started to downplay my womanhood in order to be taken more seriously. If being perceived as "pretty" meant a focus on my appearance and not my brains or skill level, then screw pretty. I slowly eliminated most things considered feminine from my world—skirts, dresses, jewelry, makeup, you name it. I convinced myself I was rejecting societal standards of beauty and what it meant to be a woman. It wasn't until my early thirties that I realized these choices weren't changing the gender bias, they were catering to and reinforcing it. Rejecting my own femininity wasn't liberating me, it was internalizing sexism.

It took some time to shrug off my own conditioning and get a clear sense of what *I* actually wanted, regardless of others' expectations. Turns out, sometimes I love running around in the woods in homemade buckskins that still smell of smoke, other times throwing on a pair of coveralls and diving elbow-deep into deer blood or motor oil. I also still enjoy wearing dresses, lipstick, and big dangly earrings. I'm perfectly capable of tanning a hide, swinging a hammer, or changing a tire regardless, and I don't need to dress in any particular way to prove it.

It's a little chilly out here for just a skirt and leggings, but I pull on my thigh-high socks and feel considerably toastier. I still have a big gap between the skirt and the socks, though. I have an idea—socks are the least-limited item in my wardrobe. I was allowed six pairs, so I can afford to sacrifice one. I cut the socks at the ankle using my Leatherman and toss aside the foot sections. I use the magic needle I made from the shard of metal I found in my tarp to hem the edges so they won't unravel. Now I have long tubes instead of socks, which I can pull higher up my legs and which close the gap between my boots and my skirt.

I feel like the most fashionable *Alone* participant in history as I set up a paracord laundry line in my knit miniskirt and leg warmers and hang my freshly washed buckskin pants up to dry.

I actually asked the production team last summer if I could switch out the allotted T-shirt for a dress. I find dresses comfortable and practical, and I loved the idea of confronting the stereotypical image of all survivalists necessarily wearing technical cargo pants. I got a firm "no." I understood it: a dress has more material, and therefore could be considered an advantage. But I'm thrilled that, without even planning it, I have found a way to represent not just women, but femininity on *Alone*.

Every gender, everywhere along the spectrum, has its own gifts and challenges. Big masculine people have more strength for certain projects but also burn through calories faster. Hauling a moose back to camp might take me more trips, but food goes further in smaller frames like mine, so that moose would last me significantly longer. Femininity can also come with the kind of intuition, deep listening, and relational skills that have characterized the most beautiful parts of my time out here. After so many years of denying my femininity, I'm thrilled to be living wild and loving it, not *in spite* of being a woman but partly *because* of being a woman.

35

THE TIPPING POINT

t's a special day, clear and beautiful, with rosy dawn light filtering in from the east. I'm excited about it from the moment I first open my eyes.

Every morning I film myself talking about my plans for the day and reporting anything of note from the night before. Today, I decide to film my morning log outside, so I head to a lovely backdrop of birch trees on the edge of the rock arena, painted pink by the rising sun.

I feel as lit up as the trees as I hit "record" and look into the camera.

"Today," I say, staring directly into the lens, "is a magical day. The day that everything changes."

And it's true. It isn't just the morning light and clear weather I'm excited about. This is the fall equinox. It's the tipping point of the year, the day the dark and the light are equally balanced, right before the Northern Hemisphere plunges decisively toward winter. My Celtic ancestors took note of and honored such seasonal markers—equinoxes, solstices, and the midway points between them—and I try to do the same. Each holds their own special energy, and the equinoxes, as a day of balance, outside of the momentum of growing or fading light, is one of untapped potential. Just as it's the tipping point of the year, I'm confident it's going to be my tipping point as well.

I believe the intentions we carry on these seasonal holidays hold extra weight, fortified by the momentum of the planet and the seasons. I also believe that, though intentions alone are powerful, they are more likely to come true if you really believe them. And for some reason, this morning, I do. Maybe it's that I've learned to make peace with my hunger, pushing past that physical limitation and learning to thrive while living on beauty. Today I have a deep sense that something else is coming, and now is my time to start not just surviving, but sur*thriving*.

I turn my face into the rising sun, gathering up as much of its glow as I can. Then, with conviction, I turn square to the camera and say, "Just like the changing seasons, today is the day when my luck here changes. Today, I start bringing in real food."

Though this is officially the first day of autumn, and often still tank-top weather where I come from, up here it's winter I feel in the air, not fall. I can almost taste it, subtle but unmistakable—a metallic tang on my tongue.

Most winged creatures are following a primal urge to rush south toward light, warmth, and steady food before it's too late. And here I stand, with no fur, feathers, or stores of food, digging my heels in thousands of miles north of the land I call home, as arctic winter draws in.

I head out to fish the peninsula's furthest point. The recent storm has stripped most of the leaves from the birch branches. Instead of rustling overhead, they now make brilliant golden confetti under my feet, thick as a carpet and deeper still in the crevices between the rocks.

I do my best to hold firm in the belief that my fishing luck will change today. My optimism wanes as I cast, reel in, and cast again, seeing no ripples, splashes, or signs of life.

A breeze picks up, gentle at first, but before long my hair is fluttering against my cheeks.

Finally, the glassy surface has turned into foamy whitecaps and my line is getting driven back to shore as fast as I can throw it out. I'm forced, once again, to pack up, empty-handed.

Trudging home, disappointed but determined to keep faith, I hear chattering from a tree ahead. There's a squirrel in a low branch yelling at me. By now I have lost enough arrows to be cautious of even the low shots. This branch, though, is backed by solid rock. There's no way my arrow can disappear.

I've missed too many hunting opportunities because setting up the big camera has alerted the game to my presence. This time the GoPro on my head is already running, so I leave the other camera in my pack and hold my breath as I feel around my pack for an arrow with a small point that won't cut the squirrel in half like a broadhead would. My eyes never leave the squirrel as I find the right arrow, draw it quietly from the quiver, and fix it in place.

I inhale as I draw the bow in one fluid motion, exhale and hold as I steady it, aim, and release. Time slows as my awareness flies toward the branch with my arrow, and I watch in stunned amazement as the point catches the squirrel in the chest, swipes it off the branch, and pins it to the moss below. *Oh my god! I've done it! I got the squirrel!*

My sense of time and place returns as I rush to it. Flecks of blood—foamy with air bubbles and brilliant red from being freshly oxygenated—dot the green moss and confirm that it's a lung shot. Its chest is warm and vibrates under my hand as I pour gratitude through my fingers; but gratitude isn't a big enough word to express what I feel in this moment. Awe comes closer. This small life will have more of an impact on my own than anything I have ever eaten. My hands shake with emotion as I pick it up, and my eyes sting as tears of relief and gratitude well up.

Then I remember the date. *It happened! It actually happened!* My luck has finally changed, and on the equinox itself, just as I said it would. The tipping point indeed!

I pick up my quiver, stroking the bobcat fur along its edge. The promise of last spring—inviting the huntress into me as I consumed the bobcat's body—has come to fruition. "Thank you, beauty. It worked," I whisper and kiss the spotted fur as I tuck the squirrel into the quiver alongside my arrows. I head back toward the cabin with my head held high and a new sense of vitality in every step, as if I can already feel the energy of the coming meal.

I'm just reaching the boulder field near the cabin when I hear an unfamiliar sound. A flutter of wings draws my eyes to a large, round shape close to the trunk of the spruce tree up ahead.

It's a grouse!

You are kidding me! Wow, equinox, you aren't messing around!

I had expected the approach of winter would mean birds leaving but hadn't realized some would also be arriving. Thus far there's been no sign of grouse whatsoever, and I had come to believe the peninsula was devoid of game birds—just as it was devoid of fishable waters, large game, and most other food prospects. Yet here it is, another equinox gift.

Once again, I slowly lower the pack to the ground.

Please, I ask the universe. *Please, please, please!*

I can tell by its muted colors and markings that it's a female, and she seems contentedly roosted, so I take the time to quietly set up the camera and tripod and aim them at the branch.

I've still got the same arrow I shot the squirrel with on the bow string, so I take aim and release. My arrow goes high, just over her head, and disappears into a thick cluster of trees. She fidgets but doesn't take off.

I shift position so I'm shooting toward rocks, not a spruce grove.

I draw out another arrow, raise the bow again, and release. *Aaargh! Low!* She cranes her neck down and looks at her feet, curious about what happened, and I hear my arrow clatter on the rocks.

I'm overexcited—too much adrenaline. I need to slow down. I'm down to the last arrow I've got with me, a broadhead. I've been saving them for moose, but it's better to use it for a grouse that's here than a moose that might never come.

I hold the arrow to my heart, breathe deeply to calm myself, and draw again. I hold my breath until I know I'm still, and release. The arrow flies straight toward the center of her chest. As it hits she explodes into flight in a spray of feathers, and swiftly disappears behind the trees of the spruce grove.

What? She took off? How could she take off?

There's no way I could have missed. I watched the arrow pass right through her, but she's gone.

I find the second and third arrows on the rocks behind the tree. The shaft of the last one is tacky with blood and countless small, downy feathers cling to it.

I scan the ground for sign, but there's no blood trail, nothing to follow. Bird skin is elastic and closes around small wounds. Beating wings would vaporize blood that managed to fall into a fine spray, impossible to see against the speckled rocks and moss.

I take stock. She's perfectly camouflaged, and airborne. *If I was a grouse, mortally wounded and feeling in danger, what would I do?* I would head to where I felt safest—the thicker trees between here and the lake.

I leave my gear where it lies and head that way. No camera, no distractions. The idea of taking a life and letting it go to waste would be repulsive to me even if I wasn't starving, but I *need* this grouse. I'm deeply appreciative of the squirrel, but I'm not kidding myself about how many calories are in an animal roughly the size of my fist. Less than I've spent this morning. The hunger that I had learned to live happily with has shifted at the sight of that bloody arrow and is now rising up in me. I can feel it inside like a tense hand gripping my belly, pulling me forward toward wherever the wounded bird may be.

The feathers on her chest match the gray blotches of lichen on the granite. She could be anywhere on these rocks; I could almost step on her before I see her. My heart is beating hard against my ribcage. My whole system is flooded with adrenaline, and I'm hot and sweaty even though it can't be above forty degrees. Tunnel vision is one of the side effects of an activated nervous system. I can feel it happening; my visual field is closing in. I push myself to shift my focus from what is right in front of me to the broader vision we call "Owl Eyes" in tracking and nature awareness. With Owl Eyes, one can take in the greater patterns of the landscape and more easily spot anything that looks out of place.

I circle the grove, walking the rocky ledges, but see no form breaking up the angular lines of the rocks, no cloudy pile of fluff and feathers.

I elbow my way into the grove, where the spruces grow so thick their branches touch one another. The ground is scattered with blocky boulders carpeted with sphagnum moss five inches deep, and underbrush that grabs at my legs and boots. In every ten square feet of forest there are probably fifty places a grouse could disappear. I'm methodical, looking into the branches of every tree, underneath every fallen limb, and behind every boulder. I keep my eyes open for the bright pink fletching of the lost arrow as I look, but I see no more sign of it than I do of her.

I reach the far side, come back around, then continue spiraling inward until I have searched the whole thing twice. Nothing.

I can't give up, but the squirrel has been sitting for a while now, and I need to tend to it.

Back at the cabin I skin it carefully, then lay each tiny, precious organ into the cook pot. I tuck the rest of the carcass in, place the skin next to it, and lock the lid down tight. For the first time, I actually have something I need to protect from mice and scavengers.

When I'm done, my panic about the grouse has passed. I'll find her. I'm sup-posed to find her, but maybe the universe requires that I share this moment with the world in order to receive its gift. I start up the big camera and hold it out at arm's length, pointed at my face as I search. I let myself see the land as she would—having burst from the tree, full of adrenaline.

How far would panic drive her?

I've thoroughly searched the rocks and the trees. Now I walk the edge between them, peering between birch trunks into the thick forest.

I muse out loud as I search, "I just don't know how far a grouse can go wounded. I know a bear can run thirty yards after it's been shot in the heart."

Then, I see a rounded shape against the green ground cover and gasp—*are those feathers?*

36

NAMING ARTEMIS

O h my god it is! It's her! I've found her!

I'd swear I already looked here, but this time there's a ray of sun shining through the trees. The grouse is glowing as I pick her up, and the light catches the white feathers of her breast and head. She's the most beautiful thing I've ever seen, so sleek and graceful. Her head lolls and one bright drop of blood dribbles from her beak. A perfect lung shot, yet she flew another fifty yards to die in this peaceful stand of white-trunked birches, where I can hear the waves lapping the shore.

What an incredible turnaround. I can hardly believe I have been so blessed. It's all too perfect. My throat swells and I'm crying before I know it. I can hardly contain myself. I'm overwhelmed by it—to have searched so hard and almost given up, but to have held faith; to have felt hunger so deep in my body, but still been utterly grateful for every second here; to have laid my life on these rocks and asked this place to feed me and then when it didn't, to say, "That's okay, I'll find something else to live on"; and to have found sustenance in beauty. It was all meant to be and has all culminated in this.

This is the moment when I know I belong. My chest swells with the knowledge. My breath feels bigger—no, *I* feel bigger, my lungs and heart taking up more room, my shoulders wider. The land has tested me every step of the way—tested my resolve by covering me in snow only three days in, tested my body with oozing welts and raw lips, tested me with hunger by giving me a rocky, barren peninsula with no fishing spot on a lake people travel across the world to fish on.

"She says she's here in gratitude and connection," the land had asked, "but does she really mean it?"

And I did. I do. I stare down at the bird in my hands, the details blurred through the flowing tears. *The land has seen me. I have been deemed worthy.*

The scale has tipped. I'm no longer a visitor waiting on the doorstep to see if I'll be let in. Now I *live* here.

I pluck two particularly striking feathers—boldly patterned with black and white stripes—from her breast, and thread them through my pierced ears. I'm part grouse now, as well as part bobcat, and I want to look the part.

I try to wipe my weeping eyes, but my fingers are sticky with blood. Soon, I'm messier than when I started, my cheeks still wet with tears, but now with feathers and blood mixed in as well. In this moment, it strikes me as incredibly funny. I'm brimming with so much joy and exaltation that it all feels both wonderfully blessed and ridiculously comical. Tears of wonder, gratitude, and relief keep running down my cheeks, tickling as they drag the feathers down with them. Everything about this morning, this bird, this triumph, and this life is so utterly beautiful, magical, and hilarious that I might never stop laughing and crying about it. I'm woozy with the swirl of so many intense emotions. It's hard to talk to the camera through my tears and laughter, and impossible to sum up all I'm feeling, so I just say, "What a freaking morning," and head back to camp.

I stop on my way home and gaze out over the lake, realizing that this is a big deal, and it's about more than just the squirrel and grouse. I have hunted a little with rifles, and I have shot my bow a lot, but this is the first time I have ever *shot and killed* something with my bow. Today isn't just the tipping point of the sun's arc and the seasons; it's a tipping point in my life. Now I'm a real hunter. *No—a huntress*, an important distinction. It matters to me to embody all that's beautiful about the feminine in this pivotal moment. And I have been—I'm wearing the wool skirt and leg warmers and am hunting from a place of love and connection.

This time, I let the land and my body's deep knowing draw me to the grouse, rather than use the more masculine approach I took earlier—charging after her in my adrenaline rush and thinking my way through. Neither is better or worse; they are equally valid, but different. As the masculine approach to hunting and outdoor skills is what our culture generally thinks of and celebrates, I'm thrilled that it was the feminine approach, using softness and deep listening, that brought me this success, and that I get to share it with the world through the camera. After so many years of pushing my softness down to illustrate my toughness, it's a joy to feel utterly in love with who and what I am and, over two decades after I started making my first wooden bow when I was nineteen, to finally have become a bow huntress.

I know what I need to do to mark the occasion—name my bow! As soon as the thought enters my mind, I already know its name. Artemis, of course, goddess of the hunt, animals, and the wild. Walking home with my bow and my bird in hand and adorned with grouse feathers, it isn't just my bow that is Artemis, I am also embodying the ancient goddess myself.

37

SPRUCE GROUSE COTTAGE

The sun is warm on my back as I lay my birch bark "cutting board" on the ground outside the cabin. As I pluck the grouse, clouds of her tiny feathers, too small to catch, reflect the bright sunlight and swirl around my head in the light breeze. I can smell the spruce needles scrunching under my feet and the animal scent of her body. All my senses are heightened. Everything feels different—stronger, brighter, more real—now that I belong here more deeply.

I save everything, peeling the fat from around her organs and intestines and saving the congealed blood—rich in protein, iron, and salt—from her chest cavity.

With her organs in the pot lid and her body wrapped in birch bark, I tuck her next to the squirrel, feeling like the wealthiest person in the world. Wealthier, because those rich only in money, who have never known lack, will never appreciate food in this way. Money can't buy this kind of gratitude, but true hunger can.

Surprisingly, now that I know I have food, I don't feel compelled to eat it right away. It isn't that I'm not hungry—I'm ravenous—but I'm used to that. It's far too beautiful a day to sit inside, though, and I can cook just as easily in the dark. These two generous creatures have changed everything. If I continue this trend, and staying and "surthriving" here are possible, I'm doubly determined to harvest more cabin-winterizing materials. I bring my "scarf" (actually a wide piece of wool cloth I got from a fabric store) out to an area of deep sphagnum moss and spread it on the ground. I heap piles of moss onto the scarf in thick layers. Sphagnum moss is one of the best insulating materials around and will be a lot harder to harvest once it's buried in snow or frozen solid. Today, while it's still easy, I'll harvest enough to improve the cabin and cushion my bed, and for anything else I might need it for this winter.

One scarf load is four times what I could carry in my arms alone. I choose a sheltered spot against my south wall and start a pile of moss, then spend the afternoon hauling countless more loads. By dusk the pile is as tall as my chest.

Satisfied with my work, I turn back to the cabin, where my meal beckons. It feels appropriate to begin with the squirrel, as it was my first kill here. Today, I decide, it will get my full attention. I'll cook the grouse tomorrow.

Flames aren't great for cooking—they make a lot of smoke and often burn the meat—so I let the fire burn down to brilliant, cherry red coals while I cut the squirrel into smaller pieces. Red squirrels are tiny, and much more so without their skins. The entire thing, nose to rump, is only about six inches long and two inches around. I separate the minute scapula from the toothpick-sized ribs with delicate flicks of my knife. Shoulders are remarkably insubstantial, just a few muscles and ligaments holding them all together. Butchering shoulders always gives me pause, making me wonder what my own look like inside.

My shoulder trouble started in 1998, when I was twenty-three and working at an outdoor education center in the northern Adirondacks. I never knew what caused it—maybe splitting the many cords of wood we used to heat the dormitories, maybe all the hide scraping I was doing in frigid temperatures. Whatever it was, by spring I had crippling pain in my shoulders. For the next decade, when temperatures dropped below freezing, the joints would sometimes seize up so painfully that I occasionally needed help getting in and out of my clothes.

I pause in my butchering and rock back on my heels—I haven't stopped to think about it, but my shoulders haven't bothered me once out here. I've been working the heck out of them in frigid temperatures with no reprieve, and they're better than they've been since I was a teenager. My lips and thighs are a mess, but my biggest issue, my shoulders, have been golden. *What an amazing and mysterious blessing!*

I take my time to cook every organ and muscle to absolute perfection. I even render the fat out of the minuscule scrapings from the hide and the fatty bits I pulled from the carcass and organs by snipping them into tiny pieces with my Leatherman scissors and heating them gently until the liquid oil melts out of the gooey adipose tissue. Afterward, the remaining tissue is browned and crispy, like a miniature pork rind, and I eat it hot right out of the pan.

I usually render fat by the quart, but the quarter teaspoon I get for my efforts now is like gold, and the rich, savory scent of the liver hitting the hot fat is the most amazing thing I've ever smelled. I place a little square of it on the ancestor plate, exhaling to warm it and infuse it with all my prayers and gratitude, then put a square on my own tongue and moan with pleasure. *Oh my god—food! I remember food! This stuff is incredible!* Looking at the carcass earlier, it had seemed so tiny. Now that I know how amazing it is, I can hardly wrap my mind around the fact that I get to eat this *entire squirrel!*

I pull out my buckskin overalls, cut off one of the salt buttons, and shave a dusting of the precious powder over everything. Each bite feels more potent than any meal I've eaten in my life. Organs are my favorite, until they're gone and I have meat in front of me. Then meat is my favorite. There isn't much that could be put in front of me right now that wouldn't instantly become my favorite. I spend a full hour slowly savoring every organ and muscle, then stay up another hour boiling down the head and the bones for broth.

When I finally lay out my sleeping nest, it's late, the latest I've gone to bed since being here, but I fall asleep from a place of deep satisfaction and contentment and sleep better than I have in weeks.

I might be imagining it, but I would swear my lips already feel better by morning. I check my thighs—scabby and rough to look at, but the skin is back to normal proportions. Even my thumb doesn't seem to hurt as much. *Animal protein, the miracle cure.*

I pack up the cameras first thing. I told myself that when I had successfully hunted, I would treat myself to a big willow harvest. Today is the day!

I know I'm strange and that a lot of people would consider collecting materials a chore, not a treat, but harvesting is what I like to do for a good time. It always was, from long before I actually knew what to do with any of it.

I was probably six or seven when I first heard that you can make tea from the bark of the manzanita bushes that grew all over the open slopes near my home. I didn't even like tea back then, but on every hike in the spring, when the manzanita bark loosened and peeled to make room for new growth, I would run my palms along the trunks and fill my pockets with handfuls of little curls of dry bark. I don't know how many quarts each of my parents must have quietly composted once I left the room, having dutifully accepted brimming bags of it with, "Oh thanks, Hon. I'm sure this will be delicious."

We evolved as hunter-gatherers, and those genes run deep in all of us. For me they have always been palpable and pushing to be expressed. I'm glad I eventually learned how to use the things I harvest and didn't just turn into an eccentric with a closet full of pinecones and pockets brimming with shiny rocks.

Willow has such a long and important co-evolution with humans that it's healthier and more vibrant when cut regularly. Everywhere it grows it featured prominently in the material culture of pre-industrial peoples, and often still does. This is as true in Western Europe, where most of my ancestors are from, as it is in California, where I was born and raised. Native basketry culture is still vibrant in California and willow is used for baskets, backpacks, trays, cradleboards, ceremonial regalia, and much more.

Many places, however, it is no longer cherished and tended like it once was, and I believe it misses the close relationship it used to have with humans. It's beautiful to feel like harvesting and tending it here offers something to this place, as well as providing something useful for me.

I harvest my way along the shore of the mainland, relishing the *snick* of my Leatherman wire cutters as they snip the tender shoots. I leave a pile of willow wands at the base of each small bush, and when I've cut as much as I think I can carry, I head back toward home, bundling up each pile as I go. It isn't ready to weave with yet, as fresh willow shrinks a lot and is prone to snapping, but I sort it by size and tuck the sorted bundles into my rafters to season in the warmth of the fire. The sight of them there is deeply satisfying—a promise of baskets to come.

My harvest methods are changing in general. There are always improvements to do on the cabin and thus more materials to harvest. At one time I had a rotation when cutting poles—first the west woodlot, then the back woodlot and eastern spruce groves. Now it's nowhere near so logical.

I picture what I'm after, feel a pull toward a place and simply let myself be drawn there. I still check in with the trees before cutting them, but that too feels different now. It's less picking out a tree and asking permission, and more holding my need in my head and sensing which tree is jumping forward and grabbing my attention. Words don't seem as relevant. Why ask a tree if I can cut it when it just volunteered?

After a lifetime of striving for this sense of connection, it catches me by surprise to realize it's happening without my having done anything specific to cause it. It's just me being really and truly *here*—and listening deeply.

Finally, after harvesting willow and building-poles, I pull the grouse out of its birch bark wrappings. The wing feathers are so beautiful that I get an inspiration. I use twigs to pin them outstretched above the door as if they're flying—the grouse is my new mascot. From this day forth, I decide, this cabin will be known as Spruce Grouse Cottage.

I peel the breast away from the ribs with my knife. It's deep red—darker than beef—which tells me it must fly a lot more than I'd realized. I think of grouse as walking birds, but when you understand animal physiology, butchering an animal is like tracking—you can tell its life history by what's going on inside its body. The muscles that work the hardest need the most oxygen and are the darkest in color. Domestic chickens and turkeys have light breast meat and dark leg meat because they rarely fly. Wild birds vary inside as well, according to their activity patterns. Some of the darkest meat I've ever seen was the breast of a Canada goose, as they migrate long distances.

In addition to clues about its life, the dark meat also tells me something about how it will be to eat it. It has more iron, and thus more food value, than light meat. *Hallelujah!* Even better, this breast alone is bigger than yesterday's whole squirrel.

I cook it with the same level of care as the squirrel, saving the second breast and legs for later. The organs feel like a whole meal in themselves, and I pan the camera over them, sharing the visual feast before the actual feast.

I make my customary offering, and all my consciousness settles into my mouth as I prepare for my first bite. It's heavenly! I revel in the texture and incredibly savory richness. Spruce grouse is *amazing*! I wasn't complaining about the squirrel, but this bird is exquisite. No filet mignon could hold a candle to it.

I alternate bites of the dense, pungent organs and the salty, fragrant breast meat. Harvesting firewood burns calories, so I'm usually conservative with it, keeping my fire so small that I'm just warm enough, but not wasting a single piece. Today, I throw caution to the blustery wind shaking the trees above and heap the wood on, letting myself be utterly cozy, and basking in the luxury of a full belly and toasty cheeks.

38

THE NORTH BAY

The next day, with calories in my system and the rest of the grouse to eat soon, I decide I can afford the calories for another scouting hike. I've explored the closest stretch of shore and gone quite a way inland to find the "lake" on my last adventure. Today I'll head straight north, paralleling the water.

Once I reach the mainland the walking is easy, as it's mostly low grass and willows near the water's edge. It isn't long before I near the end of the long, wide curve of shore, beyond which it's all new territory for me.

Before I reach it I see something strange up ahead—a little mound of green on shore. *No wait—it's a bush, but there's something not quite right about it.*

I walk closer. It isn't a bush; it's a pile of branches, each nipped off at a sharp angle and neatly stacked. *Sweet! Beaver sign!* I've been hoping, of course, for moose sign, but with no front teeth on top they leave ragged edges on the shrubs they browse, and they don't make piles. Beavers have jaws like pruning shears and make stacks like this to drag into the water near their lodge so they can feed on them all winter long. The leaves of the cut branches are fresh and bright green, not withered by the sun and wind, so the pile is probably only a few hours old.

A beaver would last me far longer than several grouse as they're much bigger and full of fat. They're most active at dawn and dusk, so I'm guessing it'll be back for this pile at nightfall. *Looks like I've got my evening scheduled.*

Now I scan the shoreline more carefully as I hike. Where there's beaver sign, there's a beaver lodge somewhere. If I'm not able to get them when they return for these branches, perhaps I can go right to the source.

I round the curve ahead, and a new tableau spreads out before me. I'm now across the water from the southern tip of the island I identified from the top of the inland peak and can see into the vast bay beyond it. I hear a far-off rushing sound to the north, just like I did on my initial scout on day one. Now I know that my guess that day was true and that it is, in fact, the direction a lot of the weather comes from, so the wind makes sense.

When I draw level with the far end of the island, I can see green shoots poking up out of the water. *That's strange; is it shallow enough there for the willows to grow up through the lake?* But I don't think that's the answer. Once I get closer, my suspicions are confirmed. It isn't the green of growing bushes. It's willow, but it isn't growing there, it's sticking up from the underwater raft of vegetation I knew the beavers were building somewhere. I can just see its blurry form under the surface.

Dang it! That means the beaver lodge must be on the island. And why not? If you're an agile swimmer, why build on the mainland where the predators are when you can grab food from the mainland and live on the island, safe from harm?

It's a beautiful hike, but the only moose sign I find all day is two shed antlers in the grass, probably a couple of years old as they are bleached, cracked, and well gnawed by mice.

I do find some deeper water, but it's still shallow enough that I can easily see the lake bottom perhaps six feet down. Better fishing than on the peninsula, I'd wager, but not enormously promising, and hiking so far for a slim chance at fish doesn't make much sense.

The biggest finds of the day are where I turn around in the late afternoon, on a little rise with thick soil unlike anything I've got near the cabin. Growing in it are not only shrubs, but honest-to-goodness herbaceous plants—the first I've seen since launch. Amongst them, I spy the feathery leaves of yarrow, one of my favorite medicinal plants. Its dried powdered leaves sprinkled on a wound help stop bleeding and fight infection, and the tea is good for headaches, stomachaches, and fevers. I sing to it as I harvest and fill my pockets with the fragrant leaves.

The other big find are soapberry bushes, which I learned to identify back at base camp before we launched but have seen no sign of until today. Their oval leaves, now yellow-green with their fall coloration, beckon to me from the woods beyond the shore. When I investigate, I see that there are a few small, yellow-orange berries still clinging to the branches. I gather all I can find, a small handful.

Saponins are a natural soap, thus the plant's name, and they are quite bitter. I try a berry and it's sweet for a second, then the saponins hit. Food is food, so I chew up several more and choke them down. *I shouldn't eat too many at once*, I remind myself, as saponins have a laxative effect. *Hey, wait a minute, that's perfect*, I think, and swallow the rest.

I figured I'd start pooping again when I began bringing in more food, but I've been eating for two days now, and my plumbing is still on strike. I can use all the help I can get.

The berries have most of the saponins, but there are no more berries, so I fill my other pocket with the leaves, hoping that they too can be used for soap, and turn back toward home.

I head back to the cabin, drop off my new finds, and suit up for a cold night. By dusk, I'm waiting for the beaver, bow in hand, by the pile of nipped branches. There's a downed tree between me and the branches, and I use it as a hunting blind, waiting silently as the light changes and the bird activity quiets to a whisper. My ears strain for ripples through the water as the colors drain from the land and darkness engulfs the shore. My legs grow stiff, and I have to alternate hands between my bow and my pockets every few minutes to keep them from growing numb. The stars twinkle into the night sky one by one, until whole constellations paint the open space before me. When the camera battery dies, I know I've been here for two hours. If the beaver isn't here by now, it probably isn't coming, and I'll soon be too frozen to shoot anyway.

It's a crystal clear night, and as I pack up I'm amazed at the number of stars. On the peninsula I'm hemmed in by trees, but now I'm looking out over open water into a vast sky, hundreds of miles from light pollution. I see the big dipper for the first time since my arrival, and use it to locate Polaris, the north star. Apparently, I've been about ten degrees off in my estimate of true north. Not bad.

I turn toward home, find the profile of the truffula tree against the peninsula's skyline, and hurry back to my hearth and the waiting grouse breast.

After another absurdly delicious meal, I cook up the grouse legs to eat tomorrow. I'm still chilled from the hunt, so when my cooking is done, I want to build up the fire. Before I can, I need to move the rocks that support my cooking pot out of the way. They're too hot to touch, so I use sticks to roll them out of the fire pit and onto the bare ground on either side of my legs. The ground is cold and hard beneath me, but now I can feel the steady heat radiating from the rocks and it's relaxing the muscles of my thighs. It's almost (but not quite) as delicious as the grouse. I want more of it, so when they're cool enough to touch, I tuck one rock under each thigh and plop the third one into my lap, right on top of my femoral arteries. It's the most comfortable I've been since launch. Food yesterday, food in my belly today, food for tomorrow, and snuggled up with three warm rocks. I'm sighing with contentment right up until crawling into my sleeping bag. A girl could get used to this.

39

THE FIRST CHILL

I n the morning, I'm hoping to feel that old urge, but the soapberries have no effect. I need to be more diligent about eating fiber regularly. Crowberries aren't very exciting, but with no edible green plants, and my system still rebelling at the idea of cranberries, they're all the fiber I've got. They're too watery to bother drying for winter, but I decide to eat at least three handfuls a day for as long as they last, no matter what.

Now that I've been successful hunting and have explored every potential fishing spot I can think of to no avail, I let go of my futile attempts at fishing. I spend a lot more time stalking the peninsula with my bow—listening deeply and letting myself wander to wherever the land draws me. I fold myself into its contours, following the seams of rock and the edges of spruce thickets.

Two ravens croak above me one morning, and I stop to watch them soar overhead. They're probably the most intelligent birds on the continent. They can't take down large game, but they can see animals from high up, and know their movements. Ravens have been documented working alongside wolf packs, alerting them to the location of caribou and other game. Once the wolves eat their fill, the ravens swoop in and clean up the scraps. Both species benefit. I call out to the ravens in my mind, inviting them to join me in a similar partnership, but they move off, doing barrel rolls over the tops of the spruces.

Days pass, and I hunt more carefully than I did at first, to conserve my dwindling arrows. I haven't lost any since being more diligent, but even so, I'm now down two more. One shattered against a spruce trunk upon impact and another had its nock (the forked piece at the back end of an arrow that grips the string), break and fall off when the arrow hit a rock. I have only four more intact arrows, a serious handicap. Now that they've learned about hunting, the squirrels watch the arrows coming and jump out of the way, fast as lightning. I haven't brought in any game since equinox, and I've only got a few more swigs of bone broth left from the grouse.

There are so many challenges and little disappointments out here. If I chose to dwell on them, my days would feel overwhelmingly hard. We tend to find what we look for. Whether it's feelings of failure and unworthiness or of success, we magnify whatever we focus on. Feeling positive or hopeless is more up to me than to my external circumstances, so rather than bemoaning my diminishing food and lost arrows, I choose to focus on small, achievable goals, and the little pleasures and successes that come with them. Today is a case in point. I've been out hunting unsuccessfully all morning. Right now, it's the midday lull with little animal movement, and the sun is shining, so I decide to bolster my spirits by pursuing something that doesn't dart away from me at top speed: tanning that squirrel hide.

It's frozen, but after I thaw it in my hands, the hide is moist and pliable and in the perfect state to tan. I've long since eaten its brain, but I need some fat to lubricate the hide so that I can soften it. I scoop up a pinch of my salve and work it well into the flesh side of the skin, then take it outside and sit on a rock in the sunshine.

Like wild harvests, hide tanning is one of my greatest joys in life. Even with my hunting disappointments and strong hunger creeping back in, with the skin in my hands I'm in my happy place.

I stretch the hide in every direction to loosen the fibers and help draw the fat deeper into the middle of the skin. I'm using the brain-tanning technique, even though the fat involved this time is salve, not brains. With this method, it's important to keep the microscopic protein fibers of the hide moving past each other constantly as they dry so they don't stick together and become hard and stiff. The texture and colors shift under my fingers—the cool, translucent, white-blue of the wet skin turning tawny, opaque, and velvety as the moisture evaporates.

By midafternoon, all but the last step, the smoking, is done. The skin is warm and dry, lusciously soft, and creamy white. The smoke will give it the warm brown color that characterizes brain-tanned leather and keep it soft and stretchy even if it gets wet. Otherwise, even after the work I've put in, water would turn it as hard as rawhide again. I tack it above the hearth with my needle and thread so it will be smoked by the hearth fire. *That's one small success!* I celebrate it by finishing off the last of the grouse bone broth, then crack her leg bones with a rock and suck out the marrow. With that, the grouse is finished.

We don't get sun like this very often, and tomorrow is Thursday, another dance party day. I've got clean clothes for it, but now that I've got those soap-berry leaves, *what if I could actually wash my hair?* Thus far I've done a sponge bath every few days, but I have yet to risk exposing all my skin at once to take a thorough shower.

I heat a pot of water and beat the soapberry leaves with my carved birch-wood spoon until the water is slightly frothy. It isn't exactly soap, but maybe it'll knock back the layer of grease in my hair for a day or two. I carry the pot, my wool T-shirt to use as a towel, and a sock for a rag to the back porch, where the sun is brightest.

This will be my first time being naked on camera. I'm a very open-minded person. I grew up in Northern California hanging out with my mom's hiking friends at the river every other weekend from the time I was a kid. I'm per-fectly comfortable with nudity, but there's something about having it on film, and not knowing who'll be editing the footage or if it'll be broadcast to tens of millions of people, that's a little unnerving.

Holy crap, it's freezing out here! I scrub down quickly with the sock, want-ing to get to my hair before the water goes cold. I'm surprised that I'm not particularly filthy, but then I've never had any skin besides my hands and face exposed out here. It's the first time I've seen this much of my body in weeks. I look at myself in the view screen of the camera. Wow. The extra belly fat that took so much effort to put on is totally gone. I turn around and show the backs of my thighs, which are still a mess from the welts, to the camera.

"My first real bath," I tell the camera. I'd like to say it feels good to be clean, but the only way it feels is absolutely freezing. I consider leaving my hair dirty and running for the shelter of the cabin, but I don't know when I'll have another opportunity to wash, so I go for it. I soak my hair in what's left in the

pot and scrub it hard between my hands. The water turns dark right away—
now that's the level of filth I was expecting. What seemed like a light breeze
with my clothes on feels like an icy wind naked and wet, and now I'm covered
in prickly goosebumps. I rinse as best I can, towel myself dry, throw on my
clothes, and run for the shelter.

The cabin is only forty feet away, but by the time I get there, my whole
body is shivering. *I'll warm up when I start working again,* I think, but my fingers are stiff and clumsy as I button up my pants. I give up and just pull my
belt tighter.

I'm not just a little cold, I realize. *I'm dangerously chilled.* I can't get my fingers or my brain to work. *Holy crap—that's stage one hypothermia.* For the first
time since my arrival, I feel a note of fear. It isn't a dangerous accident or an
encounter with a ravenous predator that's finally scared me, it's the everyday
environmental conditions combined with my own poor judgment.

There are still some coals in the hearth, thank god, so I have the fire going
again in no time. I can't wrap my brain around doing anything beyond feeding it and huddling around it. Logically, I know I'll be okay, but my emotions
have done a belly flop. The exuberant positivity that has characterized most
of my time here is gone, and I feel sad and lonely. I want to shake myself out of
it and get back to business, but neither my mind nor body are there. Instead,
I let myself be, and surrender to the waves of emotions within me. *What am I
doing out here? I could be sitting by a campfire with friends right now. It's harvest
season back there. They're digging potatoes and roasting peppers, probably can-
ning more food than they know what to do with.*

I wrap my arms around myself and rock back and forth, the only motion I
feel capable of right now.

*What if those two animals are all I'll ever get out here? What if I keep losing
arrows every time I try to hunt? How cold is it going to get? This is the Arctic—and
if I'm laid this low on a sunny day...*

Though I'm straddling the fire, holding my hands and feet out to it, it takes
forever for the warmth to reach my core and hours before I begin to feel like
myself again. Note to self—*taking silly risks and letting myself get this cold is
definitely not worth it.*

40

THE MAGICAL LETTER N

t's a different and wiser Woniya that wakes up the next morning. It isn't what the brief hypothermic episode did to my body that troubles me, but the way it affected my entire inner landscape and outlook. It isn't actual calamity that takes most people out on this show, it's the mental aspects. Positive attitude is a critical survival skill, and yesterday was a big lesson in something that clearly affects mine. Overall, it was a fairly minor incident. I'm grateful to have learned—early on and in a safe and mild way—about the consequences of underestimating one of the biggest dangers out here: the cold.

This life and place demand constant balance. Effort versus surrender, knowledge versus trust, incredulity versus deep knowing. There's only so much I have control over, and I need to be sure I'm taking my cues from the land, not my own preconceived ideas of what my time here is "supposed" to look like. Greasy hair isn't life threatening—getting wet and cold is.

I don't have power over the climate. What I *do* have power over, though, is how snug and tight my shelter is. Thus far, I've been piling cut trees against the doorway every night to close it, but the cold has been seeping in past them, and they don't keep storm winds out. It's time for a real door.

I lay four short, peeled poles on the ground, then place a row of bushy spruce trees across them, alternating the spruces tip up, then butt up, to fill the air gaps. I lay four more poles across the top, lined up with the original four on the bottom. My door will essentially be a "spruce sandwich," with the short horizontal poles as the bread and the vertical trunks and their bushy branches as the lunchmeat. To tie it all together I make one of my "paraspools," but longer than usual so it acts as a needle. I pass the "paraneedle" through the door, sewing the short, peeled poles together so they squeeze the bushy trunks into one solid unit.

It takes hours to sew it up, but it works. It's a little saggier than if it were lumber, but in the end I've got a solid, stormproof door that I can easily lift and fit into place.

I start to tuck the paraneedle into my backpack, which is shoved into the back corner of the cabin, when something shiny down near the ground catches my eye. *What is that?*

There's something on the sill log that forms the base of my north wall. The roof is too low to stand in the back corner, so I just use the space to store my gear, but now I crouch down and shuffle closer to get a better look. My eyes pop in disbelief. There, catching the light of my headlamp, I see of all things, *a sticker!* It's clear, shiny and square, is about three-quarters of an inch across, and in the middle of it is a black capital letter "N."

How in the world is there a sticker on my cabin? Or anywhere out here? There can't be. It's impossible. My skin feels tingly, and I look over my shoulder toward the entrance.

Am I being messed with? Is someone hiding in the trees filming me right now? I peer closer. No mistaking it; right there, dead center in the middle of the log is a capital N sticker. A sticker I didn't put here, on the cabin I'm building by myself deep in the wilderness. As if that isn't enough, it isn't just an N sticker—it's an N sticker on my north wall, exactly lined up with where I saw Polaris on my way back from the beaver hunt.

What? I slump down to the ground. I feel hot and shaky. This is crazy.

Okay, think this through.

I can come up with three possibilities to explain it, none of them particularly feasible.

One: The production crew did it. When I was away from the cabin, they came out here for some unimaginable reason, snuck in without disturbing any of my things, and put a sticker marking north in the hardest to reach and least visible part of my cabin. Even though the whole goal of the production team is to interfere with us as little as possible, besides the required medical checks, none of which have yet happened. And on top of that, they managed to do so silently, even though I would hear a helicopter or boat from miles away across the wide-open lake. *No way.*

Two: The sticker was already here. Somehow, on a little peninsula just south of the Arctic Circle, in an unpopulated region of one of the vastest lakes on the continent, there happened to be an N sticker on a wild tree out in the forest. The sticker hung on while I cut and hauled the tree, limbed it by whacking the crap out of it with my saw-machete, cut it to size, and dragged it into place. And somehow, the sticker survived all this unblemished, still looking shiny and new. Then, miraculously, when I laid the pole in place, I not only never saw the sticker (which just caught my eye from feet away) but also happened to lay the pole in such a way that the sticker was facing out, exactly vertical, and lined up perfectly with polar north.

Um, yeah, no. Moving on...

Three: The sticker somehow came with me. I have a bunch of camera gear and technical equipment, most of which I wasn't familiar with and didn't spend a lot of time examining upon arrival. Maybe something had the N sticker on it. I stick various gear items in this corner from time to time to keep them out of the way. At some point, while I shuffled things around, the sticker rubbed off of whatever it came on and happened to stick, upright, legible, and exactly lined up with where I just discovered polar north to be while coming back from that beaver hunt.

This, too, feels totally unbelievable. The chances are about a gazillion to one, and yet, of all three, it's the only feasible option. When you've eliminated the impossible, the remaining option, however implausible it might be, must be the solution.

I'm frozen in wonder, completely mystified. I touch it, just to make sure I'm not hallucinating. Yes, there's the slick texture of it under my fingertip— it's real.

I plunk myself down by the hearth, unable to carry on with my day. The ways this place subtly speaks to me have been amazing, but now it feels like it's reaching out directly and poking me. The sticker isn't a feeling; it's a physical object I can hold in my hand. It showing up is one thing, but the alignment? I can't shake the feeling that it was placed there by design. The only word I can think of is *magic.*

Okay Woniya, why are you so incredulous? Hasn't this journey been magical all along? The invitation to be on television came the week after I said out loud to a group of people, "I am ready to be seen," and the email showed up the very day I told the wilderness, "I want a deeper wilderness journey—far wilder, with fewer people and less stuff." I launched with a bunch of unfinished projects and plenty of extra thread sewn into my double stitched seams, and a needle blank showed up right in front of my face on day two. *Are you a witchy woman who believes in magic and prayer, Woniya, or are you not?*

The sticker here feels crazy, but is it any less crazy than the fact that I still feel strong and healthy, having eaten significant meals for only three days of the past several weeks? With all this, why *wouldn't* a stray sticker end up in the most magical and mysterious place it could possibly be?

Here's the thing—I'm a trained scientist. I have a master's degree in it. In science, we use the concept of "magical thinking" derogatorily. The understanding is that if you can't prove something—can't collect data and draw conclusions backed by solid statistics—it doesn't exist.

There's a reason I didn't remain in the field of research science. It felt wrong to me, like it was squeezing the mystery right out of a beautifully mysterious world. I know I can't prove magic and can't use solid data to back a feeling that the universe is sentient. But I also can't prove that it *isn't*, and the more I believe and trust in magic, the more it shows up.

If I can neither prove nor disprove magic, then believing in it or not is a choice. One of these choices brings meaning and joy to my life, and one deflates them. Why wouldn't I choose what makes me most happy—the version of the universe I would most like to live in? Similarly, what matters most isn't what is one hundred percent true about the sticker, but how it makes me feel.

What feels true to me is that the land is giving me a message that I'm seen and wanted here. This place, however much it challenges me, has my back— and it wants to make sure I know that. In case that wasn't clear enough with the needle or with getting the squirrel and grouse on equinox, it just got more literal. It's telling me that my compass—my north star—is right here. In the spruce poles of this very cabin, in the glimmering sky above, and in the vast wilderness of a place in which I've never previously set foot but that felt like home from the moment I stepped off the helicopter.

41

FOOD FRIDAY

ventually, I shake myself out of my reverie. I haven't forgotten that it's dance party day. I paid dearly for this beautifully clean hair, and I'm not letting it go to waste. I decide on a Latin theme and head out to the rock arena where I salsa my way to and fro long enough to get my blood pumping.

It looks like snow is coming, so I decide to start a covered outdoor woodshed to keep my larger pieces of firewood dry until I cut them up and stack them inside. I cut, haul, and stack poles for a while, but there's still one left to bring in when the light fades. After the hypothermia episode, I decide to tuck in safely by the fire tonight and leave it for the morning.

I don't have much in the way of dinner options. I've eaten every morsel of the squirrel and grouse, scraped the marrow from their bones, and then boiled them again for broth. Nevertheless, I add the bones to the cook pot and stoke the fire. There may not be any calories, but there's calcium and other minerals. The third boiling of bones isn't something I can justify thinking of as "broth," however, so I create a new dish—Starvation Soup. It's an unappetizing, milky looking bone tea, but it's what's for dinner.

After boiling the bones, I prop a thin, flat rock over the fire and toast the bones on it until they're chocolate brown and brittle, then chew them up. I can't manage to swallow reindeer lichen, but I'll be darned if I can't get down a whole critters' worth of bones in a sitting!

Tomorrow is Friday, and with my food dried up, I decide I'll make it Food Friday and focus on coming up with a new strategy for catching game.

Even with only Starvation Soup in my belly, I feel warm and content every time I think of the N sticker. I shine my headlamp at it one last time before closing my eyes to sleep. The dream beasts hardly rouse me in the night, but somehow in my semiconsciousness, I'm aware of the echoes of their footfalls passing through the solid rock and into my slumbering visions.

The next day the clouds, already dark, look heavier and heavier every hour. I spend most of the day working on the woodshed and hauling firewood to fill it. I'm so focused I forget about Food Friday until midafternoon, when my work is interrupted by a beep from my hip bag. I pull out the blocky, yellow GPS device to find a message on the screen.

MED CHECK TOMORROW

Wow. And so it begins. I have officially been out here long enough to potentially endanger my health. Now I'm kicking myself for not focusing on food strategies right away this morning, but there just aren't enough hours in the day for all of my necessary projects.

I don't actually think there's any risk of getting pulled tomorrow; I know I'm still healthy. I'm not thrilled about the serenity of my private peninsula being invaded by a crew of people, though, nor having to tell them I haven't gotten game for a week now.

I look at the nearly complete woodshed, torn between finishing it and starting a new food procurement strategy. I only need a few more poles to complete the roof. *That's right! There's still that pole from last night to haul. That decides it.*

The snow starts up in earnest just as I head out for it. I get to the little, bowl-shaped dip in the land, a small hollow filled with sphagnum moss where I was cutting yesterday, and I freeze.

The tree is where I remember it, but now there's a pile of little green balls on the trunk. It's rabbit poop. A rabbit was here in the night, and that means it'll probably be back.

I haul the tree back to the cabin, construction forgotten. *Never mind the woodshed. It's Food Friday, and I have fresh rabbit sign!* I've seen only one hare in the weeks I've been here, but it now looks like it isn't because they're scarce, but because they're mostly nocturnal. I'm not going to start hunting all night by headlamp, so it's time to switch tactics.

Of course I've thought about snaring, but this landscape is crisscrossed with small game trails, and I've had no indications of which are active and which are unused. I have limited materials and no snare wire, so it seemed silly to waste a lot of energy and cordage on a shot in the dark. Now that I've got definitive, recent rabbit sign, it's different.

I throw my thick wool shirt on over my sweater and put every camera I've got into my backpack. I search the cabin for everything useful: paracord, paracord innards, traps pieces, tools, and fishing line.

Fishing line! That's it! It isn't snare wire, but it'll hold a loop a lot better than the limp paracord innards. It will have to do.

The ground is already turning white, and snow is obscuring the trails, but I see a rabbit hole that looks well used and two branches of trail leading away from it.

These are rabbits—they chew for a living. I can make all the fishing line nooses I want to, but if a rabbit can reach the line, it'll snip through it in a heartbeat. For my snare to work, it'll have to be a power snare that can lift the rabbit up and off its feet.

I have a good understanding of animal behavior, and this summer I read a lot about trapping, but I've never set a snare in my life. The sun is going down and it's snowing like crazy, but I'm damn well setting one now!

I want the noose right in the middle of the trail, a trigger sensitive enough to be tripped by the rabbit's own weight, and a lifting mechanism strong enough to pull it off its feet. There's a springy young spruce near the hole that will do nicely for the lift. *Now what do I use for my trigger?*

It's getting dark. No time to hesitate—just come up with something, Woniya!

Let's see. I can use two branches as uprights on either side of the trail, and a straight crosspiece between them. The uprights will need to have side branches that I can carve into little hooks to hold the crosspiece in place. I'll bend the spruce sapling over and tie it to the middle of the crosspiece, which will pull it upward against the upright's hooks. The noose will dangle from the middle of the crosspiece, right in the rabbit's path.

The trigger is the noose and crosspiece. When the rabbit's head passes through the noose, it will pull on the crosspiece, releasing it from the hooks. This will allow the sapling to unbend, lift the rabbit up and off its feet, and pull the snare loop tight.

Theoretically, it should work, but I need dead, seasoned wood, so the moisture inside doesn't freeze the crosspiece to the uprights, and I need to get this whole thing built before dark, which is almost here. *Aaaack!*

A short push through the forest brings me to the vein of willow at the foot of the sunset rocks. I cut two dead branches with little side shoots that will act as my hooks and a straight one for the crosspiece.

A little carving gives me my uprights. I drive them deep into the bouncy moss and cut the crosspiece to size. I then bend the sapling over and use a piece of paracord sheathing to tie the tip of the sapling to the middle of the crosspiece. But as soon as I let it go, the spring of the tree unbending whips the uprights out of the ground. *Too much tension!* I need enough to lift a hare, but not so much that it destroys my setup. I try again, giving the tree more slack to lower the tension, and slowly release it. The uprights hold, but the crosspiece rolls, releases from the hooks, and gets flung up by the sapling again.

How do I make it stable while still sensitive? I try flattening the ends of the crosspiece and making a little divot on each side of it for the hooks on the uprights to fit into and grip. *Perfect!*

Now for the noose. I pull out the fishing line and tie a loop about fist-wide—big enough for a rabbit's head, but not its shoulders—that slides closed easily, then tie it to the crosspiece so it's fist-high off the ground. Which would be perfect if the noose was snare wire. This is fishing line I'm dealing with, not stiff wire, though. It droops down, dangles limply and turns from side to side in the wind. Unless it happened to hit it just right, a rabbit would nudge past the noose, which would swing politely out of the way—*after you, my good sir!*

I need something to keep the fishing line steady in the middle of the trail and hold the noose stiff and open, but also weak enough to give easily when the trigger releases and the sapling springs up. I look around. There is no grass anywhere, and no understory plants except cranberries and Labrador tea—no plants with fiber I can use for cordage. Then, in my peripheral vision I notice some ragged strands of hair sticking out from under my fur hat. *Bingo!*

I pluck them, but can barely feel the hairs with my cold fingers, so I stick my hands in my armpits to warm them up enough to function again. And I thought tying knots with *fishing line* in a snowstorm was hard...

I stick a few strands of hair in my mouth and crouch down to noose level. It's almost impossible to see the white strands against the snow, but that will just make it more invisible to a rabbit. I carefully tie one end of the hair to one upright and the other to the noose, but it snaps as I pull the knot tight. I grab another strand but drop it and lose it in the snow. I pluck additional hairs and after three more failed attempts am nearly at the point of deciding it's impossible. Then I manage to get one side tied and taut. I heave a sigh, afraid to move and disturb the delicate balance. I finally get the noose tied to both upright stakes, but it still moves back and forth, so I tie another hair to the bottom of the loop and attach it to a third stick that I bury in the snow under the trail. The noose is stable, round, open, and right in the middle of the trail.

I step back, cramped with the cold and so much crouching, and critique my work. *If I didn't know better, I might almost think whoever built this snare knew what they were doing.* But it's one lonely snare, quickly thrown together, and made with inadequate materials. I really need more and better ones to have any chance at a rabbit. It's now completely dark and the lower legs of my pants are soaked through from kneeling in the snow. My hands are too stiff to tie any more hair knots, so this is all I can manage tonight.

I'm proud of myself for trying, but not convinced that I really achieved my Food Friday goal of a legitimate new food strategy. As I head back home to warm up by the fire, my doubts about the snare far outweigh my hopes for success.

I lie awake for some time, praying to whatever rabbits are listening, asking them to come to my trap, explaining my need, and promising to honor them and use every part.

42

ENJOY YOUR BREAKFAST

The morning light has a different quality than usual when I wake up the next day. *That probably means*—I pull the door aside and—*yes! The storm delivered!* It's a snowy world out there.

I'm too excited about the snow to feel the cold as I shrug into my pants. I reach past the bulky sweater, my daily go-to, and grab my fur parka instead. It's the perfect occasion to wear this behemoth for the first time. Finally, the hours I poured into making it are about to pay off.

It's a little bulky and awkward, and the antler buttons don't quite line up with the buckskin loops, but I'm lucky it's wearable at all, given how little time I had to complete it before launch. It wraps around me like an embrace from dozens of fuzzy little critters at once—which is pretty much what it is. I feel instantly warmer and subtly held, by the buckskin and the deer that it came from, and all the people and places I love and associate with the smokey smell of the home-tanned leather and furs.

I've been dreaming of the first snowfall that really accumulates and sticks, eager for it to reveal the previously invisible stories in the landscape all around me, but now a million worried thoughts snowball in my head.

I'm going to need more covered firewood storage.

That roof insulation needs to happen ASAP.

How quickly can I finish the front wall of the cabin?

Oh god, the berries are all covered up.

How do I pick and store a winter's worth of berries, if I never see the ground again?

And then my thoughts are interrupted by rhythmic crunching—*what in the world is that?*

It's not my imagination; it's the sound of boots on snow! I throw my boot liners on in a rush and step outside without bothering to pull on the boots themselves.

Is this the med check already? They're supposed to warn me well in advance. I haven't even had time to pee yet!

Our GPS signals are constantly monitored, but besides a brief text check-in morning and night that reads simply, "ALL GOOD," there's a strict hands-off policy on *Alone*.

Solitude is part of the challenge. Camera batteries are replaced and footage is collected via "blind drops," where participants leave their dead batteries and filled footage cards on the shore in waterproof bags for collection.

At the same time, they can't let anyone actually starve to death out here. For safety, after a certain amount of time—the amount in which someone could start running into serious health problems—they begin doing medical checks. If your blood pressure or BMI (body mass index) are too low or your pulse is too weak, they can pull you for medical reasons and your *Alone* adventure is over, just like that.

I'm not surprised that they're here, but I'm shocked by the timing. I would probably have been nervous about the med check had it come when I expected it. Now, instead of worried about it, I'm annoyed they showed up unannounced and are interrupting my morning routine.

"Aren't you guys a little early?" I ask as two men, Dave, the survival consultant, and another man who seems to be a member of the safety team, squeak up my front walk. *How have I never noticed how deafening humans are before?*

"We didn't get your morning check-in," Dave tells me. "We're just here to make sure you're okay."

My stomach sinks. I sent my check-in well before I crawled out of bed, as I've done every morning. But last night was the first time I pulled my new door totally shut, so there were no air gaps. I hadn't thought about what that might mean for sending my morning check-in. The message couldn't get through the thick spruce boughs of my walls and door. This isn't the med check—it's a needless rescue mission. Their being here without warning isn't their fault, it's mine. *Damn it!*

I'm cursing myself, but I try to take it in stride and not let it show.

"I'm fine," I tell them. "I'm so sorry you wasted a trip. I sent my check-in as soon as I woke up, like usual. It's been working up until now, as I didn't have a solid door in. I forgot I need line-of-sight to the sky to send it."

They're kind, but brisk, already turning to go before it's really sunk in that they're here. When interactions like this can't be avoided, production tries to minimize them as much as possible.

"Enjoy your breakfast," Dave says, turning back toward the shore, where I can hear the boat engine idling.

I laugh, assuming he's messing with me. I haven't had breakfast in three weeks. Then I choke the laugh back, reading in his face that he wasn't trying to be funny.

"You'll get a message when we're headed out for your med check," they tell me, then they're off toward the waiting boat.

As their footsteps fade, I sigh and feel hollow inside. It isn't just being reminded by people with round cheeks and full bellies how long it's been since I've really eaten—I got the grouse a week ago and already the idea of waking up to food is so foreign that I automatically assume it's sarcasm—it's also the shock of human voices and faces magnifying my solitude.

I know I shouldn't, but I can't help myself—I creep out to the open rocks to watch them go, feeling slightly guilty but not guilty enough to stop. I'm just in time to see the boat turn around and accelerate as it hits the deeper water far from shore. I watch it dwindle into the gray distance, missing them and wishing they had never come at the same time.

Enjoy your breakfast, yeah right, I muse, as I get back to preparing for my day.

First things first—the snare. I know I couldn't have caught anything overnight. It's the first snare I've set in my life, with no real idea what I'm doing, and using only fishing line and hair. What I *do* know is that any trapline, even this one, is a commitment. It's unethical to let it go unchecked—something could be tangled up in it, alive and suffering. It's also impractical, as a struggling animal could call in predators from every direction, and there goes my hare.

A trapline should have a minimum of ten to twenty snares to have a good shot at catching a rabbit a day. With only one, mine is more of a dot than a line, but that doesn't mean I'm off the hook from checking it.

My remorse over the botched check-in fades as excitement about the glittering world before me returns. It's about much more than just the snow's shimmering beauty. Bare granite tells no stories—a herd of caribou could waltz down my front walk twice a day, and if I wasn't here to see them, I'd never know it. Fresh snow is a canvas, though. Everything that passes, from wee mice to lumbering bears, paints its story upon it. If I have any shot at trapping—and without wire, I might not—the snow cover is what will make it possible.

Sure enough, not fifteen feet from the cabin, I see just what I'm hoping for. Four footprints in the snow shaped like the letter "Y." A classic snowshoe hare track, with the enormous hind feet first and the dainty little front feet in between. *Sweet!*

I head toward my snare, babbling excitedly into the camera, when I come to a stop. *Where is it?* My snare should be right here, but I don't see the bent spruce sapling anywhere. *What the heck?*

And then I draw in a reflexive gasp and the cold air stings my lungs.

YOU ARE KIDDING ME!

The sapling isn't bent over because it's been sprung. Dangling from it in midair is the mottled brown and white form of a snowshoe hare. It's so camouflaged against the snowy trunks that I didn't see it at first glance.

This. Is. Amazing.

I cannot freaking believe it! I caught a rabbit! *Me*, never having trapped before! The first snare I have ever made, and with no snare wire, and *I CAUGHT A RABBIT!*

I wade into the trees, laughing with surprise and wonder. The rabbit is cold and stiff, as it has probably been here for hours, but I hug it to my chest, beaming with delight. My cold fingers disappear into the long silky fur, and I can't stop stroking it.

"Thank you, thank you, rabbit gods," I yell aloud to whatever is listening.

This little, bowl-shaped dip in the woods has changed my world. *I'll call it Rabbit Hollow*, I decide. My body and soul sing as I tromp home.

It worked! My prayers, determination, and ingenuity came together, and now the land has spoken and deemed me worthy.

The morning's to-do list falls by the wayside.

I lay a square of birch bark, my wilderness butcher block, in the snow where I can get a good camera angle on it. I sharpen my knife, make the initial cuts, and ease the skin off as gently as I can. Most wild rabbit hides are too thin to tan without tearing them, but they're still useful. Cutting them in spirals turns them into long furry ropes. I've read that before central heating and down jackets, the Paiute people of the Great Basin Desert survived the harsh winters by weaving blankets out of such ropes. I've never done it, but there's no better time to figure it out.

I gut the rabbit with my usual care, separating every precious piece of fat from the organs and laying them all on the birch bark tray.

In my nightly prayers as I lie in bed, I've promised the rabbits that I'll use everything, absolutely *everything*, if they come to me, and that's what I intend to do.

I pile the intestines on a piece of bark to use as ice-fishing bait once the lake freezes. I tuck the ears into my pack, for who knows what, and I dry the huge back feet, the "snowshoes," over the fire as good luck charms.

I sing to myself as I strike a spark and start the fire, then spread a fresh piece of bark on top of the camera case. The table is all set.

I take my time cooking, then place a piece of heart—cooked to perfection in the scant half teaspoon of oil I rendered from the organ fat—on the ancestor plate.

I exhale onto it, adding my warm breath as part of the offering. "We are in this together," I tell the ancestors. "You saw me and my need, and you fed me. I see you too, in everything I do out here. Thank you. I remember and honor you."

Then I dive in. I start with the heart, the center of its small, vibrant body, and eat it in slow motion. I work my way in rapt delight through every morsel of the other organs. I feel the strength of the rabbit bounding in my system, as it bounds through these spruce forests. I can almost feel its feet slapping the granite rocks outside.

I grab one of the back feet and tap it on my hand, feeling something tickling the edge of my consciousness. I beat out a rhythm on my leg, a soft staccato resonating against the pole walls. *What am I missing? What do these feet remind me of?*

I've got it! The rhythm that's been haunting me, and big snowshoe hare feet slapping the granite? *That's it—the dream beasts! They were hares! They've been hares all along.*

I never pictured myself as a trapper—obviously, or I would never have left behind snare wire—but this land has been telling me over and over how it was prepared to feed me; I just wasn't getting it. Weeks of trying everything I could think of to bring in fish was nothing but wasted time and calories. Countless hours stalking with my bow, and I lost more arrows than I brought in animals. All the while, snowshoe hares have been *rat-a-tat-tatting* right through my camp, dipping their big fluffy toes into my dreams. Now, I've caught one in my first-ever snare, improvised on the spot just as the sun was setting. The message seems pretty clear.

Whatever ideas I might have had of myself before, I'm a trapper now. The sight of that dangling hare has changed my life forever. I lay my hand on my bow—not that I won't love you forever, Artemis, but it looks like you're going to have share me with my new trapline.

As I stand up to head back out and set more snares, I get an alert that the medical team is on its way.

Holy crap! I realize. It happened. They called it. I actually *did* enjoy my breakfast!

43

A POUND A DAY

When the medical check is over, I resist the urge to go out and watch as the boat carries the medical team away. I'm chilled from stripping down to my long underwear for the weigh-in, so I straddle the fire in the cabin instead.

My first medical check, a big hurdle, is over. I've been weighed, measured, photographed, the whole gamut of tests, and finally given a hale and hearty bill of health. There's significantly less of me to be hale and hearty though. The looseness of my pants hasn't been my imagination. I've lost roughly *a pound a day* since I've been out here. All that effort to stuff myself with calories my body had no interest in over the summer, and poof—every ounce of extra fat gone in less than a month.

I sit shrunken into myself, shaken. I'm still absorbing the news long after the sound of the boat engine dies away.

It will be okay, I tell myself, *because I'm living off more than just beauty these days.* I ate breakfast this morning, and there's still an entire rabbit carcass wrapped up in birch bark in the corner. The tide has turned. Trapping means bringing in game while I'm tucked in by the warm fire, not trudging around in the cold, burning more calories than I'm gaining. The weight loss will slow. I know it will.

As far as the welts on my thighs, the medical team was as stumped as me.

"Anything else to report?" they'd asked.

"Well, um...there's this little issue," I answered as I turned around and lowered my pants to my knees.

Several audible gasps.

I know how bad they look. The old welts are partly healed now, but are still deep purple, like bruises that never fade. The fresher ones are pink and shiny with brand-new skin around the outside, but the centers, while no longer swollen and weeping, are still crusty with scabs.

The medic scribbled in a spiral notebook and the survival staff took photos. Spider bites? Rash? Abrasion?

"Spider bites," was the verdict. "They must be spider bites."

But there's no way they are. They're in only one place on my body, but the same spot on both legs. Legs which are always covered. The welts have popped up over and over, without any holes or signs of bites. I've shaken my bedding out every night before bed and always cinch the hood of my sleeping bag down tight. There's no way spiders are getting in there.

At any rate, they're healing. I'll have to be satisfied with that.

Like this morning, the transition from several murmuring voices back to the stillness of the forest is jarring. I haven't been lonely out here—how could I be when the land speaks to me more and more all the time?—but it's a serious adjustment to go from so much human interaction back to none.

I rake my dirty fingers through my hair. It always sheds, but these days I get a full palmful with every finger combing. I've had hair fall out from rapid weight loss once before, when I had a long-lasting, high fever that consumed a lot of my body fat. So while it is very disconcerting to lose so much now, at least I'm not surprised by it. I'm just about to toss the wad of silver and brown hairs onto the coals when I stop myself and shove it into my pocket instead. It's time to get to trapping, and I've already lost half the day. With my tools, paracord, and new secret weapon—my own rapidly shedding hair—I head out to Rabbit Hollow.

It's absurdly difficult setting snares in this environment and with such insufficient equipment. It would be challenging anywhere, but far more so here. Given the lack of soil, there aren't many places where I can drive the stakes into the ground.

Here is what I'm up against: I need to find soil over six inches deep, near a good rabbit trail, and close to a small sapling. Even with all these criteria met, I need the sapling to bend just the right distance to end up in the middle of the trail and to put the trigger stick under the right amount of tension—so it can be sprung easily by a hare but not by the wind. At the same time, it can't apply so much force that it pulls the stakes out of the ground. Then I need to secure it all with the relatively weak, thin, and slippery inner strands of the parachute cord so I don't blow through my paracord too quickly.

If I manage all that, I still need to get the fishing line noose tied on just right, the perfect width and height off the ground, without triggering the spring pole myself. Then, because fishing line is floppy as heck, I need to tie it open and anchor it with the one cordage strong enough to keep it in place but weak enough for rabbits to break easily—my own glorious hair, which is volunteering for the task at an alarming rate.

I'm still crouched on my knees, the snow slowly melting into my buckskin pants from my body heat, when dusk finds me. My swiftly numbing fingers are having a harder and harder time tying knots in the nearly invisible hairs.

By dark I've added two more snares—just enough to officially make it a trapline, not a trap dot. Each took over an hour to create, but looking them over, I see they are masterpieces. *This could work*, I think. *I could start eating substantial calories again daily.*

Hope fills my chest as I look the traps over one last time in the glow of my headlamp. The clear fishing line and the silver hairs are hard to see, even knowing exactly where they are. And I always thought "hair trigger" was a metaphor!

44

PRIME NUMBER DAYS

y first weeks here were characterized by constant choices. Fishing or hunting? Simple shelter or winter-worthy shelter? Scouting farther afield or conserving calories?

My trapline changes all that. It's no longer a matter of, *How will I spend my time today?* but of, *How early will I get out to walk the trapline? Where will the next string of snares go?* and, *How many snares can I put up before it's too dark to see or the cold forces me to quit?*

Every day is a slight variation of traps and firewood, firewood and traps. Occasionally I add in construction or filling my new harvest basket—a willow-weaving project that has improved life dramatically—with cranberries. Sometimes I play little games with myself to break up the monotony. *Hey,* I think to myself one day, *it's day twenty-three. That's a prime number, a number only divisible by itself and one. That's pretty special. I bet something special will happen today.*

I go about the business of the day, harvesting cranberries that have emerged from under melting snow on a bluff a little east of camp. I've got my head down, following the veins of berry bushes along the rocks to an area I haven't picked before, when I turn a corner and my eye is caught by a flash of bright pink. There's a perfectly straight shaft sticking out of the ground with hot pink feathers at the top. *It's one of my lost arrows!* This is worth more to me than a basket of cranberries, but now I've got both! I'm so thrilled I do a little jig, holding the arrow to my chest. *Hot damn!*

Later that night, I remember my prediction—prime number day! And something special *did* happen!

The next sunset I walk down toward the lake to sing the sun down. It's been overcast all day, but there's one ray of light shining through the clouds and hitting a spot on the shore. Why sing under dark skies when I can stand in a ray of light for the evening lullaby?

I work my way down to the rocks below. The warmth on my cheeks is well worth the effort. After the third round of the song, I turn to go and see that the sun ray has moved and now falls on a patch of soil a stone's throw away from me. It's one of the only places on shore not covered in rocks. I walk over and feel a soft squelching and slick texture under my boots when I reach it. *It feels like clay!* Though ice crystals are spreading over the land in the dusky shadows elsewhere, the warmth of the sun has kept this spot thawed. I dig in my fingers and rub the tips together. It's smooth and slippery. *No question— it's definitely clay.* I've only got a narrow window to dig it before it freezes solid.

I claw up a few handfuls and hurry back to the cabin, grabbing the stuff sack to my sleeping bag. My mind is racing. If I play my cards right, this could be the best resource I've found yet—it means mortar for a chimney, pottery, cooking vessels, and a water vessel. It could be the key to many of the things that would make my life complete and more functional.

It's almost dark by the time my hole is a foot deep, and I'm starting to hit more rocks than clay. My legs are cramping from crouching for so long and my hands are frigid and seized up. The stuff sack is about two-thirds full; that's probably twenty or more pounds of clay. To make a strong cooking pot, I'll need to mix in sand to help it resist thermal shock. For mortar for the chimney stones, I'll want sand plus vegetation to give it tensile strength. I can use sphagnum moss as the vegetation, but the beach is all rocks. *Where am I going to get the sand?*

No matter, it's time to get home and warm up. I throw the stuff sack over my shoulder and trudge up the rock ledges toward the cabin, feeling like the luckiest woman on earth.

If I hadn't cared enough to sing the sun down or followed that ray of light when it beckoned, I would never have found the clay. My offering of gratitude led to me receiving yet another gift.

Living on beauty. Conversing with light. The blessings are reciprocal, and the magic continues.

45

EATING DREAM BEASTS

find a second rabbit in my trapline two days after the first and a third not long after that. I'm getting better all the time at predicting where the rabbits will move, and faster at setting my ridiculously complex snares.

I develop a rabbit-eating routine. Preparing and eating them has become the most important and meaningful thing in my life, a ritual every time. I can feel the calories singing to me as I process the carcass. Food has never tasted or felt like this in my entire life.

The first meal is the organs and the backstraps—the muscles that run along either side of the spine. This is where filet mignon comes from on larger animals. The next two meals are one front leg and one back leg, and the fourth is a soup of the ribcage, pelvis, and head. Roasted game is tastier than boiled, but roasting it over the fire is the worst thing I could do in my situation, as any fat it might contain would melt, drip into the fire, and be gone forever. Boiling is more practical, but much less delicious, so I develop my own technique that is somewhere in between roasting and boiling. It's a wilderness style of braising employing a browning method I dub the "Steam-Sauté."

My technique is this: Sautéing the organs usually uses up most of the fat I've rendered from the hare, but after them I add what little I have left to the pot. I sauté my leg pieces until the fat is absorbed and the meat is on the edge of burning, then I add a teaspoon or so of water—just enough to keep scorching at bay and loosen the stuck bits. When the legs are browned all over, I add more water and clamp the lid down tight, braising them in their own juices. After the first round of cooking, I use my knife to scrape the edge of one of my precious salt buttons until there's just enough salt to bring out the flavor, then do one or two more rounds of braising until the meat and tendons are well caramelized and absurdly tender.

Julia Child never gave any dish the care and attention I give each and every part of these rabbits. Everything in my world revolves around these scanty meals, so I settle for nothing less than absolute melting-off-the-bone perfection.

I always save the best for last. Every hare-eating saga ends with the boiled head—"for dessert."

When I raised meat rabbits on the homestead, I saved the organs and rendered all the internal fat, but the heads went into the compost bucket. Now I'm appalled to think of how many I wasted.

Rabbits are lean creatures—dangerously lean, from a survival perspective. Your body needs a certain amount of fat to be able to process the protein from meat. Most animals store fat in their muscles, thus the marbling of fancy cuts of beef and the richness of pork. Not rabbits. What little fat they have is either under their skin, in the connective tissues around and between muscles, surrounding their organs, or in their heads.

This makes living on rabbits a dicey prospect. If you don't carefully save and eat every morsel of fat on them, you can fall prey to rabbit starvation, a kind of protein toxicity. Without fat or carbohydrates to balance them, the toxins from eating lean protein build up in your system to dangerous levels, leading to fatigue, nausea, diarrhea, and eventually death. You can literally *starve to death* eating all the rabbits you can hold.

My domestic rabbits, fed twice a day and not working for a living under harsh winter conditions, had enough subcutaneous fat that I rendered it and stored it in the root cellar in pint jars. I never bothered with their heads. These northern hares are entirely different—I get a scant *teaspoon* of fat from the organs. Carefully peeling every bit of fat off the intestines and scraping the skin thoroughly with my knife, I get another tiny dollop. Enough to brown the liver and heart. This means the only thing standing between me and rabbit starvation is the head. My body seems to know it and responds accordingly, thus every morsel of this delectable treat—which at one time I would have considered grisly and disgusting—feels like dessert.

The cheek meat is rich and delicious, and the eyeballs and fat behind the eyeballs are even better. I can feel my body absorbing the nutrients almost before they hit my stomach. But what it's really all about is the brain. Brains are almost entirely fat. That makes the two bites of the rabbit's head more valuable than the rest of it put together.

I don't let myself go right for the brain, though. I eat every scrap off of the skull first. I've eaten a lot of deer tongues, so I knew to expect rabbit tongues to be delicious, but miniscule. I'd never considered that I'd relish the upper palate, though. What surprises me more are the sinuses—delicate mazes of paper-thin bone and dark red tissue, thick with capillaries and nerves. I wouldn't go so far as to call them delicious, but they are fascinating and different, crunchy and rich, and certainly tasty.

After I've sucked the last edible bits off the skull, it's time for the brain. It's milder in flavor than the meat or organs, but rich and creamy—like butter, only firmer and more substantial. Rabbit truffles, I call them—not actually sweet, but with the same kind of melt-in-your-mouth texture you'd only find in a high-end chocolate shop.

The first few hares are pure sensory experiences, and I'm too overwhelmed by flavors and sensations of eating real meals to think about much else. Over time it goes deeper. I come to understand rabbit biology in a new and more meaningful way—from the inside out.

Taking their bodies apart helps me understand how perfectly adapted they are to survive out here, and their stomach contents show me how they go about it. Eating their sense organs shows me the way they experience the world. The tender tongues that sample the spruce boughs, the intricate sinuses that smell every nuance of their environment. Their ears, the most important sense organ they have, are an entirely different texture than the rest of the skull. More like rock than bone, they never get any softer from boiling, whereas the rest of the skull falls to pieces.

I eat everything but their digestive systems, piling their stomachs and intestines in the back of the cabin to one day use as bait for ice fishing.

Every week out here more and more of my previous ways of being—the ones honed by human civilization—are slipping away. There is no routine but this routine, no moment but the present one. My ancestors feel increasingly present with me, as every day I live more and more like them. Over time I'm also becoming more and more rabbit. With each one I eat, more of the cells in my body are built from the molecules of their muscles and organs. The mysterious creatures who haunted my dreams have become flesh and blood, but are still the animals of my dreams in a whole new sense. My life is intertwined with theirs in a way that feels far more intimate than anything I experienced in my years of raising meat rabbits. It feels deeply satisfying and, given that I was also born in the year of the rabbit in Chinese astrology, utterly perfect.

Some days, I would even swear I feel my nose twitching when the wind shifts.

46

HAIR TRIGGERS, HARE TRIGGERS

Some days are leaner than others, but it's been over a week since I've had a hungry day. Eating regularly is such an amazing gift that I'm staggered by it. Unfortunately, this new way of being takes care of one major concern of life out here, but it underscores another.

It was one thing not pooping when I wasn't eating, but now that my body remembers about regular meals again, the fact that it's forgotten about getting the food out the other end is an increasing concern. I'm not keeping careful track, but I think it's been nearly two weeks since my last squat in the bushes. Keeping the fiber coming in and vigilantly avoiding dehydration are all I know to do for it, there being almost no edible plants on the peninsula, and certainly no laxative ones like I found on the mainland.

I don't know if it's the lower temperatures or my system adjusting, but now the cranberries aren't only palatable, my body craves them, and I haven't had a sour stomach from them since the cranberry surprise my first week. They aren't sweet, but they're flavorful and juicy, contain the fiber I desperately need, and besides spruce needle tea, are the only vitamins I'm getting.

When the sun answers my prayers, as it sometimes does, I prioritize berries. I spend hours on my knees, my little harvest basket tied around my waist with buckskin strips. Every morning I eat as many as I can manage, before my mouth gets so raw from the acid that it bleeds.

As the overall temperatures continue to drop, I stop counting on thaws to pick berries and instead paw the snow off, frantic to harvest and store enough to see me through the winter.

As I'd hoped, my weight loss seems to have slowed significantly, and my lips are whole again, thank god. My thighs are still discolored, but the skin is growing back over the scabs. I don't know how, but I seem to have finally vanquished the throbbing welts.

Every night is colder and I get closer to the fire, until eventually I spend the evenings straddling it, with my legs as close as I can get them without burning my pants. Too much of its heat is going right out through the smoke hole. Countless times a day, I walk past the piles of stone I've hauled from all over the peninsula and look at them longingly. It's well past time to put them to use for the chimney I planned, but I've got to keep my trapline up and that takes all the time I have and then some, so there the stones sit.

Maintaining snares made from fishing line is harder than I ever imagined, even after the hurdle of finding suitable spots for traps and the gymnastic act of setting them. They require constant upkeep. Snare wire stays where it's put. Rabbits may learn to go around it, but they can't remove it and eventually one will be distracted or unwary and get caught. Not so with fishing line. It's easier to snip through than a willow twig, and snipping willow twigs is what rabbit teeth are made for. Every morning when I walk the trapline, two-thirds of my snares have been snipped clean off by the rabbits in the night, and many of those that aren't have been nosed out of the way, snapping the fragile hairs that held them open. Just resetting the snares I've got takes half the day, and I need to be adding more if I want to keep eating, not just maintaining them.

I'm constantly scanning the woods for areas dense with rabbit tracks that are tucked into forested areas with low spruces where trapping is possible. I develop systems. I barb the bases of my stakes, so they hold better in the thin soil and resist the upward force of the bent saplings. I modify my trigger sticks so they'll be more sensitive where they're protected from the wind, and less sensitive where strong winds could set them off.

Before my first week of trapping is over, I've got three forest hollows covered in snares, and it's taken everything I've got. The right young saplings are few and far between, and as temperatures drop they're less springy, so I'm starting to innovate. I cut saplings and lash them to sturdier trunks if they aren't growing where I need them. I substitute rock weights for saplings where I can, securing them with paracord and throwing them over branches to give me the upward pull I need to get the hares off of their feet. Where there isn't enough soil to hold stakes or saplings for spring poles, I rely on the lifting pole system I learned from Mors Kochanski, a bushcraft legend, and use a swiveling pole to tighten the noose and lift the hare.

With all my innovations and techniques, every snare I set is still completely dependent on those three fragile hairs that hold each noose open and in place.

My system gets more sophisticated day by day, and soon I'm sorting the hairs from my head. Brown strands are for where soil is exposed, so they blend into the darker background. The silver ones are for when the ground is covered in snow, where they're so invisible I can barely see them myself. As much as I've tried to make peace with it, I'm not going to lie—frosty hairs starting to appear at age twenty-five was a little rough. Now, being able to suit each snare to its environment is a godsend.

Who would have thought? Premature graying—my secret wilderness superpower.

47

SNUGGLE ROCKS

My sleeping bag, enormous and fluffy as it is, feels thinner all the time. Finally, one night I shiver for hours before getting warm enough to sleep and then wake up cold, stiff, and feeling unrested. The bag is rated to minus forty, and I doubt it's even gotten below zero yet. This doesn't bode well, and I need to do something about it before I burn through my remaining calorie reserves by shivering all night.

It's time to implement phase two of cabin construction—ceiling insulation. I've been avoiding it as long as I can, since a lot of my light is coming in through the green plastic of my tarp roof.

Hot air rises though, and I'm losing too much heat through the thin plastic to wait any longer.

The quickest and easiest insulation I can think of is bushy treetops all over the roof. I head out to harvest, remembering as I do that this is another prime number day. *Hey, maybe something magical will happen!* I cut and haul the bushiest young black spruces I can find, always cutting where the thinning will help the neighboring trees.

I plan to pile these on the roof, but I need more structural supports before I do. I have an idea of where to go for the poles I need, but it doesn't feel right. I follow the impulse to go elsewhere, letting myself be drawn to where the pull is strongest. It doesn't make any sense, but I find myself going out past the rock arena to the grove of spruce trees, where I searched for the grouse on equinox.

I see the perfect tree and approach it to lay my hand on it, when a tree to the left of it grabs my attention. It's a little crooked and less convenient to reach with my saw, but the message I'm getting is "Take me," so I cut it instead. I stand aside as it tilts toward me and falls to the ground. As it does, it reveals the tree behind it. My eyes rise up from the trunk to its tip, drawn by a splash of color. Sticking out of the trunk, well above my head, is an arrow with bright pink fletching.

I can't believe my eyes. I feel like turning around to see if someone is playing a trick on me, just like I did when I found the letter-N sticker, but I know I'm all alone out here. This looks like my arrow, but how could it possibly be?

Holy crap—the grouse! I lost the first arrow I shot at the grouse when it disappeared into this grove of trees. *This is that arrow!*

I looked and looked for it, that day and after, but never found it. No wonder. I wasn't looking above my head. I'm almost too stunned to be excited about it. *This is crazy—what are the chances?* This is the second long lost arrow that has come back to me. It only happened because I chose to let go of the logical place to cut a tree and follow an urge I couldn't explain, then did so again to cut this unlikely looking tree instead of the perfect one beside it.

And of course I found it on a PRIME NUMBER DAY!

I hurry back to the cabin with the tree over my shoulder and tuck the arrow back into my quiver, next to my other prime number arrow, still incredulous. Over and over the miraculous happens out here, but I'm blown away with surprise and wonder every time. I'm still shaking my head about it as I layer the roof with young spruce trees. I shingle them around the smoke hole, hoping they'll let smoke out while keeping my precious heat in. *I'll get to the chimney soon,* I tell myself, *once I have the whole ceiling insulated.*

It's now dark enough inside the cabin that I need my headlamp on during the day. I'm scrambling in my backpack for parachute cord to secure more rafters for my now heavier roof, when my light falls on my buckskin overalls. These are what I continued to furiously sew when I should have been leaving for the airport to fly north, and are the main reason I missed my first flight to Yellowknife. In that way, they have already been invaluable, because accidentally missing that flight gave me another day and allowed me to put together the fur lining of my parka. I couldn't have predicted that result at the time, but back in that other lifetime I obviously considered them important enough to risk my trip to complete. And yet, I still haven't worn them.

But here's the thing—*I never had any intention of wearing them.* I know overalls are standard gear in cold climates, but for some of us, they also mean taking our parkas off to pee, thus letting out more body heat than they save. Knowing this, like the world's largest sweater, I made them more as a source of raw material than a garment. I originally planned not to bring paracord, so I thought I'd likely be cutting up most of the buckskin outer layer of the overalls for cordage, patches to repair clothing, and similar purposes. By the time I changed my mind about the cordage, I was at base camp, and it was too late to think about other overall options. I used some of the leather for the slingshot I made early on, and the salt buttons I put on them have been invaluable, but other than that they have just sat here. They've got me thinking though, and now I'm certain that they can keep me warmer at night than any amount of ceiling insulation.

I dig out my precious buckskin bundle and the magic needle from day two. I turn the overalls inside out to reveal the liner—heavy wool cloth from a fabric store, which I triple washed in hot water until it was as thick as an oven mitt.

Since the day I first placed a hot rock in my lap during my evening tea, crotch rocks have been my best friends and constant evening companions. They keep me warm and comfortable by the fire, but they cool quickly, and once they do, it's into the chilly sleeping bag for me. What I really need are rocks with enough mass to hold the heat much longer and a way to take them into the sleeping bag, without melting it or burning me.

I pirate thread from the overall seams and use my multitool scissors to cut the wool lining out. Some quick lines of stitches and slits cut around the top for a cinch closure and *bingo*—now I've got a thick wool bag to insulate a hot rock, so I can safely snuggle with it all night.

Some of my hearth rocks are already cracking from the hot fire. If this keeps up, I'm going to need a good number of stones to have enough snuggle rocks to last all winter. The only round stones of the right size that I've seen are down by the water. The shore is already icing up along the edges, so I'm guessing the rocks I want will be locked away beneath the ice soon. I head down and find several perfect candidates. I'm staring into the water looking for more, when I notice a spot right off the ledge that isn't solid with cobbles like everywhere else. It's a light colored, opaque surface that doesn't look like granite. I grab a stick and give it a good poke. The stick sinks in and comes up with a few small grains clinging to the tip. *Sand! The sand I need for my clay mix!*

To reach in, I take my coat off and push my sweater sleeve all the way up to my armpit. My hand is still two feet from the bottom and my skin is burning from the icy water. I'm not about to wade in there. How can I get to the sand without giving myself another case of hypothermia?

I've got it! My rusty tin cans and parachute cord! I head home and lash a can to the end of a long stick, then try it out. Even with the stick, the can barely brushes the bottom. I need to get a few inches deeper. There's nothing to do but strip. I put my sweater down on the icy rock ledge and lie flat out on it, naked from the waist up. I plunge my arm up to the shoulder in the frigid lake and bring up half a can of clean lake sand.

My fingers are so numb that I can barely grip the stick by the time I have a small pile harvested. It will have to do. I make a carrying bag out of my T-shirt and haul the sand up, place it next to the clay and heap moss over both to keep them from freezing solid. The effort of hauling the rest of the rocks up the hill keeps me from getting hypothermic, but the skin of the submerged arm is flushed and tingly for the next hour.

After dinner, I build up the fire and carefully heat the best-looking stones. Stones from lakes and rivers can explode when heated, as any water that might be trapped inside expands as it turns to steam. I heap heavy logs on top of them to absorb the impact should that happen, but they heat without incident.

Once the best of the bunch is too hot to touch, I use a stick to roll it out of the fire so it can cool in the open air. When I pop it into the wool bag, my "snuggle rock cozy," the smell of burning hair floods my nostrils. *Too soon!* I manage to dump it out before it does more than char the surface of the wool. When I can touch it with a bare finger for a fraction of a second without burning myself, I try again. *Perfect.* It steams but doesn't smoke. I tuck it into the sleeping bag while I drink my tea and prepare for bed.

I've been shivering for at least half an hour, often more, upon crawling into bed each night. The cold nylon sucks up my body heat until it's finally warm enough to be comfortable. Tonight the lining is silky and inviting, wrapping around me like welcoming arms. *Amazing!*

I use my feet to push the rock down into the bottom of the bag where I can rest my feet on it all night. Before long they are too hot, and I move the stone around, distributing the heat to different places. I don't fall asleep any faster than usual, but it's a delicious, rather than an agonizing process. I finally nod off in a fetal position spooning the rock, and the comfort of it goes beyond just its temperature. There's something so soothing about a solid weight, a substantial mass to wrap my arms around, that seems to multiply the warmth it radiates.

When I wake up in the middle of the night for my customary sleepless hour or two, I'm almost too warm for comfort, but this is such a new and alien sensation that I relish it, and my late-night survival strategizing is calmer and more content than the usual frenetic hamster wheel.

It takes several nights to perfect my process, moving the rock around the fire so I don't get hot spots that will burn the wool, while achieving the perfect temperature to maximize heat retention. Once it's just right, I pop it into the cozy and watch the air-dampened wool steam until it's dry, so I'm putting warmth, but no moisture, into my sleeping bag.

Instead of dreading the icy nylon, crawling into a warm bed to snuggle with my woolly darling becomes my favorite part of the day.

48

MOON MYSTERIES, MOON WISDOM

A lot of people wonder how bleeding women deal with their moon time on *Alone*. The answer is that a lot of the time, they don't. The body pays attention, and it knows that famine conditions aren't optimal for starting new life. When calories are truly scarce and the body isn't getting enough to have resources to spare, it stops ovulating and shuts down the reproductive system until things improve. I've been eating steadily for a while now, but it isn't enough to sustain me long-term, and certainly hasn't made up for the near total caloric deficit of the first several weeks.

That's why I can hardly believe it when, just like clockwork on the day it's due, I feel a deep, familiar ache in my midsection. *Phantom cramps*, I tell myself, and continue to walk my trapline, but I'm getting nervous. I haven't reached the third hollow before it's clear that there's nothing phantom about them and that I have a situation to deal with. Participants who will be menstruating while on *Alone* are provided with sanitary supplies and strict instructions not to repurpose them in any way. Before I make it to all my snares, I abandon the trapline and head back to the cabin for some of those supplies.

I'm not someone who goes about their normal routine while bleeding with nothing but minor inconvenience. My cramps didn't start in earnest until I was a junior in college, but when they did, they made up for lost time. They were so out of the blue that I had no idea what was happening and thought something was terribly, terribly wrong with me. Until that moment, although I'd had a cycle for many years, I'd had only an occasional ache in my belly during my period and never really understood what some people complained about with menstrual cramps.

By the time I was twenty-one, they regularly crippled me with excruciating pain, diarrhea, nausea, and sometimes vomiting. The more I resisted the pain and cursed my body, the worse it became. I went from someone who avoided medications of any kind to someone who kept ibuprofen within arm's length for at least one week each month. I judged myself for my weakness and my body for betraying me so cruelly.

It wasn't until my thirties that I started to look deeper into the source of my cramps—why some months were almost manageable and some beyond excruciating. For the first time, I realized there was a pattern. My cramps were always the most intolerable when I wasn't listening to my heart and didn't have my own back. They were debilitating when I was unhappy in my relationship with Chris but felt too guilty to do anything about it. When, after our divorce, I became increasingly aware of the abusive behaviors of my new partner but moved across the country with him anyway, the pain was beyond anything I had ever experienced. My body was telling me, *No! Stop! You can't do this!* But I wasn't listening, so it kept saying it louder until finally I did.

It took years to turn that epiphany into action. I realized that how I treated my body throughout the previous month had a huge impact on my cramps. I got better at loving my body and found that if, instead of willing myself to resist the pain, I relaxed and breathed deeply into the very source of it, it would ease. It wouldn't go away, but its grip would lessen enough for me to fall asleep, and I would wake up more comfortable. It took the Weaving Earth program, where those who were menstruating were honored and encouraged to nurture themselves and celebrate their body's cycles, to help me stop dreading my bleeding time. I came to look forward to it as a time of rest, renewal, and letting go of what no longer serves me.

I'd love to have the luxury of spending my first day of bleeding here doing nothing but resting and self-nurturing, but I don't see how I can with all my pressing survival needs. Once I've tended to the necessities, I hike back out to the trapline, slightly bent over but relieved that the pain isn't truly debilitating.

No rabbits in my snares, and for the first time ever, I'm relieved. *I've got more than enough blood to deal with already, thank you.* I haul water and tuck myself in by the fire.

Today is Thursday, Dance Party day, but even though I have yet to miss one, I don't have a dance party in me. I sit by the fire, cradling a snuggle rock to my belly, and sway a bit to the crackling of the flames in the hearth, just enough to feel I've given dancing an effort. I do my best to speak lovingly to my body, but I'm horrified at my blood loss, which ironically, is significantly more than normal for me. Even with my hunting and trapping I'm losing weight—I don't have any extra blood or protein to spare.

The next morning, as I toss my used pad into the fire to be sure it won't attract any predators, a different kind of sensation grips my midsection. *Jackpot!*

There's nothing like prolonged abdominal cramping to unstick what's been stuck. The hormone that causes the uterus to cramp isn't site-specific. Everything in the general vicinity often experiences cramps as well, thus the low back pain and loose bowels that often accompany menstrual periods. This is the one situation I can imagine where I'm thrilled at the prospects of intestinal cramping.

With my fingers crossed, I head down the hill to my latrine site. I pull back the sphagnum moss to dig a hole and, *thank god, my bowels are actually moving!* I crouch in the underbrush, Labrador tea tickling my thighs, and in just a few minutes have finally achieved the unachievable. *Thank you generous moon time! Thank you cramping belly!*

As disturbed as I am at the blood loss, it's well worth the trade-off. I want to leap with joy. I've finally had my first poop in weeks, and I'm putting myself back together when I remember the GoPro camera on my head. I was recording in the cabin before I headed out to my latrine spot, which means—*dear god, I just recorded a first-person perspective of myself pooping, changing my pad, and wiping. Audio and all.* I don't know who I feel sorrier for: myself, for having accidentally filmed one of the most intimate moments of my life out here, or the poor, unsuspecting video editor who will eventually screen this footage for the show.

I take the camera off and point it toward my face. "I forgot the camera was running," I say to it. "I am really sorry you had to see that, and if you even think about airing this footage or showing it to *anyone*, I will never forgive you."

By the time I get back to the cabin, I'm so thrilled to have finally pooped that I find the accidental filming more funny than horrifying.

After walking my trapline, I take the rest of the day to weave another basket, one for cranberry storage rather than harvesting. The rich red willow weaves up beautifully, and I'm adding the spokes to start the basket's sides when I notice the back of my legs itching. I rub at them absently and keep working. By the time I've woven another section—with a lovely, peeled willow spiral design—I'm squirming, and the itching has turned to burning. After starting to heal and thinking my trials were finally over, now the backs of both of my legs are on fire, and I can feel them pulsing with my heartbeat. I drop the basket and pull down my pants and long underwear. Hot welts are already rising on both legs, worse than ever. *Damn, damn, damn!*

My body was finally coming back online—my lips healed, my legs healing, food coming in and now coming out again too. *Can't I get a break here? What is going on?* And then it hits me—it's been over two weeks since I had a new welt. The same amount of time I've been totally constipated. What is the only thing I ever do out here where my pants are down and my thighs are exposed to the elements? *Poop!* I want to smack my own forehead.

I remember the Labrador tea tickling the backs of my legs this morning. It all makes sense. *How did I never make the connection? There is Labrador tea all over my latrine site and I'm squatting down into it every time I poop. I'm allergic to Labrador tea!*

As painful as the new welts are, I'm more grateful for finally solving the mystery than upset by the pain. I'm getting good enough at trapping to eat every day, my digestive system is working again, and I know how to avoid more welts in the future. *I finally have my body back!*

Over the next few days, the welts build and crest. The sores open and weep. There are long nights of tossing and turning as my legs itch and burn. Instead of cursing, I praise my body and its wisdom for helping me finally learn how to keep myself whole and well from here on out.

49

IN IT TO WIN IT

t still takes everything I've got, but with the trapline producing, my body healing, and my moon time and first medical check behind me, I'm feeling strong, capable, and determined. I'm in it to win it again, and for the first time in a long while, it actually feels possible.

The cabin looks like I've decorated it for a lynx's birthday party—furry streamers stretch back and forth across the rafters everywhere I look. With every hare I snare I add to the celebration, carefully skinning and cleaning the hides, cutting them in spirals, then twisting them into rabbit rope. I hang them up and they sway in the heat thermals above the fire until they're perfectly dry, then I wind them into a big ball of ridiculously fuzzy yarn. Occasionally I find a squirrel in one of my rabbit snares, and I tuck their tiny, tanned hides in with the rabbit yarn. With each one I picture the furry parka pockets I hope to make with them.

I think about snowshoe hares constantly. (In all transparency, I usually refer to them as rabbits, even though I'm a biologist and have studied mammalogy and know better.) They're in all my waking thoughts, and many of my sleeping thoughts too.

As the temperature drops, the wind, which has been mostly out of the north, also shifts.

One morning after a good eastern gale, I walk down to the shore for my morning tea to find the southeastern shore iced up several feet out into the bay. Just like that, arctic winter is no longer a looming threat on the horizon; it's here.

After so many years of judging trapping as far less humane than other hunting methods, my perspective is shifting rapidly. There's nothing about this process that feels like I'm tricking defenseless creatures—far from it.

Even with my big human brain and its capacity to think complex thoughts, it's all I can do to try to stay a step ahead of these sly critters. Given how often they nip my loop out of the way rather than pass through it, it feels clear to me that every time I manage to bring one in it is a gift—an offering. I feel it's the hares and the land seeing me, my need and my wide open heart, and sharing just enough to keep me going, but only if I keep up my end of the bargain.

Some people think that hunters must be cruel or disconnected from animals in order to hunt them. For me the opposite is true. I feel closer to my prey every day, as well I should. I don't believe the fox hates the hare it kills; I believe it loves it like life itself—because it *is* life itself. And in turn, every hare out here knows deep down that it isn't going to die of old age. One day it's going to get too slow and be eaten.

It's the fox that keeps the hare population strong, ensuring that only the smartest and swiftest pass their genes on to the next generation. And the fate of every snowshoe hare is to one day be consumed by, and thus turn into, a predator. Their lives are intimately entwined; they can't be separated. It's a beautiful relationship and a privilege for me to step into this ancient dance, just like the goddess Artemis herself.

I am slow and bumbling compared to a fox, so my gift to the rabbits certainly isn't helping to keep their population strong. It's that, in offering their lives to me, they are showing a world of viewers that the natural world responds better to humility, love, and connection than it does to brute strength and domination. I'm also giving the rabbits the opportunity to live a new life in my body—to travel to places and see things no peninsula-bound snowshoe hare could ever dream of. As I lie in bed for that nightly hour of restless hunger before I fall asleep, I remind them of all this and offer them my love and praise.

The hours I spend crouching in the snow, struggling with the impossibly small knots in my nearly invisible hair, would probably feel incredibly hard and frustrating if I didn't give myself pep talks throughout them: *The land wants you here, Woniya. It's teaching you how to make it. Keep showing up and doing your part. You've got this.*

I think I would have continued to feel like I could make it—that I could go the distance and potentially even win—if the rabbits hadn't mysteriously disappeared from the whole peninsula.

50

THE GREAT RABBIT EXODUS

Though the shore is iced in, the lake to the south, where the deep water surges with choppy waves, is still open as far as I can see. That's why I'm caught off guard when I walk to the far end of the trapline one day to find the shady, sheltered north bay iced up completely. Two days later, the shore there is piled high with chunks of ice and the water is open again, from storm waves breaking up the ice and tossing it onto shore. Overnight, this freezes solid, and the tumbled ice stockade becomes a permanent feature of the winter landscape, making it harder to access the north bay and reminding me daily of the ever-changing and turbulent nature of this wild and rugged land.

As the deep cold settles in, we get lake effect snow. The sky is socked in with clouds from morning to night, and all day a dusting of fine powder sifts down from it.

The constant snow is rough for berry harvesting, but fabulous for tracking. I regularly see lynx, wolverine, and ermine tracks. There are less hare tracks than ever, though—not just in the areas I frequent, but all over. *What is going on here?* I walk my trails with growing unease—nothing about this makes sense. How can the rabbits all disappear at once?

The bird populations are changing too. The swans are long gone, as are the ducks, but a new bird species arrives. Small and pinkish, with red spots in the middle of their chests, the new birds are roughly sparrow-like, but their behavior and calls are distinctive. They cling to the bare birch branches in flocks, calling back and forth all day, keeping me endlessly entertained. I name them "Zoinkers," after the hilarious one-note noise they make.

I'm grateful for the joy the Zoinkers bring me, because I need every bit I can get right now. Trapping, my lifeline, is getting much harder, and not just because there are fewer rabbits. The frozen ground is impossible to drive stakes into, so now I have to seek out thick sphagnum moss that's frozen enough to hold my uprights. It's working, but barely.

One hare is not even a day's worth of calories, and as I bring in less of them, I decrease my portion size to stretch each one out for two or more days. Eventually, I have my first hungry day—nothing but berries and chaga tea—since I began my trapline, and it shakes me to my core. I eat berries for breakfast and rose hips for supper, then dig the pile of old bones out from the corner of the cabin. There's nothing but tiny scraps of gristle on them, but I boil them, yet again, for my first pot of Starvation Soup since I ate the last of the grouse. The result is a slightly opaque, pale-colored liquid. The sight turns my stomach, and it cools to lukewarm in the minute I sit staring at it, convincing myself to drink it. I gulp it down in one big chug before it can get any colder, then sit quietly for a long time holding my felt boot liners over the fire and watching the curls of steam rise off them and up through the smoke hole.

Long after they're dry, I stare into the coals. *Can I handle living on beauty again now that I've broken the habit?* I honestly don't know, but it's looking like I might need to start trying.

I pile the thrice boiled bones into a rusty tin can, to distinguish them from the much more exciting *twice* boiled bones, and tuck in for the night.

The next morning, I find a rabbit in one of my lifting poles snares and stop worrying about the diminishing tracks.

It's a brief respite. I make the rabbit last three days, and none come in to replace it. Now I'm certain I'm not just making it up. Tracks are sparse everywhere, and in many areas there are none at all. I see maybe a tenth of the rabbit activity I used to. *Are they onto me? Has word spread from group to group, prompting all the rabbits to clear out for the mainland?*

One morning I head out to check traps and see a fresh track just twenty feet from the cabin. *Sweet!* But soon it's obvious it isn't a rabbit track. *Oh cool. It's a fox track.*

In my normal life, I love predators. Coyotes standing in a meadow sniffing the wind, gray foxes dashing across the pavement in front of my headlights on country roads, the occasional mountain lion track in the forest behind my house. Out here, it's a different story. The local predators, while not my enemies, are certainly my competition. Their lives—just like mine—are dependent on small game, and they're a lot better equipped to catch it.

My mind pivots from, *Oh cool, a fox track*, to, *Oh shit, a fox track*.

The first thing I see at the trapline is a jumbled pile of paracord sheath and innards with one of my rabbit-lifting rocks on the ground. There are tufts of rabbit fur on the snow too, and at first I think a rabbit must have chewed its way out of my trap. Then I look at the cord. Rabbit teeth bite things off cleanly. This cord is frayed and jagged. Fox teeth, no question. This is cataclysmic. Not only did a fox steal my rabbit, but now I've taught it what to look for.

I can't blame the fox. If I found a rabbit it had dropped, I would snap it up without a second thought, too. But how am I supposed to bring in food with a fox—nocturnal and with ears that can hear a struggling rabbit from hundreds of yards away—checking my traps before I do? I heave a huge sigh and sit for a while staring at the rock on the ground. I don't have the heart to reset the snare.

I see almost no tracks in the two northern sections of my trapline, but in the southeastern section I find another of my lifting rocks on the ground. The trigger stick attached to it is broken in two, and the noose is completely missing. Stolen and dragged off. Two rabbits I could have eaten are gone, and my traps destroyed—*Aaargh!* I don't reset anything. Why should I? The more rabbits I snare, the more I teach the fox that this is a gold mine.

Foxes are not on our game list. It isn't as if *Alone* participants can hunt anything we'd like at any time just because we have no other food to rely on. We still have to follow local game restrictions and bag limits. In this area, we're allowed to shoot (but not trap) one wolverine, but martens, foxes, wolves, lynx, or anything else not on a very specific list, are off-limits. If I trap or shoot the fox that is raiding my snares, I'll be disqualified and sent home. There's nothing I can do to reclaim my trapline from it, and I want to scream in frustration. Maybe that would be a more helpful response than letting myself feel so defeated, but I don't do it. I trudge back to the cabin silently, my boots heavy, and the cold biting deeply into my hunched shoulders.

I eat a handful of frozen cranberries and stare at the thrice boiled bones from my last Starvation Soup sitting by the fire. These bones are more spent than the last batch I ate. There are no calories left in them, but there's calcium and they are something for my belly to work on, so I toast them on a flat rock. When they're golden brown and brittle, I crunch them up and swallow them with a swig of water.

Day after day, I walk the few traps I have left. I see fox tracks a few more times, but not much else. I can't decide whether to be relieved the fox hasn't stolen any more hares or horrified that there's now no hare sign at all. *Has the fox cleaned them out in just a few days? Have they been scared into hiding?*

My world is shattered, my confidence dashed against the rocks like the toasted bones. Rabbits and my trapline are my everything—without them, all I've created and the life I'm building out here crumble. There's nothing else for it. I disable my remaining snares, hoping the fox will get discouraged and move on.

51

THE SECOND BIG CHILL

'm at a loss, but I refuse to give up and let despair take me, so I do the only thing I know will bring in some calories. I head out to my cranberry zone, a south-facing slope where the tops of a few bushes are poking up above the snow. There are Zoinker tracks all around them, and on the snow beside the tracks are weird little red things that look like plastic. I crouch down and look closer. I put one in my mouth. It's tart. *Not plastic—cranberry*. It's the hollowed out skin of a cranberry. *The Zoinkers are eviscerating the cranberries! Nooooo!* These berries are the one resource that doesn't run away or outsmart me, and now they're disappearing too?

I paw the snow off of the bushes and pick frantically for hours, pushed by the fear of losing the one food I can still count on. As I work my way down the peninsula to new berry patches, I scare up flocks of the strawberry-pink Zoinkers. Even now, I'm amused at their silly antics and ridiculous noises, but I'm still frustrated at the competition.

Come on buddies, I love you, but you can fly, and this peninsula is all I've got. Lay off the cranberries!

Though light is fading, I want another full basket before heading home, so I keep picking, belly down on the snow, until my fingers are stiff with cold.

When the sun slips below the horizon and I stand up to sing to it, I realize my legs won't hold me. My knees are buckling, and my balance is off. *Oh crap.* I try to touch my pinky to my thumb, a test for finger dexterity, but it just tells me what I already know. I'm hypothermic. Again. And far from home with dark settling in. *Shit, shit, shit.* I should know better than to stay still in these temperatures for so long.

I wobble my way through some shallow squats to get my blood moving, until finally my legs come back online. I don't have the fine motor skills right now to turn the camera off, so I toss the whole thing, extended tripod and all, over my shoulder like a club and head to the cabin, praying I can get a fire going.

There are a couple of coals buried deep in my ashes, and with the help of some thin pieces of birch bark, which work like natural lighter fluid due to the volatile oils they contain, I'm able to blow the coals into flames. I sit huddled by the fire, warming first one side then the other, as sensation returns to my hands. My breath is tight in my chest and my shoulders are up around my ears. I can feel the frigid air and the darkness pouring in from the empty door frame, but I'm too cold to get up and close it and all motivation seems to have left me. I try to muster a song, a positive thought—anything. But they don't come. I'm too damn drained from working so hard every day to keep the cold, dark, and hunger at bay, and barely managing it, to sing right now.

I can see the firelight dancing on the pile of stones outside. My "chimney stones."

Haha.

My stomach is leaden as I realize there's no way I'm finishing that chimney. *It's too late, far too late,* I think dully, feeling numb with disappointment and overwhelmed by all the important tasks I have yet to do—and that will likely never be accomplished. I screwed up. I should have prioritized it as soon as I found the clay, but now that's a frozen hunk, as is the sand that I nearly froze my arm off to drag from the bottom of the lake. I could thaw them bit by bit in front of the fire to mix up my mortar, but that would be a tremendous effort, and as soon as I'd built with it, it would freeze solid. When it did, the ice crystals would break it apart and crumble it to pieces. The same is true of my plans for a clay cook pot and water container. Even if I could manage to make them, dry them, and fire them without their freezing in the process, any water I put in them would expand when it turned to ice and destroy them anyway. These were the mistakes of a woman from a warm climate, who didn't fully grasp the stark reality of arctic winter and how quickly it changes everything.

I am defeated. My shelter is incomplete, my food is drying up, and animals far more skilled at arctic survival than I am are gobbling up my resources.

As soon as I'm able, I struggle to my feet to pull the door into place and shut out the sight of the stones. I don't want to have to look at them. They no longer look like hope and possibility to me, but like a tremendous pile of wasted calories. *How many of the pounds I lost during those first weeks went directly to hauling that pile of now useless stones? Three? Five? More?*

I'm despondent as I look out the doorway and into the inky darkness. Normally thrilled at the vast wild space around me, now I feel naked and vulnerable when I think about how many miles it is to the nearest human or source of physical comfort.

Tonight I was lucky—the coals were still alive. But what if they're out the next time I get this cold? My mind races. *What if I can't get my Leatherman out of its sheath to strike a spark? What if I get injured far from home and can't get back to the cabin?* If I'm careless again and can't warm up on my own, I'll have to call the production crew and have them take me out.

I have yet to feel frightened of any creature or circumstance out here, but right now, the power of the cold is terrifying. And it isn't only the sensation of cold. Sure, I'm uncomfortable, but what scares me most is the idea of being unable to handle it on my own. As challenging as life here is, having to go home because I've done something stupid and preventable is the thing I'm most afraid of.

52

LETTING THE GRIEF THROUGH

Once I'm warm enough to function, I heap not one, not two, but *four* snuggle rocks into the fire. As many as I have cozies for. I crawl into bed with one at my feet, one at each hip, and one right on top of my chest. Though it makes breathing harder, the weight is comforting, like a warm hand placed on my heart. I let the tears squeeze between my eyelids and puddle in my ears, not sure if they're from sadness, or relief at starting to warm up and knowing it's going to be okay. I'm pretty sure it's both.

I don't understand what happens to me when I get hypothermic. Fear of getting so cold that I'm unable to take care of myself is logical, but why does it also make me sad and lonely? Solitude has been one of the biggest gifts of this experience—I've been loving it. I'm a social person, but my development was shaped by being an only child. I'm used to a lot of alone time—I crave it, I need it. I wouldn't be able to feel so connected to the wild creatures, plants, and spirit of this place if I was here with someone else, and I wouldn't trade that connection for anything. So why do the thousands of miles between me and everyone I love feel so heartbreaking right now?

Positive thinking and gratitude are habits I've worked hard to cultivate. I didn't always have them. It isn't easy feeling like you were born in the wrong time and that you value the lifestyles and skills our culture considers outdated and no longer relevant. My teens and twenties were characterized by deep angst and isolation. I worked hard for most of my thirties, through a lot of soul-searching and countless hours of therapy, to get to the healthier emotional state I mostly enjoy now. Those hard-won habits are vital out here, where it would be so easy to focus on the hardship and deprivation.

Part of me feels like I've failed myself in experiencing this sadness now, but the wiser parts know that there's no real joy without grief. They are the opposite sides of the same coin, and letting myself feel this challenging emotion without talking myself out of it is its own kind of strength.

Instead of fighting it or willing it away, I breathe into the ache in my chest and let the sadness wash over me.

Right there, just under the surface, is an all too familiar grief. As lovely as it is not having anyone back home drawing me away from this experience, there's also sadness in knowing I'm so alone in the world. Besides my mother, there's no one whose world isn't complete without me in it—no one counting the days until I'll be home.

For most of my life, I felt like I didn't belong. As a student of environmental science, I was aware of the impacts of the extractive culture I was born into—one that takes and takes from the earth regardless of the consequences. I questioned whether I was good enough to justify my existence. I felt guilty taking up space and having needs. As I grew up and reached my teens, I was desperate for love to fill the emptiness within me, to prove that I was worthy. I made some bad choices based on this drive. My horrible guilt at leaving my first marriage added to my perennial self-doubt and was part of how I ended up in an abusive relationship that emotionally gutted me. As terrible as it was to go through, it was ultimately life changing as it opened my eyes to the healing I had to do and the need to make far better choices in the future. I learned the same lessons over and over until they started to stick. The years I lost to the learning process had consequences, however, and those are the real source of my deepest grief. It isn't only about being partnerless—there is no time restriction on love, and I believe I'll find it again. On a woman's fully functional reproductive system though? There are some limitations there.

I've wanted to be a mother all my life. It was never something I questioned—I always knew it. I did my best to build a life that could support the children I dreamed of having. I hand-built my cabin on the Oregon homestead with the goal of a family in mind, and started my skills school partly so that I wouldn't have to leave the land for work.

I did all the things I knew to do, except for choosing partners who were good candidates for the task. Each relationship that fell apart meant more years lost, which increased the pressure. The *tick-tick-ticking* of that unrelenting internal clock snowballed and led to more impulsive choices that ultimately pushed motherhood even further away. I thought about having a baby on my own, but how could I? I was living well below the poverty line with no safety net, in an off-grid cabin without indoor plumbing, where basic daily living took considerable effort. It didn't feel right to force a child into that if it wasn't happening naturally and if I didn't have more support.

When I'd left the homestead in Oregon after my second divorce to pursue another relationship, it had been an act of desperation, not one of empowerment. I grieved the idyllic rugged life I'd left behind, but I clung with a claw-like grip to the idea that this was my last shot at the family I'd spent so many years longing for. As it turned out, this partner told me he had changed his mind about having children (just as my second husband had done two years before) on the same night I was preparing to tell him I believed I was pregnant. Things went downhill swiftly, and I miscarried a few months before my fortieth birthday.

This loss, coming just before a milestone birthday that signaled the end of my youthful years, led to such crippling grief that I realized things simply had to shift. The desperate drive to start a family had made a mess of my life and brought only heartbreak. I couldn't keep doing this to myself. I wasn't ready to let the idea of motherhood go, but I needed to give myself a reprieve from my angsty obsession with it. I decided I wasn't going to think about babies for two years. When I was forty-two, I would revisit the question of whether I should try to have a baby on my own.

My forty-third birthday is just around the corner. *That means I've got roughly a month left to decide.*

I feel no clearer about it now than I did back then, and maybe that is its own kind of answer. I fall asleep still contemplating it, hugging a warm snuggle rock to my chest.

53

THE CRANBERRY CLEANSE

wake up feeling like myself again, *thank god*. Resolve hardens inside me. *I will not get that cold again*. If I want to stay here long term, I can't afford to tank like that. The deep chills are thus far the only things that make me think of leaving. That makes them the most dangerous thing I face.

My resolve returns with my normal body temperature, but the effort required to make life possible here is monumental, and with the fox around and the rabbits gone, plunging back into starvation mode again is far harder than I would have predicted. It was one thing before I knew I could trap, but now that my body remembers what it's like to eat every day, everything is different. I still appreciate the beauty immensely, but I seem to have lost the ability to feel fed by it as I did before. This new hunger is different—deeper, and far more desperate. I can't shut it out or distract myself from it. The first weeks, my hunger was painful, but peripheral—habitual hunger based on being used to eating regularly and the shock of stopping. I felt weak even though I had plenty of stored calories in my body. Now, I feel strong and capable, but I'm no longer flush with extra fat; I'm all lean muscle and sinew. This hunger is visceral, from somewhere inside I can't explain or define. It's deeper than my stomach—it's in every cell of my body. Not a moment goes by that I'm not aware of it.

I return to stalking with my bow, my eyes peeled for hare tracks, venturing out to every edge of the peninsula and then the mainland, but there's nothing. No sign anywhere. *What is going on?* Even if the mysterious absence of hares on the peninsula could be explained by fox predation or the hares learning to avoid my snares, it wouldn't affect the mainland populations. *What gives? Rabbit conspiracy? Alien hare abduction?*

There are only a few bones left rattling around in my rusty cans. I know their food value is minimal, but they are something, and I look forward to them every night. I point the camera at myself as I toast the last batch.

"Hey kids, you left some toasted bones on your plate," I say in my best mom voice. "If you don't eat your toasted bones, you won't get any dessert."

"Okay, Mom," I answer, crunching on the bones and staring into the camera. "Hey Mom, what's for dessert?"

"Your favorite," I answer, "*toasted bones!*"

When I haven't seen fox tracks for a couple of days, I start up my trapline again. I still haven't solved the mystery, but I know you can't catch hares in snares that don't exist. If the hares are laying low waiting for the fox to leave the peninsula, I intend to be ready for them when they poke their heads out again.

The challenge, already significant, is far greater now that I'm working to outsmart foxes in addition to hares. I can't stop at lifting the hares off of their feet; I need to lift them high enough to get them out of reach of marauding foxes—no small task. It takes three days, working every second of daylight, to get the trapline back up and as fox-proof as I can manage. *Please, rabbit gods, let it be enough.*

But so far, it isn't. Days pass in empty-bellied monotony. Traps, firewood, construction, and traps again. Neither feverish prayers nor all my new innovations bring rabbits to the table. My long underwear, once skintight, now flaps against my legs as I walk. In the last week, I've caught and eaten exactly one squirrel, which got tangled in a rabbit snare.

It isn't working. I'm not making it. I'm starving. The sentence runs on a constant reel as I tend to my many chores. *I'm starving, I'm starving.*

I'm no less in love with this life, but I'm increasingly frightened about my long-term prospects. All my hopes are now pinned on freeze-up, that magical time when the liquid lake turns to walkable land—when I can reach the deep waters for ice fishing, and all the islands and far shores open their mysteries to me.

How much longer now? One week? Two? Can I pass more medical checks if they happen before ice fishing begins? How skinny do I have to get before they pull me?

I'm retreating into my mind more and more. I would never have dreamed food fantasies could consume so many of my waking hours. I can almost taste the rich, fatty goodness of the furry inhabitants of the beaver lodge I could reach if only I could walk out to Beaver Island, just as I can almost smell the sizzle of tender lake trout on my coals. It's one thing to dream of the foods I could possibly eat here, but before long it snowballs and I'm fantasizing about other foods in vivid detail—cheese fondue, flaky pastries, and all things rich, sweet, and salty.

I'm halfway through my trapline one day when I realize I'm not even noticing the woods around me. I haven't been here; I've been in Chiang Mai, Thailand, where I spent two months on my Southeast Asia travels. In my mind, I've been walking the crowded, humid streets of my favorite night market there, not these frozen rocks. In normal life, I don't remember its details, but somewhere deep in my psyche I apparently have an indelible map of the place—every food stand on every corner—and the deep body hunger brings it all back. I'm almost tasting the rich curries and fragrant coconut dumplings, the grilled fish wrapped in banana leaves, and the sweet sticky rice steamed in bamboo stalks.

I shake myself. *What are you doing, Woniya?* The point isn't to just endure being here, it's to bring all my heart and soul to it and to be totally present. *I don't want to be in Thailand*, I remind myself. *I want this life, this place, and this wildness*. I just want it with food.

And that's when I get the dreaded message from the production team on my yellow brick communication device.

MED CHECK TOMORROW

My mouth goes dry and my pulse thumps in my temple. *Oh god. Why now? Why not when I was eating every day?* Instead of fantasizing about being somewhere else, now I'm consumed with the fear that I'll be forced to leave here before I'm ready to.

I grit my teeth and do the thing I never do—pull up my sweater and three layers of wool underclothes and look at my own belly. The skin is shriveled and droopy. I'm incredibly skinny, but I don't think I'm truly emaciated. I'm not in the danger zone yet. *Or am I?*

No, I tell myself. *I'm not*. After all, I don't actually feel weak. Sure, I'm moving a little slower, but I feel strong and healthy. Come to think of it, I feel better physically than I have for a lot of my adult life. I think back to that moment in the chiropractor's office where he made it clear that someone "in my condition" shouldn't dream of an adventure of this magnitude. Yet I've been doing hard physical labor in frigid temperatures, and I've been completely free of the nagging aches, pains, and injuries that have plagued me for decades. It isn't just my shoulders, it's everything—no ache in my Achilles tendons, no tight piriformis muscles putting pressure on my sciatic nerve, and no obvious inflammation in my system. I may not be eating, but by other counts, I'm thriving.

Health is real, but it's also a mindset, and I've let my mindset get away from me. Don't people do ketogenic diets and long-term fasting for healing? *There you have it! I'm not starving, I'm doing a cleanse. A cranberry cleanse.* There's probably a fancy spa in some Nordic country offering the same thing for a fortune per day. And there's real science behind it too. Digestion takes a lot of energy, and when the body gets a break from it, it's able to do some repair work it can't tend to otherwise. The process is called autophagy. Additionally, most environmental toxins—those from petroleum, plastics, pesticides, and such—are fat soluble, so they're stored in our body's fatty tissue. Burning through all my body fat, I'm cleaning out toxins I've been storing since before puberty. I'm also drinking a ton of chaga tea, which has anti-tumor properties. *Heck yeah—I'll be leaving here healed, toxin-free, and cancer proof for the rest of my life!*

The simple shift in mindset, from starving to a healthful cleanse, changes not just my perspective, but how I feel physically. I'm suddenly stronger and more energetic than I've been since the rabbits disappeared. As my enthusiasm and the vitality of my body return, Thailand couldn't feel farther away.

54

WALTZING THE SUN DOWN

The next morning, the medical check crew tromps up my walkway with serious faces. I explain how good I feel as we run through the gamut of tests.

"My chronic issues are clearing up," I explain. "And I've figured out the welt issue, so even though my thighs look horrible now, I know I'm finally past the worst of it."

"Okay great, so you're having regular bowel movements again?" the doctor asks.

"Well, not exactly."

Damn. I hadn't planned on mentioning it, but no, that morning during my moon time was the last time I pooped.

I wait nervously as they scribble in their notebooks and confer with one another. They seem a good deal less convinced than I am of the benefits of my cranberry cleanse.

And then the bomb drops. "We're concerned about your weight loss," the producer tells me. "You aren't in the danger zone yet, but you're approaching it, and if you cross a certain threshold, we'll have to pull you. You simply *have* to start bringing in more food."

I stand in numb silence as I watch them walk up to the rock arena and file into the boat. I pull the furs of my parka tighter as the news settles.

My mind is reeling. *A weight warning? So soon? It's only been about six weeks. I just got here.*

Though the day is icy cold, the sun is bright on my face as I watch the steel-gray water swallow up the wavering outline of the retreating boat. My limbs feel leaden and despair pushes in around my edges, but I do my best to shake it off.

It isn't true, I decide. They're wrong, that's all. All they have to go on is the numbers on their scale, but those are just one measure of health. I'm the one who lives in this body, and while I'd prefer it still had a little more meat on it, I'm amazed at how much more vital I feel than when I was eating plenty but dealing with chronic injuries back home.

I've finally taught myself to trap and was hitting my stride before the rabbits dried up. There is no way I am ready to leave this place. *I'll try harder. I'll figure it out. I'll do everything I can possibly do.* But if I'm honest with myself, I know that I've already been doing all I can think of to do. Ultimately, how long I stay isn't up to me. It's up to the land and the lake. I walk down to the rocky shore and dip my fingers into it.

"I'm not done learning about you, Tu Nedhe," I tell it. "I know we have more dances in store for us."

I also need to be realistic. If I'm already on weight warning, it's time to let go of my hopes of winning this thing. I can handle that. I want to win, but it isn't why I'm here, and I've still got my biggest motivations—wildness, beauty, freedom, and connection. I might not get to be the last one out here, but that doesn't mean I can't succeed on my own terms.

If winning is out, what does success look like now? How many weeks would make me feel successful?

Eight weeks, I think. Two full moon cycles. Living here that long would be significant, and far more uninterrupted time than I've ever spent in the wilderness. It won't be easy, but I'm determined to make it.

I can't afford more hungry days though. Not any, not ever. I head back to the cabin and carefully portion out the pemmican I've got left, cutting it in half, then in half again and again until I've got a bag full of equally sized, perfectly rolled pemmican balls. One per day, right up until day fifty-six.

That done, I think about other measures of success. I don't want to leave without making something incredible from my pile of rabbit rope. I'd hoped for a whole blanket. I don't have anywhere near enough for that, but I've got enough for a smaller project. Time to figure out how to make something warm and beautiful from them.

The project is going to take more space than I've got in the cramped cabin, and this is the clearest, brightest day we've had in weeks. *Very well then. I believe it's weaving day.*

I carry the ball of rabbit "yarn" out to the open rock of the arena. I wedge two peeled poles into my laundry line, giving me two stiff vertical supports about a scarf's length apart. I wind the rabbit rope around them, and it gives me a fuzzy rectangle about five feet long and ten inches wide. *Perfect!*

The inner strands of paracord are slippery against the fur as I twine it around each length of the rabbit rope, weaving them snugly together on my makeshift loom. It's delicate work, and my exposed fingers turn bright pink and ache with the cold. I have to stop several times to go warm up and make hot tea—*because Woniya doesn't take risks with the cold anymore*—but I keep at it.

Even with the sobering news, I can't help but be jubilant. I live for crafting; it's what my hands were made for. I'm standing in a wild paradise in the buckskin pants, fur parka, and boots I made myself with hides I tanned. Now I'm also weaving with furs from animals I caught with my own cunning—it's a dream come true.

My cheeks are sore from smiling as I pull the scarf off the loom and wrap it around my neck. Now I'm cozy, gloriously fuzzy, and beaming at having finally fulfilled my promises to the rabbit gods. I've used every part, further intertwining my life with theirs and, this time, making it literal. I feel like a superhero who's just been given their costume.

Between the med check and scarf project, the day is already gone, but it's Thursday, and I've got a lot to celebrate. Every week I come up with a different theme for my weekly dance party. Last Thursday, during my moon time, it was one of slowness and self-care. Tonight, I want to dance not by myself, but with this place—in surrender and partnership. A waltz, I decide. At first I think I'm dancing with the lake, but as I close my eyes and dip and sway to the rhythm in my head, I feel the bright sun, such a rarity, across my eyelids. *The lake is always here, my constant dance partner*, I think. Today I'm waltzing with the sun—a fleeting but potent romance in this land of ice and snow.

The gray skies and lake effect snow have meant little color at sunset lately, but tonight the lake is calm, and the sky is rich with color, all of it amplified in the lake's reflection. It's well below freezing, but I want to feel this dance fully, so I shrug out of my thick parka and baggy pants and pull my kidney warmer down to make a skirt. I want to feel free and feminine and beautiful, to lean into the fullest expression of myself and my relationship with everything around me. A woman, alone, in love with this life.

I place one hand over my heart and one on my belly and count out the rhythm—one, two, three; one, two, three—in my head, my eyes closed and the bright sunlight painted across my lids as my boots squeak on the bare granite.

I open my eyes just as the last dazzling rays of light are slipping away across the vast water. I let the departing sun lead and twirl me around the granite dance floor then laugh, breathless, and give it a little curtsey. As it disappears below the horizon, I blow it a kiss, thanking it for the dance, and then I sing it all the way down into the lake.

My quiver made of home-tanned leather with bobcat fur ruff. This came from the bobcat shown on page 38.

TOP: Some of the crafts I made on the peninsula, clockwise from bottom left: 1. Waist-tied willow basket for harvesting berries. (buckskin ties visible on back of basket and left corner); 2. Berry storage basket with spiral of peeled willow; 3. Birch bark container; 4. Empty paraspool; 5. Spoon with handle shaped like a grouse feather; 6. Spatula with handle shaped like a trout. BOTTOM: The knife sheath cover I made from the equinox squirrel, my first game on Season 6 and the first animal I shot with a bow.

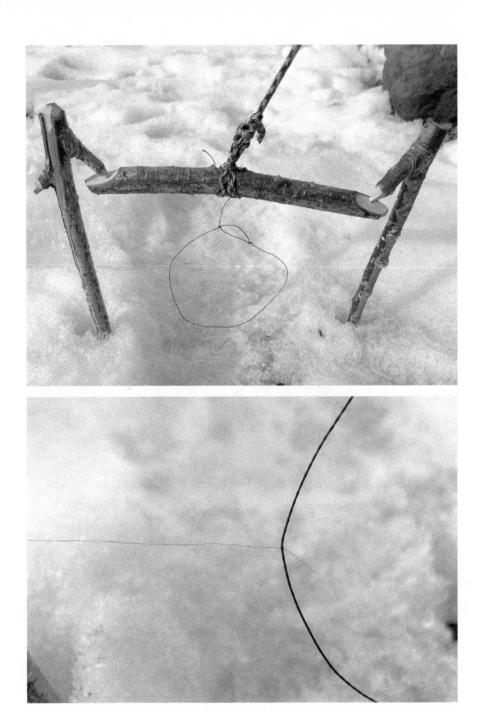

TOP: Reproduction of my improvised power snare with fishing line loop. This loop is braided line, which shows up against the snow, but I had only clear monofilament line on *Alone*. The loop is tied open with three of my own hairs, one tied to each vertical stick and one to a partially buried stick beneath the snare. BOTTOM: Detail of one thin hair tied to the snare loop.

Me in my rabbit rope scarf, January 2023.

PART FOUR

BECOMING
ANCESTOR

55

SURRENDER

Building a bedstead is another of those projects I'd planned to do "once I have all the food I need and some time to kill." *Haha*. Like the scarf, it's a project I don't want to leave here without completing, so it had better happen soon. A bed doesn't just help make a hovel into a home, it also has very real survival benefits. I'm wasting time and calories laying out my bed every night and packing it up every morning. Even more significant is the fact that sleeping above the ground is far warmer and more comfortable than sleeping directly on it, so I'll get better rest and burn less calories to boot. Saving calories is kind of like bringing in calories, so it'll be like virtual rabbits—not that different from dream beasts!

To save space and materials, I plan to build the bed right into the wall, which means tearing down the wall and rebuilding it. While I wait for a window of good weather, I get my materials prepped—peeled uprights for the legs, long horizontals for the sides, and the shorter crosspieces that will support my spruce bough mattress.

The next clear day, I start at first light and have the south wall torn out by midmorning. A wide-open shelter is a powerful motivator. My hands fly as I notch and lash, and then round the ends of all the pieces, so I'm less likely to bruise myself on pokey edges in the confines of the narrow cabin. By nightfall, the bed frame is solid enough that, if there was room for it, I'm certain I could jump on it. It looks like something you could buy in a rustic homes catalog for thousands of dollars.

It's another few hours to make the mattress—spruce boughs of descending size with tiny branch tips on top and a layer of sphagnum moss over everything. Settling onto it, my parka and sweater neatly hung on one bed-post and my headlamp and bow in arm's reach on the other, is like heaven. Plus, with all the space under the bed, I've quadrupled my covered storage space. *Why did I wait so long for this?*

And that's it. My rabbit rope project is completed, and while there's always more I could do, the last major project of the cabin is now finished too. My life here is all coming together, cozier and more comfortable all the time. The only thing between me and total wilderness surthrival is, of course, food.

I've done all that's in my power to do. I've fulfilled my promises and shown this place my dedication. Whatever happens now is what is meant to be. Beyond watching and waiting, harvesting firewood, and walking my perpet-ually empty trapline, the only job that's left to me is the one I find the most challenging—*surrender.*

It's not my strong suit, but I do the best I can, opening myself to all the possible outcomes, from achieving food sustainability to being pulled at the next medical check.

Then, incredibly, something shifts. I'm checking my trapline one morning when I see movement and a hunched white form against the brush. *A hare!* The first I've seen in weeks, and while the others were all brown, this one is white as snow. I take aim and my arrow strikes near its feet, sending it run-ning. My aim is slipping, and no wonder. I'm far too happy to worry about it though—because *rabbits are on the peninsula again!* And if they're on the move, they're trappable. The sensation in my cheeks reminds me that the last time I smiled this wide was the day I made the scarf, but now I'm beaming all the way through my trapline. Not because there are rabbits in it—there aren't—but because I see their tracks in the forest for the first time in well over a week.

It's been a while since I bothered to set a new snare, but suddenly I'm brimming with enthusiasm. With a pack full of matched sets of uprights and crosspieces I can cut to length, spools of paracord innards and fishing line, and, of course, tangled wads of my own hair, I trudge out to a new area I scoped out just before the Great Rabbit Exodus.

Sure enough, there's fresh rabbit sign here as well. I use every trick I've got—lifting pole snares, rock weighted mechanisms, and spring poles snares—and hair triggers for them all.

Please, please, please let me have a feast for Samhain!

Though Halloween has now been co-opted by candy and costume companies, its origins are in the Celtic holiday of Samhain, which recognizes this time of year as the one when the boundary between the worlds of the living and the dead is blurred. If you're paying attention, you can feel it in the landscape all around you in late October. The leaves turn color and fall as the trees go dormant. Plants everywhere scatter their seeds, die, and compost into fresh soil to feed the next generation. Those creatures who are already too old, weak, or ill to make it through the lean times ahead are taking their last breaths. Their bodies will fall prey to those stronger and will help their predators survive the cold season.

I pay homage to the ancestors all the time, but never more than at Samhain. There's a reason that traditional Halloween images are those of ghosts, skeletons, and gravestones. They aren't meant to be terrifying; they're meant to remind us of those who have come before and to encourage us to honor them and make peace with the fact that we will eventually join them.

Honoring the cycles of life and death feels more important than ever this year, and getting a rabbit feels like a critical part of that.

Then one morning, it finally happens. Trudging out to one of my lifting pole snares, I see a strange white blob against the brighter white of the snow. *It's a hare!* My first hare in almost two weeks—perfectly intact and frozen solid. My hands are shaking with excitement as I extract it from the noose. I let out a deep sigh, and my stomach untwists itself a little. No sight could be more beautiful. *I have food again! I'll eat tonight!*

All along my trail, there are fresh tracks that weren't here yesterday. I reach my farthest trap and my heart leaps into my throat. Tucked under a log, in a perfect natural funnel in the rabbit trail, is another snow-white hare. I have achieved my dream! *Two in one day! I can't believe it! It's a two-rabbit day!*

But then, maybe I can believe it. It follows the pattern. This land has shown me that it loves my surrender. It's constantly testing me—Do you mean it? Are you as committed as you say you are? Even when the food dries up? Even when the temperatures plummet?

When I fought the cold, rather than recognizing its power and changing my behavior accordingly, I got hypothermic. When the rabbits got slimmer,

I worked harder. Then the fox came and I had no choice but to let go. Every time things get hard and I resist, nothing shifts. When I finally say, "Okay then, Tu Nedhe, you call the shots. I'll do my part and show up in every way I can, but ultimately it's up to you," I find my joy and gratitude again. That's when the land starts to give. I don't think it's coincidence.

I comb the bright fur of the second hare, watching my fingers disappear into it. It's far longer than the brown fur of my earlier rabbits, I notice. And then boom—it hits me! *I know why the rabbits disappeared!* It wasn't the fox at all; that was just coincidental timing. Every rabbit I caught before the Great Exodus was brown, and every rabbit I've seen since is white.

It was the molt!

I know most northern animals molt to blend in with the snow, but not having lived this far north before, I always assumed it was a gradual thing. Apparently not, because in two weeks, every rabbit out here has gone from lovely brown to solid white. It's got to take some serious energy to grow a whole new coat of hair, and being pure brown against the snow or pure white against the dark soil and forest would make them incredibly vulnerable. Of course they lay low while molting, and only get active again when they're well matched to the backdrop.

My feet dance their way home. Eating my fill today and still having food tomorrow *and* the next day is huge, but the hares returning doesn't just mean eating again; it means my luck is changing, it means the ancestors are with me, and most of all it means *not getting pulled.*

56

FEASTING WITH THE ANCIENTS

As I pull the silky white hairs apart to begin skinning the first rabbit, I see brown hairs beneath them and another jolt of realization hits me. Apparently, they don't just lose their summer coats and grow in winter ones; the winter coat grows out through and beyond the short summer fur until it covers it completely. No wonder these incredible creatures can survive in arctic temperatures: they're wearing a fur parka *on top of* their down coat. Just think how warm and fluffy my next rabbit rope project will be!

With hares on the move, my hopes for a long-term stay are rekindled. If the rabbits keep coming and I keep my weight up, this thing isn't nearly over, it's just getting started.

Instead of other projects, this afternoon I simply sit by the warm fire, cook, and eat. I revel in the sensation of food in my belly. I sigh deep contented sighs and picture the nutrients pouring in everywhere, filling up the places that have been hollow and empty for too long.

This life is the most real and beautiful thing I've ever experienced. The lows are so hard, the joys so complete. It's always been my goal to *live* for a living, rather than work for a living so I can pay someone else to create the things I need. I worked hard on the Oregon homestead—building my own home, tanning hides to make my own clothing, subsistence farming, and hunting and gathering for my food, but I always had a cushion. It did exactly what the name implies, cushioned me from the realities of what survival and surthrival really mean. It kept me from feeling the full depth of the human experience. Having endured true lack and true hunger out here, I now know what real abundance, gratitude, and blessings are. That knowledge will change my life forever. Food in the belly, the cook pot, *and* the larder? Enough firewood to last for days and an entire afternoon to sit and relax? That is true wealth. As is the other thing I'm getting to experience right now—eating two rabbits' worth of organs in one sitting, can you imagine it? And eating more than half of a rabbit in one day? *Unbelievable!*

I tuck away the backstraps and front shoulders—the best cuts—for my Samhain feast. I go to sleep warm, comfortable, and blissfully full.

Samhain arrives cold, snowy, and gray, and I get a squirrel in a snare to add to my feast. I manage to find a patch of cranberries largely untouched by Zoinkers. Cranberries will have a special place at the feast, and I'm glad to have some fresh ones.

I'll be celebrating someone else, in addition to the ancestors, tonight. October 31 is my mama's birthday as well as Halloween, making her a proper witch and a magical lady. She'll be celebrating it somehow, but she'll also be thinking of me and wondering if I'm okay. Being sure that I'm well fed and content on this day is a gift I can give us both. Cranberries are her favorite, and she always makes a big batch of homemade cranberry sauce to last through Thanksgiving and Christmas. I've never really liked cranberries, but I've choked them down most of my life to please her. I look forward to eventually being able to tell her I've finally come to appreciate them.

I spend hours cooking everything to perfection, using an entire third of a salt button—enough to have the food actually taste salty, a rare treat for me. I drag the camera case to the center of the cabin for a banquet table and set it with three plates—one for me, one for the ancestors, and one for my mama. Then I realize I forgot to make a costume for the party. *What shall I be?* But I only have to think about it for half a second. I mean, what does my world revolve around right now, and who showed up to celebrate with me? *Rabbits!* And given my arctic diet, I'm more and more rabbit every day, so let's make the outside match the inside. I fashion some ears out of folded birch bark and tuck them into my hat, then paint a nose and whiskers on with a piece of charcoal. I check myself out in the viewfinder of the camera. *Pretty good for a wilderness costume!*

I lay out the feast on three squares of birch bark. Squirrel organs done just right, rabbit backstraps steam-sautéed (the house special), and rabbit soup—the meat tender enough to slurp right off the bone—with cranberries and a pemmican ball for dessert.

The second place setting is for the ancient ones—those of my own blood-line, the ancestors of the people of this place, the rabbits that grace the woods, and their brethren, all the way back to the bacteria fossilized in the very rock itself. The presence of the ancestors is increasingly palpable every day, but never so strongly as tonight.

The third plate is for my direct ancestor—my mama.

I move around the table, eating first from my own plate, then sitting in and eating as the ancestors, and then my mother. I'm all of us, all at once, and somehow that doesn't seem like a stretch. It makes perfect sense. Why wouldn't I be, in this place where I'm living as my ancestors did? When my muscles and bones are now made mostly of rabbit, and those rabbits are made of the forest, and that forest is made of the minerals in the soil and the waters of the lake?

When I get to the last course, the pemmican, I'm not even hungry for it, but I eat it anyway as a special treat. *Hey—with other food coming I can start saving my pemmican again!* That pushes my count way beyond day fifty-six. *I think I've got this; I've really got this!*

Then, when I head outside to send my evening check-in, I get a response back.

MED CHECK TOMORROW

Gulp.

57

DAY OF THE HEAD

wake up full of nervous energy. I'm on the watchlist, so any medical check could be my last.

It's going to be okay, I tell myself. *They didn't say pulling you was imminent; they said you need to eat more, and you have been.*

I'm feeling strong, and I don't think I'm any skinnier than I was before the last check. Plus, the cabin is decorated with long strands of fur again—I've got ample evidence to show them that my trapline is back up to snuff.

The only issue with having food again is that my pot can only hold one thing at a time. I can cook and store food, or I can fetch and heat water for tea—I can't do both. Prioritizing food and letting myself get dehydrated in my early weeks was a major factor in the first big constipation. I'm stopped up again, so I need to be more vigilant. With the crew on its way, it's even more important, as extra hydration will keep my blood pressure and vitals looking good.

The frigid air burns my nostrils as I traverse the rocks. Down at the shore I can see thousands of ice crystals, long and jagged, floating around and shimmering under the surface of the water, like someone dropped flakes of mica into the lake. I believe freeze-up is happening right before my eyes. I'm guessing today will be the last time I see a boat on my shores.

Samhain yesterday makes today the Day of the Dead, so I decide to feast with the ancestors yet again. Yesterday was amazing, but the portions were mostly lean meat. Today, I'm going the decadent route. After tea, I haul more water and get three heads boiling—two rabbits and one squirrel—before heading out to the trapline.

I would be more excited about the feast if I wasn't in such pain, though. Not pooping wasn't a big deal when I wasn't eating anything, but for the last four days I've been eating like a champ. Things in my midsection are finally shifting and I'm feeling the urge, which is an answer to my prayers. Clearly, I should have been more specific about those prayers, as the urge without actual evacuation isn't helping.

I'm halfway through my trapline when mild discomfort turns to deep abdominal cramping. I definitely have to go. I carefully choose a place—a deep crevice in the rocks of the boulder field east of the cabin, with no Labrador tea in sight. Things are moving, but the movement goes only so far and then stops. I squat there until the skin on my bum goes numb with the cold. I can feel the pressure low in my colon, my guts are cramping like hell, and I'm groaning with pain, but no amount of pushing or straining gets things any further along. I can't wait here until I get frostbite on my butt, so eventually I give up and stand doubled-over until I'm finally able to walk.

I'm headed back home when I hear the boat engine in the distance. I cross my fingers they won't ask about the poop situation. The one bonus is that the extra weight in my intestines will keep my BMI up.

I answer their questions and tell them about how well I've been eating, describe the feast I had yesterday, and show them my cook pot and the meal I'm preparing for the Day of the Dead.

"The Day of the Dead?" Dan, the producer, asks. "Looks more like the Day of the Head." *Haha, he's right. That's exactly what it is.* A whole new holiday and way to celebrate it leaps into being.

This time there's no hushed conference about my condition, thank goodness.

"Well," Dan says, once I'm put back together. "It looks like your weight is holding. Keep doing what you're doing."

Yes, yes, yes! A reprieve! The molt is over and I'm eating again. If this one teensy issue in my body can resolve itself, I still have a chance at being here long term. From what I could feel this morning, though, I'm not sure that teensy is the word for it.

58

HOLY SHIT

Sure enough, the next morning there's an icy crust on the water of the south bay as far out as I can see. A good whack with the pot busts right through it, but I get the sense that isn't going to be the case for long, as it already feels ten degrees colder than yesterday.

I give the trapline everything I've got, kneeling in the snow for hours every day setting and resetting snares. At every snare, my body heat melts the snow beneath my knees, soaking my pants, which then freezes as soon as I get up and move. The hours I spend thawing and drying my buckskin every night are wearing on me, so I pull some of the beaver fur out of the back of my parka and sew it to the fur ruff on my boots. Now instead of cold snow, I'm kneeling on thick waterproof fur. *Thank you, beavers!* I'm glad there's something to feel encouraged about, because even with the molt over, the trapping hasn't improved as much as I'd hoped. It doesn't go belly up as it did before, but it produces in fits and starts instead of a steady stream. I'm guessing that's mostly due to the weather. Storms whip through the peninsula, which is so narrow that the small patches of forest don't provide much protection from the gales. The swaying of the trees springs my traps, and on stormy nights the hares must sit tight because I rarely see tracks the morning after a storm. As time goes on, there are fewer nights that are neither stormy nor windy.

I still haven't pooped, and every day my body tells me more strongly that I can't carry on like this much longer. There's something wrong down there, beyond just constipation. Once or twice a day, the cramping brings me to the rock crevice. Sometimes I strain, feel nothing happening, then give up. More often I strain and feel something happening, but it's not the "something" I'm hoping for. When I wipe after these episodes, the moss is red, not brown, and when I stand up, there's a wide swath of frozen blood on the rocks. Sometimes I reach around and can feel the stool right there, distending the skin. It's enormous and rock hard, but no matter how hard I push, I can't budge it.

I'm kicking myself for eating those toasted bones. Had I eaten actual food along with them, I don't think it would be an issue. I hadn't, and now I seem to have a ball of solid calcium impacted in my colon—far larger than any bone, and nearly as dense. Occasionally things rearrange in my intestines, and I manage to pass a few small brown boulders, so hard a stick barely dents them, but when the big obstruction leads the way—nothing doing.

Overnight the lake ice goes from a thin crust to a few inches thick. I bust through it with the back end of my saw to gather water, keeping my ice hole open with several visits a day. At night when things are still, I can hear the groaning of the lake surface as it makes ice—an eerie, dark sound that echoes over the whole peninsula and rumbles in my chest. My own groans from the cramping in my guts echoes the sounds from the lake. At least I'm in good company.

Most of my bathroom attempts happen in the daylight hours, the only time it feels safe to have my pants down for so long without risking serious frostbite. One evening though, I'm sitting by the fire and my guts won't let me put it off, so even though it's a clear night and biting cold, I head out to the rock latrine.

It's getting worse, with less time between the intense cramping. I'm increasingly terrified that I'll end up having to call for medical intervention. Of all possible scenarios, I never imagined that the state of my intestines would be what takes me out. I guess this is the flip side of surrender, and as such, I'm careful not to blame myself or my body for what is happening. I do my best to use only loving, encouraging self-talk.

You've got this, I tell my colon and butthole. *I have faith in you. I'm right here with you—we're in this together.* Tonight, the dark pressing in on all sides compounds it all, and it's hard not to feel hopeless—hunkered down in the dark and cold, with intense pain I can't relieve twisting in my midsection.

I'm huddled inside my furs, staring down at the dark ice and snow beneath me when I see it start to brighten. I look up at the sky above and gasp at the turquoise and magenta ribbons dancing against a backdrop of glittering stars. Blue curtains of light fade in and out behind them and the ice crystals in the air make everything shimmer like it's painted in glitter. The pain takes a backseat to awe and wonder.

Clear nights are the most bone chilling by far, so I haven't even been outside at night on one for some time, but now I'm almost grateful for the pain that forced me out here. The magic of this celestial light show wraps around me, buoying me up. Sure the pain is excruciating, and I'm losing a lot of blood, but *damn—look at that sky!* A beautiful blessing, when I need it most.

Nothing is moving tonight, and I can't let myself get frostnip on my tender nether regions. I wipe the blood away with clean snow and put myself back together. I whisper my prayers to the northern lights before sealing the cabin door behind me. *Thank you, Tu Nedhe. I hear you. There's beauty on the other side of this suffering. It's going to be okay.*

Keep the faith, I tell myself throughout the following days, remembering those glorious lights. *Keep the faith.* And mostly I do, though it's getting to the point that I'm having a hard time walking upright as I go about my routine, and judging by the passing of days, the next med check is imminent.

The good news is, I'm starting to figure out this bleeding issue. Sometimes, the straining is horribly uncomfortable, and I bleed profusely. Sometimes, it's just the normal pain of an incredibly impacted stool that I can't evacuate. This kind of pressure and prolonged straining can cause the blood vessels down below to balloon out—that's what we call a hemorrhoid. The sharp pain and truly bloody episodes, I've determined, are when a bleeding hemorrhoid is being forced out in front of the obstructed stool.

At those times, I can't push through it without tearing the vein, and my body clearly knows this and won't let me try. Other times, I can feel a difference and I know that the stool is there without the swollen blood vessel in the way. If there's any way to move this thing through without medical intervention, it's then, though it's clear that the process will be akin to giving birth. If I don't grit my teeth and make it happen, I fear I'll be on the next helicopter out of here.

Not many days after the dancing aurora tells me I can do it, my chance arrives. I get the urge and head out to the rocks, a sterile pad from the first aid kit and a wad of sphagnum moss in hand. I push and strain and the impaction moves to the very edge of my body and then stops fast, as always. The pain tells my body, "Stop pushing, you can't do this." But this time, I know I can. I have to, or someone in the ER in Yellowknife is going to have to do it for me, and neither of us will be happy about it.

I inhale deeply and hiss the exhale out of pursed lips, willing myself to push harder, even as I feel a sharp, tearing pain. The extra blood adds lubrication and I feel progress, actual movement. I dig my fingers into my stomach, pushing from the inside, as well as with every internal muscle I've got.

I don't let up and with each exhale I push a little harder. After what feels like an eternity of agony, the bulk of it passes, and I fall to my knees in the bloody snow, overcome with relief. *I did it, it's over. I'm going to live!*

I hold the sterile pad to my anus and it stings the raw tear, but I'm so overjoyed at my success that the pain seems nominal. There on the ground is the horrifying lump that has plagued me for the last sixteen days. (Yes, you read that right, *sixteen days*.) It's almost perfectly round—the size, shape, and general texture of a cue ball.

"Holy shit," I say out loud, looking at it. It's no wonder I couldn't move this boulder without tearing myself apart. I feel so much sympathy for my poor, dear body. I'm beyond relieved to have accomplished this grisly task, and frankly—seriously proud. That was hands down the hardest thing I've undertaken in all these weeks out here.

"*Holy shit*," is right.

Walking back to the cabin, fully upright and what must be at least a pound or two lighter, is a religious experience. My body is the most amazing, capable, and beautiful thing in the world, and I suddenly love it with all my heart.

I'm a little tender in the posterior as I settle myself in by the fire to heat water for a good wash and some serious self-care. I haven't felt this kind of deep calm and ease for weeks. Even the sight of the blood-tinged water in my cooking pot as I lovingly clean and tend to myself can't shake it.

59

REDEFINING SUCCESS

The thickening lake ice is a reflection of the swiftly dropping temperature. I'm guessing that we're hovering just below zero degrees Fahrenheit, and it's cold enough all day that I don't want to risk letting the fire go out. I need to know I can always get warm in a hurry, so I start to collect rotten birch logs as well as seasoned trees and limbs. When I head out to walk my traps or cut firewood, I toss a few onto the fire to keep it smoldering.

The cold affects everything. Basic self-care falls by the wayside. It's too cold to bathe, too cold to do laundry, too cold to have my hat off long enough to comb my fingers through my ever-thinning hair. A couple of times after butchering, I scrub the blood off with snow, but now my skin is chapped and raw from it, so even this level of hygiene is out. The painful chapping in addition to the deep cracks that have opened up all over my hands makes it painful to even bend my fingers. They don't heal unless they're covered, but I'm almost out of plastic bandages, so I prioritize the nastiest cracks. I work my spruce pitch salve into the deepest ones and keep them covered with a combination of little pieces of bandages, medical tape, and strips of buckskin.

We're losing almost ten minutes of light each day, over a full hour a week. There aren't enough daylight hours to maintain all my snares, and I've promised myself I won't work on traps after dark—the risk of hypothermia is too great. I weigh my options and strategically choose to let go of my least productive snaring zones. A rabbit every two or three days keeps me eating, but it isn't enough to sustain me, and it sure isn't "surthriving." The time of my next moon cycle comes and goes, with no hint of a symptom and no bleeding at all—my body is catching up to the reality of my situation.

The trapping isn't just waning, it's also changing. I used to have my best success in brand-new areas, where the rabbits hadn't yet learned what to look out for. Now it's as if there's a rabbit intelligence network infiltrating the area and word spreads before I get to new spots. I'm bringing in less food, but at least I feel its impact more. Because they are few and far between, each squirrel snared is a victory, and each rabbit, an indescribably potent gift.

Always, always, the thickening of the lake ice and the transformation of the world before me tantalizes me. A vast, unexplored world, and the new resources that it could offer (*let me get lake trout, let me get lake trout*), hovers just out of my reach. Perhaps just one more cold day will give me access to it, perhaps two. The hope of it lifts me even as the cold presses me down. But even that is less oppressive than I'd imagined.

Now that we're in the dry-cold phase of winter instead of the wet-cold, I'm actually warmer in my homemade boots and fur parka than I was early on in my rubber boots and commercial rain jacket. My gamble paid off, and there's no longer any part of me that regrets what I went through to bring homemade gear. I've never been so warm in such a cold climate. *Thanks for your crazy ambition, Woniya! You did it!* Through my felt and furs, and being thoughtful and deliberate, I feel less threatened by the cold even as the temperature drops. Like any challenge, it comes with its own gifts. The cold is a scythe, cutting away the unimportant and leaving only the most vital elements of life. Shelter, water, firewood, food—*how did I find so much to worry about in my life back home, when I always had these four things in abundance?*

The scythe of winter is trimming my body down to its simplest elements as well. Every day I pull the leg warmers—which were once tight above my knees—a little higher up my thighs. Eventually, they're all the way up to my crotch. I convince myself that it's the wool that's stretching, not the fact that my thighs are approaching the diameter that my knees once were.

Something more profound is also shifting, something within me that I don't have words for. My chattering mind slows to the pace of the spruce trees dancing with the wind. I no longer feel like a welcomed guest here; I feel like a part of the landscape. And given that everything I eat now comes from it, that's the literal truth.

The eight-week mark, the one I set as "success," comes and goes, but I remain. I continue to feel strong and vital, and I still have a reserve of pemmican balls.

Okay, I ask myself, *I made it to eight weeks and am still going strong, so what is success now?* Ten weeks, I decide. Two and a half months living on my own, in one of the wildest places on the continent—that would definitely qualify as success.

I count out the days—seventy days would bring me to November 17. That's three days before my birthday! There you have it—spirit has spoken. Getting to spend my forty-third birthday living the life of my dreams in the most magical place on the planet would be true success and an incredible birthday gift.

Plus, my situation could also improve by then—if I can get out onto that ice and bring in some fish, I could still win this thing. It'll be all systems go.

Speaking of all systems go—yes, I'm going again. The first two times after the "holy shit" are painful and bloody, opening the tears back up, but less so each time, and I seem to be healing well. Finally, a day comes when I go out to my latrine rocks and have what seems in every way like a normal, healthy bowel movement. No pain, no straining, no blood, and no rock-hard little balls stuck together. I cry like a baby afterward, tears of joy because I'm so indescribably grateful for a simple poop, something I've taken for granted most of my life.

The lake ice is no longer groaning as it forms. Now the noises are sharp pops and cracks, like someone is standing out in the middle of the lake beating a piece of sheet metal. It's disconcerting, but a good sign, as the cracks relieve the pressure of the ice as it grows thicker and stronger.

A day or two after the popping starts, I walk down to the shore at dusk—you know, 2:30 in the afternoon—to fetch water and find that the ice is now four inches thick. Perfect! It's time! Three inches should hold a small person like me and four is thick enough for all but the heaviest people, but I have to give it a little longer. Thick enough to walk on near shore is one thing, thick enough over the deeper water where currents can make the ice inconsistent is quite another.

Every morning I pound my way through the ice with the back of my saw to reopen my water hole and haul a pot of water and as many ice chunks as I can carry back to the cabin to keep my tea water close at hand.

I look out toward the small island to the southeast as I fill my pot. *Soon*, I promise it. *I'll visit you soon.*

60

THE HARDEST THING

While I'm dressing the next morning, I get the message that I've been dreading. The one that could potentially make me break that promise.

MED CHECK ON ITS WAY. STAY CLOSE TO SHELTER UNTIL IT ARRIVES

Panic seizes me. My weight was good last time, but back then I'd been trapping well and feasting for days before my weigh in. Now I have one more serving of squirrel left, and while I haven't had totally hungry days, it's only because I've been stretching every rabbit out for far too long.

Not today, I pray. *I'm not ready. Please give me enough time to get out onto that ice.*

While I'm thrilled to be able to report that I have a normal digestive track again, it means I no longer have the extra pounds I was packing in my intestines to help pad my weight. I'm all muscle and bone now, and probably less muscle than I want to admit.

I drink a full pot of tea, and then desperation sets in as I hear the thumping of the rotor blades. *There are those small rocks I harvested back when I made my slingshot; maybe I could hide some in my bra to add weight?* I take a step toward the corner where they're stored and then catch myself.

For god's sake, Woniya. Who are you? The med checks aren't out to get you; they're for your own protection. I consider myself an extremely honest person. The kind that gets all hot and sweaty with their voice pitched too high if they have a carrot stick in their pocket while going through the agricultural inspection at the California state line. *Now I'm considering duping the people whose job is to look out for me?*

I sigh and let the idea go. I'm not going to stay here like that. I can't imagine being forced to leave, but I'm not putting my body or my integrity on the line. It's up to the animals, the ancestors, and the medical staff how long I get to stay here. I'm in their hands.

The boat motor was loud, but the roar of the helicopter as it settles down onto the rock arena is deafening. It sets the treetops thrashing around, and I would probably find it terrifying after so much quiet and solitude if I didn't see Dave climbing out of it. His presence, as always, is calming to my nervous system. He and the cameraman walk up while the medical staff gathers their equipment.

"We saw a wolf out on the lake ice," he tells me. "Not far off your shore."

"No way, really?" I ask Dave, who knows me well enough to know I'll be thrilled, not frightened. "I've been hoping to see one! Do you think it will still be there? Can I go see it?"

"No, the helicopter scared it off."

Damn—but still, a wolf! Right here! What a lifetime achievement it would be to see a wild wolf. And on the lake ice too. I add it to my new definition of success. Make it out here until my birthday, and until I see a real, wild, arctic wolf.

"I thought about padding my weight," I admit, as I step onto the scale. "I would be beyond heartbroken if you pulled me. But then I realized that you guys are here to have my back. You're on my team, and I'm entrusting the choice and my health to you. I'm not going to be anything but honest with you."

The cameraman asks me to share a little more while the medics and producer confer. "This has got to be incredibly hard," he says, pointing the lens at me. "Want to talk to the camera about how hard it is? How it's the hardest thing you've ever done?"

The hardest thing? I ask myself, but it doesn't ring true.

I'm silent for a long minute. It takes his question for me to see the truth myself.

I've never had what one would consider a life of ease. On the surface my life out here is far more physically demanding and uncomfortable than anything I've experienced before—does that mean that it's necessarily harder? I don't think so.

I've known loss and grief that felt like they would tear me apart. I've had my dreams shattered in myriad ways, and harder still, I've shattered another's dreams.

I'd known I wasn't happy in the relationship with Chris before I married him, but I was young and naive at the time and didn't realize that you can love someone without it meaning that you're meant to be together. We'd been engaged, then broke up and got back together, as I mucked my way through figuring out what I needed to be happy. I was too sad at the thought of leaving him to carry through with it and didn't trust myself enough to believe in my own heart's deepest truth. And so, both of us hoping that my cold feet were just my commitment issues, I married him.

It turned out I did have commitment issues, but not the ones we'd thought. My issue was agreeing to commit to something I knew in my core wasn't right for me, and placing my desire to love and be loved, to please someone and avoid hurting them, over my own happiness.

By the end of the first week of our marriage, I was terrified I'd made a mistake. In another three months, I was certain of it. The guilt was paralyzing. I was consumed by my own grief, horrified at his suffering, and deeply ashamed of all I'd dragged him through. From the deep hollow of my pain and fear, I always acquiesced when he begged me to stay a little longer. For eight months we lived in hellish limbo, pretending to all the world we were happy newlyweds. I started having panic attacks; it felt like my chest was seized in an iron vise and was unable to expand to take a full breath.

Breaking the heart of the wonderful man I loved, but wasn't happy with, was incredibly hard and excruciatingly painful.

Years later, I finally saw that prioritizing his emotions over my own was what had gotten me into that mess, and that acquiescing further had dragged out the agony for both of us. Being wracked with guilt and beating myself up over it, instead of treating myself with compassion, were part of the same pattern. The next major relationship I got into was with an abusive partner. Coincidence? *No way.* He was emotionally abusing me to the same degree I'd been beating myself up since leaving Chris. It wasn't until the new partner's abuse turned physical that I did something about it. Making plans to get away without alerting him, for my own safety, and biding my time until he was in one of his "happy and sweet" spells, was both incredibly challenging and terrifying.

I look up at the camera.

Leaving Chris was the hardest thing I'd ever done. And there were no northern lights dancing just for me back then, no rabbit fur scarves, or wild wolves in the background—no beauty and sweetness to balance out the pain. Strategically extracting myself from the abusive relationship that followed was no picnic either. But this? The hardest thing ever? *Not for a second.*

"It isn't," I finally answer the cameraman. "Not remotely. I love this life, with all its challenges, and I plan to keep on living it for as long as you all will let me."

61

MY GREATEST SORROWS, MY GREATEST STRENGTHS

hold onto my hat to keep the helicopter from blowing it off and screw my eyes up tight against the driving ice from its blades, but I don't mind the wind and the noise this time, because *they are letting me stay*. The producer told me, with his sternest face and most serious voice, that it was by a narrow margin. They're getting concerned about me, but it isn't so dire that they've opted to pull me. I've survived another medical check.

I sit on a rock in the arena and watch the helicopter dwindle for the first time since launch day. I felt so alive and full of hope on day one. Today I feel raw and vulnerable thinking about the suffering in my past—suffering I helped create by not trusting myself. I feel again the angst that has plagued me since the end of my second marriage and my miscarriage two years later, knowing I'll probably never hold my own baby in my arms and that it's my own damn fault because of the choices I've made.

And yet, even though I feel sadness when I think about it, this time the thought doesn't come with the deep, crippling grief I've carried for so many years.

At this moment, when I think about not raising a family, not being surrounded by grandchildren in my old age, I'm not gutted to my core with sorrow. The realization is shocking. It's been such a constant presence for so long that it's hard to imagine who I am without it.

Then again, I don't have to, because it's part of me. I don't have to carry it with me forever to have been shaped by it. I think back over the last year, the loaded forty-second year, when I'd determined I would decide either to have a baby on my own, or to let the idea go. I was in no kind of place to consider becoming an older, single mother—my life was less stable than it had been back on the homestead. My anguish about being childless had been pressing for much of the year. And then at some point, it has shifted—not just disappearing, but becoming easier to bear. *Of course—* I realize. *The doe!* It shifted just after the doe arrived.

The road-killed doe that showed up last spring came just in time to give me content to film for my *Alone* application. That would have been enough, and yet she was far more magical than that.

Elbow-deep in her body cavity as I was gutting her, I was confused when I felt something big and hard in her belly. *What hard thing would a deer have been eating?* And then I realized in horror that it wasn't her stomach I was feeling; it was her uterus, which then fell, glistening and slippery, right into my arms.

The doe had been pregnant when killed on the road that day, with not just one but two sweet baby fawns. They were so close to birth that the only part of them not fully formed were their hooves—still translucent and soft under my fingers.

"Wow, those would make amazingly soft pelts," my second housemate said of their tiny, spotted hides. But I knew I could never do that. Skinning and processing a full-grown doe was one thing, but these small, sweet ones, dead before they'd had the opportunity to take their first breath, felt incredibly sacred and inviolable.

"No way, hands off," I said, laying them tenderly in a wooden salad bowl.

While I appreciate the resources they provide, I always mourn the death of any creature meeting an untimely end on a roadway. This one was tragic on a whole other level, but I wasn't yet ready to look at why it felt so important and personal. Instead, I tucked the fawns into a corner of the living room while I focused on butchering their mother and filming the process. It was past 2:00 am by the time the meat was wrapped and put away, and the house was dark and quiet as I crept into the living room and picked up the bowl where the fawns lay.

I bathed them in the kitchen sink, rinsing the amniotic fluid from their soft hair so that their fur was unblemished and their spots shone bright white. I'd never touched anything as tender and perfect as their soft black noses and tiny whiskers. I picked out one of my favorite willow baskets and headed outside with my headlamp, where I filled the basket with a bed of ferns and wildflowers. Though I was tired, I wasn't ready to lay the baby deer in it. Instead, I pulled the rocking chair up to the woodstove and held them in my arms, rocking rhythmically and stroking their fur as it dried. It was in that moment, with the cadence of the rocking chair and their weight in my arms, that I realized why it felt so significant.

In the morning I was headed for our next five-day session at Weaving Earth, where the first-year students would be presenting their year-end projects, called "Wild Witnessing." That meant it was the one-year anniversary of my own Wild Witnessing project. I had created a ceremony for myself and asked to be witnessed in sharing about—and grieving—the wounds of my womb and then making peace with the children I never had. The two most potent wounds were two pregnancies that had never come to fruition, one through my own choice as a young woman who didn't feel ready for motherhood, and the recent miscarriage when motherhood was what I wanted most in the world.

I had intended the ceremony to be healing, but in actual fact, I hadn't been able to let go and grieve fully while in the spotlight, so it hadn't achieved its purpose. As a result, I'd been stuck in a grief spiral for months afterward. Perhaps I'd been trying to force the healing, which needed to come in its own time. Now, one year later, these two beautiful, wild babies had come to me in the flesh, for me to hold and grieve and bury, and thus finish the ceremony I had begun. After taking the time I needed to rock and cry and kiss their wee noses and shower them with love, I laid them in their basket until sunrise. In the morning I buried them under wild rose bushes while golden Wilson's Warblers flitted to and fro all around us.

Suddenly, it all makes sense. From that time on I was so busy thinking about the show that I was too distracted to notice, but after the spontaneous ceremony with the fawns, I no longer felt the pressing weight of sadness and loss in the same way.

And look at me now—this adventure is beyond anything in my wildest dreams.

When I left Chris, and that rare creature—the little *Aplodontia*—brought me a bouquet of wildflowers to help me through my grief, I made a commitment to prioritize living the wilder life I loved.

Perhaps if I hadn't gone through that suffering, I wouldn't be here now. And if I hadn't experienced that level of grief and misery and let it change me, I would likely be having a much harder time with the challenges of solo survival in arctic winter. It probably would, in fact, be the hardest thing I've ever done.

The hardest steel goes through the hottest fire. If I'd had the things I wanted and if they had come easily, would I be the strong woman that I am today? Not likely. If I'd had siblings to play with, both parents in the same house, or my mom waiting for me when I got home from school, would I be this fiercely independent? If I hadn't almost lost her to cancer when I was only seven and learned I would survive even that, would I believe so firmly that I can survive this?

That anti-hunting vegan, that nerdy, wimpy girl who got picked on in grade school, is living on her hunting and trapping out in the arctic wilds and loving every second of it. *How incredible is that?* And does it stand to reason that if I'd had a lasting marriage and children I would have been happier with that life? When this deep drive to live like I am now has always been present in me? Not necessarily. When confronted with the choice, I've chosen freedom over and over. That isn't coincidence; it's the strong compass deep inside me. I try to picture myself as a housewife or working a nine-to-five job. Would my soul have survived those intact? I doubt it, because I tried living a life that didn't feel true to me during those years with Chris, and it felt like dying.

As it turns out, not having someone to miss or children at home is an asset on this journey. Not having anywhere I would rather be is a source of serious strength.

Before leaving the rock arena I turn a full circle and just take it all in. The fall colors are all gone and everything is shades of black, gray, and white, broken up only by the green spruce boughs, and yet it's no less beautiful than when it was blazing with golden fall color. I love it. Deep down in my bones it feels like home in a way that few places ever have.

If I could take it all back and trade this experience for the family I always wanted, would I do it?

I don't know, but I'm pretty sure I wouldn't. It's time to let go of the story of needing children to feel complete and whole. Maybe the key to future happiness isn't using reproductive science to give me a baby. Maybe it's birthing myself and the life I was meant to live.

The realization floods me with peace. I never would have thought that months of starving on this stark and rocky peninsula would somehow turn my life's deepest sorrows into my greatest strengths, but now I can see that it's absolutely true.

62

THE ISLAND GIVETH

As if in confirmation, when I head back out to finish walking my trapline, I find the biggest, meatiest snowshoe hare I've trapped yet. The love goes both ways—the more I listen to this place and let it change me, the more it shows up for me.

And there's more. At dusk, the lake ice is five inches thick at my watering hole. It's finally time to get out onto it. The day I've been dreaming of for so long is finally here!

It's too late in the day for an ice-fishing venture, but the island just off my south shore—the one that has teased me since launch day—is a short walk away. I'm doing it!

My pulse races as I step out onto the ice, trepidation and excitement all tumbled together. I know it's thick enough to hold me, but it's equal parts unnerving and thrilling to set foot on what has been open water for months. To be able to walk out into this vast new landscape, utterly unavailable any other time of the year—that is the real wilderness, the ultimate adventure.

It's happening! I'm out on the ice! I made it to freeze-up!

The solidity underfoot makes short work of my trepidation and soon there's nothing but exuberant joy.

My world has just quadrupled in scope. *Imagine the islands I can explore, the distant shores I can reach, the fish I can catch.* But the light is already fading on me. First things first—that island! The lake surface is a little too slippery to feel stable on my feet, so I glide-step my way across, not quite ice skating and not quite walking. In no time I'm hauling myself up the low rocky ledge of its shore. It's thigh-high, so I leap up and do a belly flop, wriggling up onto the icy granite like an awkward seal, very glad I don't have the camera running.

It's a small island, so it doesn't take me long to circumnavigate it. The terrain is much like the mainland—open rock and scattered spruce trees. No rabbit tracks, so my hopes of a new trapping locale where the rabbits might not be as wary don't look promising. Then a weird pattern of rocks catches my eye. It's a circle. *Dear god, it's a campfire ring!* And jutting out from the snow is an out of place but familiar shape—a straight piece of metal. *Oh my god, it's a handle!* I give it a pull with awkward mittened fingers. The snow sloughs off and I'm holding a rusty but serviceable frying pan! *A frying pan? Are you kidding me? This is gold!*

Containers of all kinds are incredibly vital in wilderness survival situations, but none more so than those that you can cook with or store water in. This pan could be the key to my health and well-being. If I'd had something like this, those constipation episodes might have been far less horrendous. All those weeks of letting myself get dehydrated because I couldn't melt water and cook food at the same time, and right here, not fifty yards from shore, has been another cooking vessel! No sign of human life on my whole peninsula, and I've been staring every day at someone's old fishing camp and never suspected it.

The sun is well below the horizon by the time I'm done kicking the snow clear to be sure there aren't any other hidden treasures. I head back across the lake, a beaming smile on my face and pan in my hand, in the last of the day's light.

By the flames of my evening fire, I can tell that the pan is too pitted with rust for cooking hares, but perfect for melting snow. I prop it up on the hearth rocks. Now I can use my pot to cook on the coals and sip warm water from my pan at leisure while I work my culinary magic. Food and water simultaneously, and a frying pan just as my fishing possibilities are coming to fruition? *Total game changer.*

63

RAINING CREOSOTE

A noise wakes me in the night. A storm is whipping the trees around me into a frenzy and grabbing at the limbs of the living spruce trees I've lashed my front wall to. The noise is the whole cabin creaking as they sway to and fro. I want to peek out the front door and see what's happening out there, but the air bites my nose the second I poke it out from under the scarf I use to help seal the hood of my sleeping bag. There's no way I'm getting up. I roll over, spooning my snuggle rocks tighter, and do my best to go back to sleep.

When I wake again, the rocks are cold, hard weights in the bag. They thud against the floor as I heave them out of my sleeping bag one by one. The creaking hasn't subsided and I'm shivering just from opening the bag those few inches. There's no point in staying in bed (*minus-forty sleeping bag, my ass*), so I shrug myself out into the air and peer out the door. The snow whips past my nose in a solid wall of white. This is the kind of storm I've been bracing for since day one.

So much for ice fishing. It must have dropped another twenty degrees overnight, and with that wind, unbroken over miles and miles of lake, going out onto the ice would be a death wish. This life takes bravery and determination every day, but there's a difference between bravery and stupidity.

I put on every layer I've got and keep up a good pace to maintain body heat while I walk the trapline, but the snares are all buried in snow and there's not much point in digging them out only to be buried again. It's so cold that the water in my new pan freezes unless I have it nestled right in the coals, so I switch it out with the rabbit stew I'm warming up. The stew has a hard shell of ice on top by the time I've got drinking water. *Dear god, these temperatures are not messing around!*

For three days the storm rages over the landscape, the wind screaming up and over the peninsula. I hang close to the cabin, venturing out only to harvest and haul firewood, walk the trapline, and go to the bathroom. Several times a day I thank the folks who left this pan on the island, grateful to be able to melt snow for water while staying within the relative shelter of the little stand of trees. From the doorway, I can barely see the rock arena through the swirling snow.

Thursday arrives. It's dance party day, and I said I would dance every Thursday, but I just can't make myself do it. How can I shake my booty when there's so little of it left and when it's too cold to move properly?

Even double walled, the cabin feels like it's barely keeping the storm outside. The ceiling is sparkling with ice crystals—condensation from my breath and cooking steam that freezes the second it hits the frigid tarp. I have to straddle the fire to feel any warmth, and my back is freezing even as my legs get uncomfortably hot.

I heap wood onto the fire to give me a bigger envelope of warmth and am just starting to feel slightly more comfortable when *plink*—a drop hits my pot lid. I wipe it up and look at the brown smear on my finger. *What the heck—is that blood?* How is there blood dripping from the ceiling? Another drop hits my sleeve, then one lands at the hearthstone by my feet. They're half-frozen, sludgy, and reek of smoke. *Crap, now I get it.* The ceiling is covered in tarry creosote from my smokey fires, and when I raise the temperature above freezing up there, the ice melts and mixes with it and it all comes raining down together. *Great—I can either freeze my butt off, or have sticky, stinky creosote rain all over me and my things.* Neither option is acceptable, so whenever there's a brief break in the storm, I head out and harvest materials to insulate the underside of the ceiling. By wedging short poles between the ridge pole and the walls, I can weave spreading spruce branches in behind them as a framework, and then work bushy tips behind those for insulation. It doesn't entirely stop the creosote rain, but it slows it down and keeps the worst of it off me and the bed.

By the third day of the storm, I've finished the ceiling, tanned most of my squirrel skins, and eaten every scrap of the snowshoe hare down to the marrow. I swallow the last swig of my flavorless Starvation Soup the morning that the wind finally settles and the sky clears.

64

GETTING HUMBLE

The drop in temperature wasn't just my imagination or the wind chill. It's now reached the point where my nostrils freeze together for a fraction of a second on every inhale—which generally indicates at least twenty below, in my experience.

Just getting out of bed and dressing in these conditions takes almost an hour and is exhausting. Everything feels exponentially harder. It's so cold that a pot of hot liquid starts crusting over with ice within a minute of pulling it off the fire. It feels like a full-time job just to keep myself hydrated and to keep my digestive system up and running.

With all the tea I'm pounding, I'm peeing all day long, and I'm noticing a new and unsettling phenomenon. I usually have stellar bladder control. I'm the kind of person who can notice I have to pee and then remember an hour later that I still haven't gotten around to it. Not so these days. If I don't start unbuttoning my pants the second I feel the urge, things could get ugly. I used to try to get a good distance away from the cabin to pee, but now it's all I can do just to get outside in time. It freezes as soon as it hits the cold granite, so now I've got a growing yellow mound on the north side of the cabin—a bona fide pee slick. Fascinating as it is, I decide not to capture it on film.

The cold also makes my nose run constantly and causes my breath to freeze on my eyelashes, making blinking awkward. I've got frozen snot covering the back of each mitten, and when it gets too icy on both my mittens and sleeves to keep wiping my nose without chapping it, I just let the snot go. With the wind constantly whipping my hair into my face, before long it too is coated in frozen snot. This flakes off throughout the day, so maybe it's taking some of the dirt and grease along with it. Freeze-dried snot—the new shampoo.

One day I'm trudging along the trapline, digging it out of the snow, when I notice a strange lump in my pants, swishing around between my legs. Did I tuck my shirt in funny? I fish around but don't find the lump.

I go back to the cabin to thaw out with some tea and see what is going on. Since getting freaked out by the droopy skin on my belly a while ago, I've decided that looking closely at my body isn't helpful. I judge by how I feel, not what I look like, and I'm still feeling good. So when I drop my pants to see what is going on, it's pretty shocking to see how shrunken my thighs look and how my knees bulge out below them. *Oh my god, that's what the lump was.* My underwear, once taut across my ample rump, is no longer actually touching my butt. It's dangling loosely from my hips with so much air space between the cloth and my body that it's gathered itself up into a ball between my legs. It isn't something *in* my pants, it's the *absence* of something. My butt and hips. *Wow.*

I sink to the ground. I'm digesting my own muscles. I can no longer deny the degree to which my body is showing the strain of what I'm asking of it.

When I head back out again, at the far end of the trapline I see a sight that stops me dead in the middle of the trail.

No, no, no! Fox tracks headed right toward my best trapping zone. I've been seeing lynx tracks in the snow with some frequency, but they've never bothered my snares. Foxes are different, as experience has shown. I can feel my pulse in my ears as I follow in its footsteps, fresh and crisp in the deep snow. When I reach the far hollow, the biggest trap area with the most rabbit sign, I let out a moan. The area is torn apart with fresh dirt tossed up onto the clean snow. The fox has dug into the hillside and gutted the rabbit's home zone. My hands fall limply to my sides and my shoulders sag. This is disastrous. I need this trapping area—it's the only place I've been successful lately.

I walk down to the lakeshore, plunk heavily onto a big boulder, and stare out across the frozen lake.

I just lost a handful of potential fishing days to the storm, I've barely been eating, and now my trapline is shot. I'm already walking a knife edge out here—any medical check is the one that could send me home. Do I relent and accept that the next one will be my last?

No, I tell myself. *I'm not giving in.* I'm going to do anything it takes to stay out here. I simply don't have enough daylight hours to keep up my trapline, outfox the foxes, and ice fish as well. Okay then, it's time to stop prioritizing the trapline and focus on fishing. For serious ice travel, I need to make a safety device—a ladder or cross beam of wood so that if I fall through the ice, I've got something to keep me from going all the way down and that I can use to haul myself out of the water. Working as fast as I can to get it made, I'm still not done before the sun sets.

I know it's too close to dark to fish, but I'm feeling reckless in my desperation, so I head back to the cabin and start pulling out my hooks and hand reel—long abandoned in the back corner. I've got them in my traps pack when I look down at my bait pile—a frozen tower of rabbit guts. Every time I clean a rabbit or squirrel, I put its stomach and intestines on a piece of bark and tuck it back here. Now they are all stacked up in a disheveled pile of lumps of frozen innards.

Oh man, I think to myself looking at it. *Okay, Woniya. How much do you want this?*

Ice fishing is a gamble, but there's actual food value in this gut pile. People all over the world eat stomachs and intestines regularly. *Am I any different? Am I too proud to eat the one calorie source I've got left, even with it staring me in the face?*

Anything it takes to stay here, I told myself earlier. *But really?*

I sigh. *Yes, really.* I set down the fishing gear, pick up a stack of the frozen guts, and get some snow melting in the frying pan.

Alright, I tell myself and the camera as I set myself up under a spruce tree with a pot of warm water. *It's time to get real humble.*

It's freezing cold and almost too dark to see without my headlamp, but this isn't a job for inside the cabin. I take a frozen gut puck and thaw it in the hot water, then snip the intestines open with my Leatherman scissors and spill the contents onto the ground. The ropey tissue is slimy under my fingers as I slide my nails along the inner membrane and scrape out the green-brown goo, but at least the smell is milder than I'd imagined. Still, it's hard to fathom putting this in my mouth. I don't have time to stop and think about it—the water is already icy cold before I grab the second puck, so I have to work fast. I dunk the emptied ropes of intestines in the pot, which turns the water a disgusting shade of brown and stings the deep cracks in my fingers. It's too late to worry about infection now; I'm committed. I shift my knees to avoid the growing pool of intestinal contents, hoping it'll freeze solid before it oozes into my buckskin. Suddenly the humor of the situation strikes me. This is the most disgusting thing I've ever done, and I'm filming it for international television. Talk about humbling—*it doesn't get much more real, folks.* Arctic survival at its finest. *Should I just have left the camera off? Too late now.*

It takes over an hour and several changes of water to clean three rabbits' worth of digestive systems, but when I'm done, I've got a pile of fairly clean-looking protein heaped on a fresh piece of birch bark.

I creak unsteadily to my feet, stiff from all the crouching, and head inside. It's not going to look any more appetizing with time, so let's get this over with before I change my mind.

The intestines twist and squeak in the pot and a bubbly foam cooks up out of them, filling the cabin with a sour-smelling steam. *Holy cow, am I really going to eat this?*

I'm grateful I've got a salt button left, because I don't think I could face this meal without it. When they're cooked through and well salted, I hold the pan lid up to the camera. "Are you ready for this?" I ask it. "I'm not sure I am."

I take a tentative bite. Chewy and strange, but actually not that bad. Not exactly meaty, but not poopy either, thank god. It turns out they're nowhere near as gross as you'd think. By the time I'm done with them, I'm wishing I had cleaned more.

65

BECOMING ANCESTOR

'm planning on just walking the trapline but not resetting much in the morning, and then, incredibly, I find not one, not two, but three squirrels in my snares—more animals than I've gotten in one day yet. The squirrels must be especially active after so many days of waiting out the storm.

I almost weep with gratitude as the first whiff of cooking organs hits my nose. Like always, I make up an ancestor plate and place it on my largest hearthstone. The rest of the organs go down so quickly they barely even touch my hunger. I get the squirrel legs steam-sautéing, and while they're browning, I find that I can't stop staring at the ancestor plate.

Do you ever hear the world speaking to you? Not audibly perhaps, not actually hearing voices, but from somewhere deeper—a knowing that springs forth out of nowhere and can't be denied? It's that way when I ask a tree if I can cut it and instantly feel the "yes" or "no." It was that way when I felt I ought to go to the far side of the rock arena to harvest poles and found my lost arrow in the tree trunk. It's happening with this ancestor plate now.

My offerings have been an incredibly potent part of my time out here, and they still feel just as important, but something is shifting. For the first time, I feel pushed to eat this offering. I pick up the ancestor plate and look around, speaking to something unseen but increasingly present in everything I do here.

"I think I need to eat this," I say out loud.

A deep feeling of "yes" rolls over me, followed by the message, "Of course you do. We've been waiting for you to realize it."

Though my logical brain hasn't quite caught up to the idea, I feel the rightness of the answer deep inside.

I take a piece of liver from the plate with tentative fingers and slowly chew it, experiencing it more deeply than the rest of the organs put together. It feels strange, but also right, to be eating from a plate set aside for ceremony. If eating food when you're actively starving isn't ceremony, I don't know what is.

As the flavor washes over me, I feel more and more that I'm eating this not just *for* my ancestors, but *as* them. I'm what my ancestors turned into, their legacy here on earth.

With every passing week I've felt myself becoming more fully human—the product of countless millions of years of evolution. The choice to clothe myself in wool and leather stitched by hand—the very materials my ancestors wore—was another step closer to them.

I love that every day I spend in this place, I'm further from the modern life of schedules and devices, climate control and walls—all the ways we shut out the living world around us and keep ourselves from being part of it—and more rooted in a timeless way of being. It's what I've longed for all my life.

This body was shaped by the need to find food, build shelter, and weave fiber into baskets and clothing. It didn't evolve for keyboards, electric lights, or whizzing automobiles. As a matter of fact, those things slowly degrade its health and vitality. What's more, my body evolved for famine. The level of deprivation I'm experiencing right now isn't something new. It's the human legacy. Feast and famine cycles are woven deep into our genetic memory—our insatiable hunger for fats and sweets is part of that. Our forebears rarely had them in abundance, and when they did, feasting on them when they could and building up their body fat meant they were more likely to make it through the lean times that were inevitably coming. Every winter my ancestors had to fight for enough food and warmth to make it through, and every winter some of them didn't manage to survive. I'm the product of those who did, and who came out more resilient and resourceful on the other side. Those genes passed on down the line until they eventually landed in me.

In more than twenty-five years of running around in buckskin and furs, harvesting wild foods, and practicing the arts known as ancestral skills, I've always felt connected to my ancestors, but it's been mostly intellectual. Out here it's visceral, and while I've certainly spoken to them before, this is the first time they've answered back.

Is it my own voice or is it theirs? The distinction is fading. The line between us has blurred until it doesn't exist anymore. I'm not just living like my ancestors; I'm becoming an ancestor. I know it, I feel it. And they feel it too. I'll still make the ancestor plate, but from now on, it will be with the knowledge that it is my own plate too. When I eat from it, the nourishment goes both ways, passing from me to them and back until that one small meal feels like a potent feast.

66

FIVE THOUSAND SUNSETS

The next day, even with hurrying through my routine, it's near sunset once I've got all my fishing things and safety equipment together and head down to the lake. Up until the storm I was keeping my little hole just off-shore open, heaping spruce boughs on top of it for insulation. The storm scattered those boughs who knows how far across the ice, and all I can now see of them is a peppering of green needles here and there. The hole is iced up, but that's okay. I don't need to haul water now that I've got my pan to melt the snow around camp.

I stand on the rock ledge of the shore, incredulous that the time is finally here. It's my moment of truth, the thing that could make or break my chances of staying longer—even winning, against all odds.

Here goes!

The surface is way more slippery than it was last time, and I have to fight to keep my feet under me. It's a whole different world out here. The storm-driven snow must have been like a sand blaster, polishing the surface of the ice for all those days, because now it's crystal clear and mirror smooth. I feel like I'm looking through the glass at an aquarium, except it's beneath my feet instead of in front of me. I can see every stone, every pebble, and every nuance of the lakebed below in exquisite detail. It's mesmerizing, and I keep having to remind myself I'm here for a purpose and don't have a lot of daylight left for it.

We took kids out ice fishing when I taught outdoor education in the Adirondacks, but it was in a shallow pond and we never caught anything, so though I've done it many times, I basically have no experience ice fishing. I know I'm looking for deep water near a topographic feature like a drop-off or ledge, so I head straight out into the lake to find an area of sufficient depth.

I keep walking. And walking. Fifty feet out I'm still looking down at shallow rocks just under my feet. A hundred feet out it is hardly different. It's both validating and frustrating to finally see for certain that, in fact, this location is every bit as bad for shore fishing as it seemed to be.

The bottom starts dropping off significantly once I am 150 feet out, and now it isn't details of the bottom I'm seeing, it's the cracks in the ice. It's counterintuitive, but I know they aren't a sign of a fragile surface, quite the opposite. What worries me isn't that I might fall through, but that those cracks look like they're at least twelve inches deep. That's a lot of ice to get through with a totally insufficient tool.

I'm finally out where I can't see the bottom anymore, just vast darkness below me in every direction. I'm well past the little island—which I now think of as Frying Pan Island—so I position myself where I think the bottom drops off from its shallows and get the tripod set up.

With my fishing gear and my last remaining rabbit stomach beside me, I kneel down and start chipping.

Since freeze-up I've been hacking my way through the ice near shore with the back end of my closed folding saw. It's far from ideal, but without an axe it's the only tool I've got for it. Before the storm I was able to chip my way through the four inches of ice to open my watering hole within five minutes or less.

Five minutes barely makes a dent in this surface. It's now the harder, denser ice that forms in deep cold, not the opaque ice shot with bubbles that accompanies initial freeze-up. In ten more minutes, I'm about four inches down, but the saw is binding up in the narrow hole and each strike is less effective. *Holy crap*, I realize, my stomach sinking into my boots. *This might not happen.*

I have to stop every few seconds to swipe the chips out with my mitten, otherwise I'm making great shave ice but no downward progress. Dread creeps in like someone pouring ice water into my veins. The hole is getting deeper, but every half inch takes more and more effort and the edges of the cracks where the liquid water starts don't seem any closer. Twelve inches thick was an optimistic estimate. I think I'm looking at something closer to eighteen. I'm warm with the work, but I've got a stitch in my side and my legs are cramped up from kneeling.

Not having an axe has been a minor inconvenience up until this point, but not a major handicap. Now it's crippling. I can't fault myself for my gear choices; I did the best I could with what I knew. Had I brought an axe and left something else, it might have meant going home sooner and not making it until freeze-up. But now there's not much I wouldn't trade for the axe I left behind.

My world shrinks and I'm aware of nothing but the small patch of ice in front of me. I go slower, taking more breaks to stretch, but it no longer feels like I'm making progress, and both the light and my hopes are plummeting.

There's still nearly a foot of solid ice between the saw and open water. Maybe I could get through it with another several hours of chipping, but at that point, I'll have burned up a good deal more calories than I can get from a good-sized fish or two, and I'd probably have to do the same thing every day to keep the hole open. That would be most of my daylight hours and mean giving up on trapping entirely.

This can't be happening! I think. *This was supposed to be my moment of triumph!*

So many weeks of waiting for freeze-up, and now in one storm the lake ice went from finally safe to walk on to totally impenetrable. Even as it's clear how futile my efforts are, I have a hard time registering it. I stand up to ease my aching back, then furiously beat at the surface again, flinging ice chips into my eyes, but not accomplishing much else.

Finally, I can no longer pretend I have any chance at success. *It's over. I'm through.* I've been depending on getting through the ice to access the fish that are this area's most abundant food resource and my best, and maybe only, hope of making it through the winter. Despair settles heavily onto me, and I can feel the descending dark and cold inside as well as out.

The crushing of the hope that has kept me going for so long is like a sock in the stomach, knocking the wind out of me. I'm bent over and a little woozy with it. I run through my options, trying to keep hopelessness at bay. I could build a fire on the lake to melt through the ice, but that would just create a water-filled pit—the fire would sink into it and put itself out. I could build it on a platform of green branches instead, heating rocks and then using them to melt through the ice, but the stones are all buried in ice and snow. Hauling rocks and firewood and keeping it all going would burn even more calories than the chipping, would still need to be repeated day after day, and would be a wet and sloppy process likely to produce both frostbite and hypothermia. It doesn't make sense, and the calorie equation doesn't pan out.

When I straighten up, the light has shifted, and the sky is lit with orange and red and every color in between—the first real sunset we've had since my waltz with the sun. I've been so focused on the work and my disappointment that I've barely been paying attention to the world above me. Now it's impossible not to notice, because the sun has hit that angle where it isn't just the sky it's painting with color—the lake ice that was dark as steel moments ago is now catching and reflecting the light above. Every warm and brilliant color imaginable spreads out in all directions, engulfing everything I can see. I'm literally standing on the sunset, and it's incredible. The sick feeling in my stomach fades and my chest swells with the wonder of it.

I want to get farther out into it. I turn around to see how far I am from shore, and there, just rising up over Frying Pan Island, is a perfect half-moon, enormous against the glowing sky, and perfectly framed by the trees of the island.

It's spectacular, and just like the northern lights above the latrine that night, it's hard not to feel a divine hand behind it, offering me the most incredible consolation prize imaginable. And it's working. I get it. I feel it. Everything is going to be okay. In a world that offers up condolence of this magnitude, how could it not be?

I push the tripod out in front of me and slide-skate my way farther onto the lake, feeling more alive and energized than I have in weeks. If my time is winding down, let it go down in a blaze of brilliance. Let me absorb all the joy and wonder that I can hold.

Farther out into the lake, the cold and wind are stronger, but the nipping at my cheeks just adds to the exhilaration. I'm sliding and dancing and sailing through the sunset. The wind draws tears from my eyes that blur the distinction between ice and sky even further. Is this what it's like for the birds, as they fly west into the setting sun?

I glide on in the frigid cold across a lake painted with liquid fire, until up ahead I can see a change of texture on the ice—jagged angles instead of mirror smooth. I slide right up to the edge, where laid out before me is a broken landscape of huge plates of ice. Out here the cracks haven't just drawn lines in the ice, they've gone all the way through and split it into pieces that have been heaved up at different angles to release the pressure of the lake freezing so hard and fast. They are enormous, each one anywhere from five to twenty feet across. It looks like an enormous jigsaw puzzle that a toddler has gotten ahold of. It stretches on as far as I can see, barring my way completely.

Each slab is at a different orientation to the glowing sky and reflects its own individual color. Now, rather than engulfed in one enormous sunset, I'm staring out at a sea of them, each one unique. It's the most incredible thing I've ever seen. I let out my loudest, rawest, wild woman yell and jump up and down. I turn in a circle with my arms thrown back, drawing in deep lungfuls of icy air. I'm weeping and laughing with joy and wonder and no longer care that I can't get through the ice. I don't care about any of it. They could sweep in with their helicopter tomorrow and scoop me up, and it would be okay because I got to experience this—this unparalleled beauty and unfathomably wild place that has cradled me so well and taught me so much. I feel that all my life has been building up to bringing me here, in this moment, and I can achieve no greater purpose than just to take it all in and let it unmake me. If my body gives out and my flesh melts away to become the soil that feeds the next generation of spruces and grouse and hares, that too will be beautiful and meant to be. I'll still feel I've been given an incredible life and gotten exactly what I was supposed to from this, the most magical and generous place on earth.

I glide along the edge staring out at the sunset sea until the color fades and the cold brings me back into body awareness, but I'm so lit up with the excitement, and probably a good measure of adrenaline and dopamine, that I don't even remember the journey home until I'm standing at the cabin, lifting the door into place.

67

BEAVER ISLAND

The next morning, I feel like I've been transported overnight to a whole new planet. Last night's sunset saturated everything I could see with more color than I thought was possible all at once, but this morning, everything is socked in with heavy, low clouds, and the entire world—sky, snowy ground, forest, and lake—are all one misty shade of gray. It's as if several days' worth of color was used up in that one brilliant blast.

I'm still shaken to my core by the revelatory evening. While I maintain the same sense that, having had that pinnacle sunset experience I'm reconciled to whatever comes after it, I'm also not going to just roll over and give up.

The air is so thick I can't see very far in front of me as I walk my trails and check my snares, all of which are empty. For some reason, I have a sense that they're going to stay empty, that my trapline is winding down. Perhaps this intuitive knowing is real, or perhaps it's that the climax of last night was so high that everything, trapline included, feels diminished after it. I do my best to disregard the feeling, determined to carry on.

I strategize about what I can do for food if neither ice fishing nor the trapline will provide it.

There's one last possibility to explore—Beaver Island. With the ice more than thick enough for safe travel, there's now nothing except the short days and minimal light to keep me from finding that lodge and trying for a beaver. As soon as I get back from walking my traps I pack up the cameras, my bow, and my big saw, and head across the ice toward it, judging I've got perhaps two hours of daylight left.

It took me about forty minutes to draw level with the island from the shore of the mainland all those weeks ago, but then I'd had to wind my way through forests and up and down the rocky cliffs of the peninsula to get to it. Now, once I scramble up and over the blocky chunks of the ice stockade that has barred the north shore since freeze-up, there's nothing between me and the island but flat ice, and I close the distance quickly.

It's all the same huge mass of water, but it feels like I'm walking on a whole different lake than the one I stood on yesterday. Unlike the clear, polished surface of the ice to the south, the surface here is dull white, and I can't see two inches into it, much less to the bottom of the lake. I push on, my eyes fixed on the island. It's eerily still out on the ice, with no wind and no movement besides my own, and the clouds are so thick I can barely see the mainland. There's none of the beauty and wonder of last night, just my own determination pushing me forward.

With the rougher surface of the lake here, it's a heavy-booted trudge to the island, rather than a slippery glide, but I'm still surprised at how soon I am heaving myself up onto the shore of its southern tip. I haven't gone far inland before the rocks change to brushy undergrowth as tall as my hips. It grabs at the rough wool of my pants and dumps snow all over me. After less than ten minutes I stop, exhausted, to catch my breath. *Damn, this isn't what I was hoping for.* At this rate, I won't even make it to the lodge at the far end, much less there and home again, before dusk. As much as I'd hoped to explore the whole island, my main goal is to find the beaver lodge, and that is going to be on the shore itself. I decide to cut back toward the open ice and explore the shore from the lake instead of the land.

I'm nearing the water's edge when I spot a dark speck flying toward me across the lake. Before it gets close enough to see clearly, I have a good guess what it is, and shortly the bold, black-and-white pattern of its head confirms it. Chickadees often fly in pairs, calling intermittently to one another and yelling at everything else with their sassy, scolding calls. Seeing this one on its own so far out in the middle of the lake gives me pause. It alights on a branch not ten feet from my face, cocks its head, and looks at me, as if it flew here for no other purpose. "Hi weensy," I say, and it looks quizzically back. I'm blinking back tears, partly because I love these little fluff balls so damn much and it's been a while since I've seen one, but also because I have a suspicion about why it's here. I feel—from the same deep place that told me it was time to eat the ancestor plates myself and that my snares will remain empty from here on out—that it's here to bid me goodbye. Feeling directly spoken to by a wild kindred spirit is usually a source of great joy to me, but now my heart shrinks in my ribcage and my throat swells up. I shake my head at it. *No.*

Even though last night I was reconciled to leaving if I had to, I don't want to hear this message. I fight back my rising tears and work to convince myself that this time, I'm just making things up and that it's here by coincidence—even though I watched it soar across the open lake making a beeline right for me.

It flits from one low branch to another for a few seconds, yelling at me with its *chickadee-dee-dee* call and looking back at me after every few hops, then it sails toward the mainland, as swiftly and silently as it arrived.

Stop being so reactionary, Woniya, I tell myself. *Every little thing that happens doesn't always have to be imbued with meaning. Focus on the positive. There's still that beaver lodge.*

Forward movement clears my head and helps me shake off the melancholy, and soon I can see the northern tip of the island. I can feel the anticipation and excitement building within me, and my breath gets faster as I round the corner. I'm almost to where I saw the beaver's raft of vegetation from the mainland, so many weeks ago.

Then I see the lodge—a stout pile of spruce trunks against the water's edge. I was right, it was just where I thought it would be. And yet the discovery doesn't come with the jubilation I hoped it would, but with a cold, hard knot in my stomach.

I don't know what exactly I was expecting—a small, poorly built heap of wrist-thick branches maybe? An open hole near the shore where the beavers come and go regularly? One look tells me those were the naive hopes of a woman from a climate where a beaver's life is easy. I wasn't reckoning on arctic beaver. Built strong enough to withstand sixty-below temperatures, eighty-mile-an-hour winds, and hungry packs of arctic wolves, this thing is a serious edifice—a fortress. Dynamite could probably bust into it, but my folding saw doesn't have a chance.

The logs it's built of are the size of my waist—the size it used to be any-way—and completely embedded in clay. Clay that's frozen solid, like every-thing in a thousand-mile radius is frozen solid. Even if I had enough calories in my wasted body to put in the effort, even if it was possible to bust into the beaver lodge—which I don't and it isn't—the beavers would be out of it and safely under the ice by the time I opened it.

What was I thinking? Did I really believe this lodge was going to change every-thing, when I've seen so many signs that my body and time here are winding down?

I heave a deep sigh and watch the water vapor from my breath—a small white cloud against the backdrop of heavy dark clouds—float out across the ice. It makes it about ten feet before freezing solid and drifting down to the lake's surface.

The cramping of my shrunken stomach has become such a fixture in my world these last months that I barely register it anymore. This time as it twists inside me, I'm deeply aware of the ache and how long it's been since I had anything to fill that empty hollow.

Clearly, some part of me was holding onto the hope that this lodge could be my salvation, and if there was an obvious breathing hole where the beavers come up to the surface, maybe it could have been. But I also know that wasn't the sole reason I came out here tonight. After the more serious blow of my failure to get through the ice last night, I'm not particularly surprised by this one, and therefore not as crushed as I thought I would be at finding the beaver lodge inaccessible.

The Arctic has taught me I can be fed by more than just food and that beauty and wildness are powerful sustenance as well, but unfortunately, the medical crew doesn't factor that into their check-ups. The dull gray of tonight's sky is no match for the beauty of yesterday's, but this is as far out on the ice and as close to the distant shores as I've ever been, and I can feel a sense of adventure rising inside me as I look out at them. I've spent so many weeks staring across this lake, waiting for the thick ice that would allow me to explore the land's remaining mysteries. With my last potential calorie source decidedly beyond my reach, I don't have many days left before they come to whisk me away. This could well be my last chance.

The island blocks my view to the west, so I can't tell if the sun has dipped beneath the horizon yet, but I know it must be nearly down. In this season and at this latitude, there are about four hours of solid daylight, with another hour of hazy, low light at dawn and dusk. The smart choice would be to turn around and head back home, get the fire going, and make another pot of the coffee-colored chaga tea that serves for dinner (and breakfast, and lunch) these days. I know that. My body may be failing, but my reason is still intact. I know too that once the sun goes down, the temperature out on the ice is going to plummet.

Home and safety, or the open lake ice and adventure—*what's it going to be?*

I cup my palms to catch my warm breath and direct it over my cheeks until I can feel them again. I give my rabbit fur scarf a quarter turn to find a spot for my face that isn't crusted with my frozen breath, and I turn away from the island—and home—and head out across the lake.

Not all the way, I promise myself. *I'll just go to the eastern shore, only a few hundred yards away, not the far-off northern shore. A few more minutes won't hurt. I can still make it back by dark.*

With my legs pumping, I don't feel cold anymore. I feel lit from within, hungry to fill my senses with all I can of this place in the time I have left.

This minute right here—staying through freeze-up and getting to walk with ease across what has been deep, impassable water—this is a win. Every day I get here is a win. It might not be the one I hoped for, but really living every minute I have left—sucking the marrow out of every second—is a victory. *Screw it*, I say to myself. *I'm doing it. Hot damn!* No actually, cold damn. *Cold, frozen damn, but halle-freakin-lujah!*

I'm still smiling to myself when I see it—there in the snow, ten feet out from the east shore. *No way!* It's four deep toe marks pressed into the snow, the blue tint of the lake ice seeping through the whole track, coloring each deep claw mark a darker blue.

Oh my gosh, my definition of success! So close!

I'm looking at a wolf track! *I've found a wolf track!*

I can see the trail stretching out before me, paralleling the shore. The fading light is forgotten, my promises to myself are forgotten. A wolf was here, not long ago. *Maybe I can follow the tracks to their source! My last unrealized dream—to see a wolf in the wild before I go!*

In another sixty yards, a second set of tracks joins the first. *A mated pair!* I'm off after them. It's getting darker and hard to make out the details of the tracks, but the divots in the snow are clear enough. They swing wide to the northwest, and I follow, walking to one side to preserve the trail. I'm so intent on the tracks that I don't even realize how far north I've come until I look up. The tracks veer off toward the east and head off the ice, but that isn't what has my attention now. I'm almost to the shore when I see something weird happening with the surface of the ice ahead of me. What has been flat white as far as the eye can see is now bumpy and ridged. The strange bumps aren't white like the rest of the ice, they're marbled with brown swirls. *What the heck?*

I turn around to check the light and judge how much time I've got. My impulsiveness is starting to catch up with me. I can feel the fatigue in my legs and the effort it's taken them to carry me here. This is too damn far from home for this hour of night, but it'll only take me a minute to explore this new mystery. A minute more isn't going to make a difference in the light.

Forgetting the wolves, who are clearly deep in the eastern forest by now, I creep cautiously toward the bumps. I'm only a few steps from the closest one when I freeze.

It takes me a second to register what I'm sensing. *I hear something.* In all this vast, frozen wilderness there has been almost no sound for hours, except for the high-pitched calls of the one chickadee and my own breath in my ears. This is totally different. Faint, low, and ever changing. There's something familiar about it—something I know but can't place. And then I'm hot all over, my chest tight against the furs of my parka—my body registering what it is before my brain does.

It's gurgling. I look down at the ice below my feet. There, not far beneath my toes, I see an amoeboid white shape fly past under the ice, and then another. Air bubbles. My heartbeat thuds in my ears. Suddenly it all makes sense.

The shape of the land in front of me—a narrow valley pointing right toward the lake.

The irregular shapes on the lake surface.

The roar of sound I heard so often out of the north before freeze-up.

Not wind through the trees as I'd imagined, but a wide and rushing river, loud enough to hear from all the way back at the peninsula. The strange shapes are foamy water and standing waves frozen in place, the brown swirls are the muddy water they carry. I'm not standing on the lake anymore; I'm standing on top of an enormous, fast-moving river, and the ice beneath me is only inches thick.

Adrenaline clouds my thinking like the descending darkness clouds my vision. Months of careful risk avoidance while living on my own in one of the wildest, most remote places on earth amidst wolverines and wolf packs, and never a second of serious danger or deep, visceral fear. Now, in one foolish moment, I've hiked myself smack on top of the biggest hazard imaginable.

I take a few deep breaths to choke down my panic. Ice over moving water is soft and weak, full of air and irregularities. One wrong step and I could go down in a heartbeat, sucked under the lake's surface by the flowing current. It's already too dark for the rescue helicopter to fly. Even if it could, if I go through the ice and manage to stay on the surface, the crew would never get to me before the hypothermia does.

Think, Woniya, think.

My eyes dart to the shore, so close I can almost feel it, solid and reassuring beneath my feet. Every animal instinct tells me to go there—run like hell for the shore and solid ground, faster than the ice can give way. But that leads me closer to the river's mouth, where the ice is likely more rotten than where I stand now.

As tempting as it is, I know heading for shore is a death wish. I force my feet to obey my will as I turn away from the perception of safety and back toward the open lake I just came from. I slowly plant one foot in my own closest track. *Solid—thank god.* I take another step, and another. The ice holds. I release my held breath.

With every step I feel a little more confident, a little less panicked. Finally, I'm back on clear white ice and snow, and flat feels like the most beautiful texture in all the world.

How could I have been so near fatally stupid? Maybe my judgment really is slipping. By the time I'm halfway back to the beaver lodge, I know I'm safe, but my whole body is still shaky. I'm clammy with sweat inside my clothes, even in these subzero temperatures.

Then I hear a loud beep from my hip bag. *Oh god, right—my GPS device!*

YOU ARE OUT OF BOUNDS AND LATE FOR CHECK-IN. HEAD BACK IMMEDIATELY

In my excitement, I hadn't even stopped to think how far out of my assigned area I'd wandered. This far north, the satellites are so low in the sky that the signal doesn't send often, so I'm only getting the message now that I'm well on my way back. I scared the hell out of myself, but at least I didn't know how much danger I was in until I was halfway through it.

Not true at production base camp, where there's a staff person watching my GPS signal day and night. Somewhere, many miles away, there's probably a group of frantic people yelling at a flashing blip on a screen, wondering if they'll be doing their first ever body retrieval tomorrow.

68

AND THEN IT HITS ME

'm kicking myself for my recklessness as I trudge back home through the swiftly descending dusk. I've never been so far from home this late. It's open ice, so I can't really get turned around, but the thick clouds obscure the stars and make the darkness feel that much more oppressive. I'm not exactly worried, but I'm decidedly uncomfortable, and it's not just the clamminess of the panicked sweat from earlier that I can still feel against my skin.

I see a shape ahead of me in the darkness and let out a sigh of relief. It's Beaver Island—I'm in the home stretch. When I round the far end of it, I can just make out the tree line of the peninsula and the profile of the truffula tree leaps out at me. It soothes my frazzled nerves as if it were glowing—my homing beacon.

Even once I'm home safe and tucked in my bag with my snuggle rocks, the unease lingers. I can't get comfortable. I think my bedding material has shifted on me; my sphagnum moss must have compacted. Then I remember the cameraman on the last med check asking, "Is it getting harder to sleep, now that you're so bony?"

I had dismissed it at the time. Sure, my legs were getting skinny, but I wasn't really bony, and it's always been hard to sleep out here. But now I remember the balled-up underwear discovery and I'm curious.

Just as I avoid looking at my body out here, I've also avoided feeling it, but now that the question is stirring, I can't let go of it until I know. I slide a tentative hand under my long john top. I can feel every rib in exquisite detail through my taut skin.

This whole time I've been telling myself that once the food really dries up, I've still got another week or two of rations in my breasts and butt. I already know there isn't much left of my butt, yet somehow I'm still shocked enough to gasp out loud as I feel my breasts. They're like two deflated balloons in my hands, nothing but empty sacks of skin. *How have I not noticed it before?*

The crew was right. It isn't the bed that's becoming pokey, it's me. No wonder my underwear doesn't touch my butt anymore. I can barely find it myself.

I didn't want to believe the chickadee was wishing me goodbye, but I knew deep down that it was.

Just let me get through to my birthday, I pray. *A few more days. Let me spend that one special day in this place that means the world to me.*

Now that I have a clearer picture of where my body is at, I'm acutely aware of it as I walk my trapline the next morning. It isn't that I'm weak exactly—I can still do what I need to do—but everything requires a bigger effort of will. Wouldn't I feel weak if I was really approaching the danger line? Then something one of the medics told me comes back to me.

"Some people slowly fade over a long period when starving," he had said. "Some just charge on, going full strength right up until their heart stops beating."

Hmmm...

Alright, already. I know I have to go, I just don't want it to happen for a few more days. *After my birthday I'll be content to leave*, I tell myself. *That's the only gift that I want, to be able to spend it here, alone, in this magnificent wilderness.*

And then out of nowhere, it hits me like a ton of bricks. *Really, Woniya? What kind of gift is that? To push yourself right up to the very edge of what your body can take before it gives out entirely?*

Oh my god, it's true. That wouldn't be monumental at all; it wouldn't even be anything new. It's what I do all the time. I always work myself up to the very edge of my endurance until I collapse into some injury or illness that forces me to stop. Look at my journey here—I pushed myself to the very brink until I almost didn't make it. My lips literally dissolved with cold sores because I was running myself on empty right up to being dropped off in the Arctic wilderness to survive alone. *Would repeating the same patterns you've run over and over be a gift, or would choosing something different—something that's actually loving to yourself?*

I stop dead in my tracks, suddenly sick to my stomach, because I can feel the truth as soon as I ask the question.

Why have I not seen it? I've been kidding myself. Staying on wouldn't be a gift, it would be perpetuating a pattern that's anything but self-loving and accepting. It would be forcing myself to prove something, yet again, before giving my body what it actually needs—food and warmth and the space to heal itself. I can't take it in. It's the last thing I want to admit. So far, success has always meant making it to my chosen day—however arbitrary—before getting pulled, not making it to that day and then simply *deciding on my own to leave.* I still always assumed they would be forcing me home against my will, it was just a matter of when. Now it seems so obvious that I've been looking at it wrong all along. Success is choosing my departure on my own terms—leaving while I'm still strong and vital, not weakened and stumbling. Or worse, on a stretcher.

So who are you, Woniya? Why are you here?

Sure, I'd love to win, but that was never my most important motivation. I came here to lay myself on the altar of wildness—to surrender to the deep wisdom of the land around me. And the land has been telling me that I'm done, time and again, and I've been refusing to hear it. I've passed almost all my measures of success—eight weeks, ten weeks, getting onto the ice, wolf tracks, Beaver Island, and I still pushed on as my body dwindled.

When is it going to be enough, Woniya?

Winning would change my life tremendously—financially and otherwise— but what would actually change it the most would be choosing myself— Woniya. Choosing to see myself as good enough and accomplished enough, just as I am.

I burst into hot tears, because I can't even begin to convince myself that I can decide to do anything else. Today is my last day.

I've got to film this, I think. And the thought reminds me that this choice isn't just about me. One day, this experience will be broadcast all around the world. Some of the people watching will be impressionable young people— including young women learning how to be in the world by watching examples like the one I'm setting now—learning how to treat their own bodies and how to let others treat them. As a survivor of sexual abuse, am I going to show them that I'll let my body suffer greater and greater harm, until finally a team of men takes my sovereignty away, dragging me out of here against my will and making my decisions for me?

No way, I think, resolve hardening like a bar of iron inside me. *I am not leaving like that.*

My fingers are shaking as I hit "record." With all the healing work I've done in my life, it is this moment that truly completes that journey. Making the right choice isn't just the best birthday gift I can give myself; it's also a gift to the world. If I'm not going to have my own children to mother, perhaps I can be a mother to the world by making this choice publicly when it matters most.

I pour my heart out to the camera, explaining my epiphany, explaining that I have to go and why, and then I sling it over my shoulder and walk back to the cabin, still dazed by the rapid turnaround within me.

There's a chaga fungus in a birch tree close to the cabin. I've been waiting to harvest it until it was my last option or I was at the end of my time out. It's a ceremonial gesture to cut it now, the ringing of the gong at the end of my last act.

I spend the evening living it up. Drinking strong chaga tea, eating a triple ball of pemmican, having a big fire and burning most of my wood. The last thing to do tomorrow is to pull my snares and use the satellite phone that is set up to call one number and one number only—the *Alone* production team.

69

THE ANCESTORS SPEAK

n the morning, fatigue and dread of what I'm planning to do weigh heavy on me, and it takes me a long time to pull my snares and erase the evidence of my trapline from the forest.

Finally, I head out to the rock arena, where the satellite phone has the best signal, and I sit with it in my lap, staring up into a cloudy sky. I look out over the vast frozen water before me. Darkness hovers on the far edge of it. I can feel dusk approaching even though it's early afternoon and it's been only a few hours since sunrise.

I'm a bundle of nerves and raw emotion as I lift the phone and turn it on. As I scroll through the menu options, my fingers tremble so badly that I can hardly select "dial production."

I have gone over this conversation in my head a hundred times since my epiphany yesterday, but as I practice it again now, one last time, to the droning sound of the dial tone, I can barely squeak out, "This is Woniya. I am calling to tap out." I try again, but the lump in my throat feels so hard and tight that I can barely breathe, much less speak. Instead of hitting "dial," I drop the phone into the snow and burst into tears.

Where did all my resolve go?

I felt so certain yesterday, but thinking about making the call now, everything within me screams out against the choice. *What is going on?* And then it occurs to me—sure, I had a deep knowing yesterday, but what if this is a deep knowing of an entirely different kind?

My thoughts start to snowball, ricocheting off the inside of my skull. *What if going isn't the right choice?* I know I'm starting to be in rough shape, but I have no idea how anyone else out here is doing. That storm, these temperatures, the minimal daylight—they've all been brutal, and they've got to have been as tough on anyone else still out here as they have on me. I've been thinking that without more food, my chances of winning were close to nil, but we're already past the seventy-day mark. The Mongolia season, the harshest season thus far and nothing compared to these conditions, was decided in less than sixty days. *Could this one be almost finished?* Is that why I suddenly find myself unable to make the call? Is something inside me reacting to an intuitive sense that I am on the very edge of winning? My gut sense is that it is.

I think I'm still in the running. I could have this thing. I could win it. That would be tremendous—for me, for women, for everything I care most about.

The whirring in my mind spreads to my limbs and I'm up and moving. *How many days will it take? What do I have to do to be out here a little longer? I just pulled all my traps and burned most of my firewood, damn it!* I look at the sun—it's not yet brushing the horizon. I head out with my saw and harvest firewood until dusk. Finally, I let the darkness and descending cold push me back inside where I drink a pot of lukewarm chaga tea. I have enough wood to keep me warm tonight, but the sight of the nearly empty firewood alcove sends me back outside again, where I work fiendishly in the feeble light of my headlamp collecting several more days' worth of firewood.

The next morning, I wake up determined, but it's as if gravity has doubled and everything I do, from pulling my frigid clothing on over multiple layers of long underwear, to melting ice for my morning tea, takes ten times the effort it did last week. *No matter,* I tell myself. *Another few days of good effort might be enough to decide this thing.* If it can be won by the power of perseverance, I'm golden. I gather up the snares and traps pieces I pulled yesterday, peel myself off of the ground by the hearth, and head out into the biting air beyond the cabin door.

It's impossible to set my elaborate snares in gloves. By moving my scarf a quarter turn every fifteen minutes and sticking my hands into my armpits when my bare fingers seize up, I manage to keep my face and hands from freezing while I painstakingly reset my snares in new locations. By dusk I have a smaller trapline set up in the woods all around the cabin. It's much closer to home than my previous trapline, so I'll burn less calories checking it.

When I send my evening check-in message, though, the reply comes back:

ACKNOWLEDGED. MED CHECK TOMORROW

Damn it, so soon?

If they're coming tomorrow, I need something in my middle when I step onto that scale. That means I absolutely must find something to eat tonight. I've finished off all the intestines and stomachs, but there must be something around here with some calories in it, right?

In the back of the shelter where I kept the gut piles for fishing bait there are still some odds and ends. I've got rabbit paws and ears, a squirrel hide I scorched by thawing it too close to the fire, several squirrel tails, and some bones that were too small to crack for their marrow. I throw them all into the pot. Whatever it takes.

As I set the pot onto the cooking rocks, the vibration jiggles the hearth-stone and my beautiful wooden ancestor plate falls into the fire. I manage to snatch it up before it gets burned and put it back where it goes.

When the skin on the rabbit ears and feet pulls apart easily and a scum of loose hair is floating on the top of the pot, I know my weird-ass soup is as done as it's going to get. It's disgusting, but it's what I've got and my only chance at not getting pulled. I peel the fur off the rabbit feet and suck the boiled skin off the base of the tufts, trying to keep the hair out of my teeth, then chew the tendons and ligaments off of each tiny bone. It's an incredibly tedious process. The rabbit ears are actually not bad—probably the best part, which isn't saying much. It takes me an hour to painstakingly eat every morsel of solid food, and more than once I wonder if I'm getting anywhere near the calories from it that I'm burning in the process of eating it. Afterward, I stare into the chalky dregs of "soup" at the bottom of the pot, trying to muster the will to drink them. Maybe if they were a little warmer? As I grab some firewood, my arm brushes the ancestor plate, still sooty from its fall into the fire, and it's like I've been stung by it—like the ancestors screaming in my ears.

What the hell am I doing?

Do I really think the twenty calories left in this pot are going to get me past a med check, when I barely passed the last one and have eaten maybe 800 calories in the several days since then? Of course they aren't.

And what does it matter anyway, because I said I wouldn't do this! I fell right into my old pattern. I knew it was right for me to tap, deep down in my very core, yet I kept pushing and pushing. *How did I let the striving and self-denial take the lead again in the most critical moment?*

But I already have the answer. It was the other sense of knowing. The one that believes I am close to the win. *What if that's also true? What if one more day could mean going home a champion and financially stable for the first time in my life?* And then I realize that doesn't change anything. I already knew that I needed to leave. The ancestors were telling me the same thing when their plate pitched into the fire; I just wasn't listening. If I stay, I'll be going against my own values for the sake of money and the arbitrary, manmade concept known as "winning." Maybe I really am on the brink of being the last person out here, just as my gut sense tells me I am. That doesn't change what's right, it just makes my choice more significant. Doing what's right when there isn't much at stake is one thing; doing it when we know what we might be sacrificing is quite another, but it's even more important.

I believe my body could keep on going a while longer, but at what cost? I may well be one of those people who can push themselves right up until their heart stops beating. This last week I've known my body was winding down and I've had to push it harder to accomplish the most basic tasks. I'm staggering blindly toward a looming cliff edge obscured by mist, and I might not know that I'm close until I take that fatal last step and it's too late. No more. Here is where it stops.

I throw open the door and toss the foul foot broth outside, scattering the gray liquid across the sparkling snow. There will be no more Starvation Soup, no more new cracks opening up on my withered hands, no more underwear sliding down my hip bones to pool at my knees. Though the thought twists my shrunken stomach up into knots and steals my breath away, my resolve is unshaken. Tomorrow, I'm making the call.

I stay up late, staring into the coals, hardly able to fathom that this is my last night here. I pick up a piece of charcoal and for the first time in weeks, I write the date and day number on my hearth rock. November 19, day seventy-two. *Oh my gosh, of course I have to go tomorrow—it's not just my forty-third birthday, it's also day seventy-three, a prime number day.* Forty-three and seventy-three, that's two prime numbers. I don't know where this whole prime number thing came from, but it seems that the magic knew all along this would be my time. My resistance is gone. Now that I fully believe I'm going and that it's absolutely perfect, I let myself actually think about what leaving means. Amidst all the other thoughts, the one that rises to the top is predictable: *The next time the sun sets, I'll be sitting down to a big birthday dinner.*

In the morning, I don't even consider pulling my traps before calling to tap. I'm not giving myself any opportunity to change my mind or back out. I wake up before first light and stagger out of the cabin into the sharp pre-dawn air, pull out the satellite phone and dial up production. My voice catches, but I clear my throat and take a deep breath.

"This is Woniya," I tell them. "Please tell the crew not to bother packing up the medical equipment. They won't be doing a check on me today. They'll be picking me up." I pause until I can push down the lump in my quivering throat. "I am officially tapping out."

70

LEAVING TU NEDHE

This time, I stand out in front of the cabin to meet them. The silence of the wintery landscape is broken by the engine long before I see the helicopter. The rhythmic thudding feels shockingly out of place against the groaning of the lake ice and the wind through the spruce branches. Even though this was my choice, I can still hardly wrap my brain around the fact that this is my last day, and the people in that crazy machine aren't coming to assess me, but to whisk me away.

As the helicopter settles down and the deep rumble of the rotors pounds in my chest, I let the raw mix of emotions pour through me—excitement and fear, joy and grief—all tumbled on top of one another. For a moment, my primal animal nervous system wrestles for dominance with my modern human sensibilities. I force my feet to remain planted as the urge to run away tugs at my legs.

Eventually, jacketed forms approach me along the snowy path, and even as I let myself feel the longing for human connection for the first time in months, a flood of tears at what I'm leaving behind engulfs me.

There are cameras trained on my face, but there's no way to staunch my tears, and I don't want to. I want to feel this, all of it, and I want the world out there to feel it too because as painful as it is, it's also beautiful.

I'm laughing even as the tears pool in the rabbit furs around my neck, making them clammy against my throat. I try to find words for the joy and the heartbreak, the gratitude and the wonder but, "Hi, everyone," is all I can manage.

The crew is as stunned as I am that I called them here. There has been zero indication from day one that I would ever leave of my own volition.

"I have loved being here with every fiber of my being," I explain to Dan, the producer. "And I don't really want to leave, but my body is done and I'm more and more aware of that."

I look out over his head to the swaying trees, the craggy rocks, and the flat expanse of ice stretching into the distance beyond them. How can I put into words that which, just like this vista, feels infinite? What has been so primal and visceral and beyond the realm of spoken language?

"I have looked into the void, touched its very rim, and come out whole," I could tell him.

"I have held hands with my ancestors, heard them whispering in my ear, and over time, become one of them."

"I have learned what it is to be an animal—to live and die by my skill and my wits and what the land has to offer me—and it is the most real and important thing I have ever done. If you would just leave me, if no one was out there watching, I would probably choose to stay out here and let my flesh become fox and lynx and let my bones melt back into the earth."

But I know they can't leave me, and the end of this journey is not mine alone to decide.

Instead, I look into his eyes and put it in terms that are easy to understand. "Today is my birthday," I say. "And it feels like the most amazing gift I can give myself to go somewhere where I have warmth, and food, and the ability to care for myself."

Back at the cabin, I pack up everything. *Everything.* It's a small helicopter, and there's a weight limit, but I'm not willing to leave behind a single piece of my life out here. The unused clay I had such plans for, frozen solid and heavy as a boulder; the bundles of willows not yet woven; balls and balls of rabbit rope; baskets of frozen cranberries; charred rounds of spruce and birch—my unfinished burn bowls. No one argues with me. They can all see what it's costing me to be willing to step into that helicopter, and no one wants to risk me changing my mind and having to wrestle me in.

Last of all is my enormous, overstuffed backpack. They offer to take it for me, but I refuse. I came out here on my own, I lived out here on my own, and I'm going to walk out of here on my own with everything I brought with me—including my intact body.

I feel strong and proud—still shrinking inside at the thought of going, but knowing that whatever other adventures await me, I'll meet those too with fortitude and strength.

My other gear is in the helicopter, and they're ushering me toward it. One foot is already on the first step of the ladder when I realize I can't leave yet, there's something I haven't done.

"Wait—I need some time to say goodbye," I tell them.

I walk over to my dancing spot and face the water—looking out at the island that gave me my frying pan and at the jumble of ice flows where I had the most magnificent evening of my life. I throw my arms out wide.

How can I say goodbye to what has been the most life changing experience I have ever known? How can I just fly away from all of this, from the ancestors, who have been with me every step of the way? It's too much. Then I realize that I won't be doing that, because I can almost feel their hands on the small of my back now, supporting me gently. And I know that's my own hand I'm feeling too, because I have the strength to listen to, believe in, and support myself, and somehow it took this experience to really see that.

"I love you, Tu Nedhe, with all my heart and soul," I tell the water before me. "Thank you. Thank you so much. I don't want to leave you, but I have to go. I couldn't do that without saying goodbye, but it isn't a real goodbye, because I'll take you with me wherever I go. You're part of me now, forever. We are part of each other."

And it's true. Every cell in each of our bodies is replaced regularly. After these months of eating from the land, I carry the hares and the spruce tips in the fibers of my muscles and the minerals of the bedrock in my bones. Keeping me alive out here was their gift to me, and now it's time to offer them my gift in return. They get to experience a new life through me, to travel to far-off places they've never dreamed of. Together, we offer a gift to the world— showing how someone coming to the wild from a place of humility, respect, and connection can be nourished in bigger and deeper ways than someone who comes to conquer and take without giving back. That is a message that the world needs desperately.

The rocks are blurry through my tears as I tear myself away and give the pilot a nod. Dave Holder gives me a hand into the cockpit and straps me in.

I sob all over again as the rotors start up and I feel the skids leave the rocks for the last time. I gasp and fight the straps and laugh through the tears as we ascend, reaching my hands out toward the barren stretches of granite as we zoom away from my peninsula, my home. I already miss it with a pain that's like a hot knife in my chest. I love it so much I feel my heart will burst. And yet ultimately, I've come to see that I love myself more. And that's the real win.

Me in my shelter during a medical check. The insulated double wall is visible on right side of the door frame. *Photo by Dave Holder, October 2018. Used with permission.*

The two fawns from the doe I butchered for my casting submissions, just before I buried them.

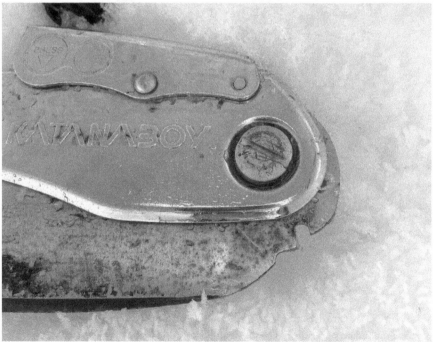

TOP: The view from the rock arena, looking southeast over the lake toward Frying Pan Island. *Photo by Dan Bree, November 2018. Used with permission.* BOTTOM: Detail of the back of my folding saw. This is the end with which I tried, unsuccessfully, to beat my way through eighteen inches of lake ice in order to ice fish.

Me and the cameraman, Sean Cable, on November 20, 2018, which was my birthday and the day I tapped out. My shrunken cheeks and protruding nose show my emaciation, but I am thrilled to be holding the thermos of bone broth the team brought me and to have human contact again. *Photo by Dan Bree, November 2018. Used with permission.*

PART FIVE

COMING HOME TO ME

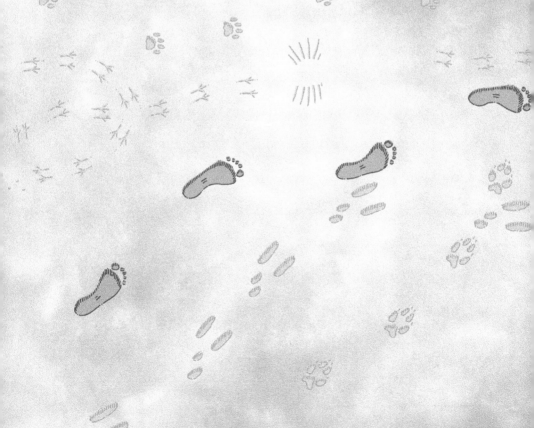

71

A DELICATE FLOWER

ven through my heartbreak, it doesn't take long for my awe and wonder at the incredible landscape spread out before me to eclipse my sorrow. On launch day, the view from the helicopter was beautiful and fascinating, but didn't mean much to me. Now that I know this place so intimately, the bird's eye view of it is overwhelming. Every rock, every trail, and every stretch of shore has stories attached to it. Seeing so much of it all at once, and my own little peninsula in the context of the larger world that envelopes it, is breathtaking, and helps me find some peace with the transition. Then we bank and head the other direction, with vast water and unknown territory in front of us.

Long before I'm ready for it, I can see something different up ahead—straight lines and right angles and other shapes that don't make sense against the forest and water. The helicopter starts to descend, and I can see a cluster of buildings—the production base camp—on the ground below.

There's a crew there waiting for us. After we land, people begin grabbing my bags and someone holds my arm and steadies me as I crouch-walk out from under the spinning blades. On the far side of the landing pad, they've set up a chair for me to wait in. The first priority is to have the doctor see me, and they're still readying a room for him to use for the examination.

It feels like a lot of fuss, and I'm confused about why everyone is treating me like such a delicate flower. While I'm grateful for the care, I'm also a little frustrated. I've just spent months taking care of myself in the arctic wilds—*haven't I demonstrated that I'm anything but delicate?* As the helicopter powers down and the excitement and the adrenaline start to wear off, though, I realize that I'm pretty tired and cold, and even a little shaky, and soon I'm glad for the chair and the blanket they bring me.

It's hot and stuffy when I step into the exam room. *Oh my god, a heated room! I'd almost forgotten there were such things.* The doctor is kind and attentive and puts me at ease.

"I need to check your weight and vitals," he explains. "To make sure you're fit for the plane ride to the hospital."

Hospital? I'm going to the hospital?

I strip down to the same long underwear I've worn for all my med checks and step onto the scale. I haven't been allowed to look at it and see my own weight since the first medical check. Reading the numbers now, I think there must be some mistake. I haven't weighed less than a hundred pounds since I was twelve. I sink onto the bed and wrap my arms around my shoulders. Even in the stifling heat of the room, I'm shivering.

It's not a mistake. I've lost fifty pounds since launch. *Fifty.* And I'm only five feet four. That is a tremendous percentage of my body weight. *An entire third of me is gone*, putting me squarely in the BMI danger zone.

"We've been very concerned about you," the doctor explains. "I'm glad you made the call, but you were going to be heading out today either way. With your level of weight loss, though, we need to run some blood panels on you before we can begin the refeeding protocols."

Refeeding protocols? What the heck does that mean?

Returning to regular eating after the level of starvation I experienced, he explains, can be dangerous—even deadly. Refeeding is the process of slowly and carefully getting the body and digestive system used to eating again and giving it time to adjust to the kinds of food it hasn't processed for some time.

I thought I was coming out to the birthday dinner I've been fantasizing about. A plane ride to the hospital is not what I had in mind.

"Can I shower first?" I ask. Now that I'm around "normal" people again, I'm acutely aware of how filthy I am. He looks at his watch. "You've got about half an hour. The plane has to take off soon to make it to Yellowknife before dark."

So much for relaxing in the luxury of being clean and well fed. There's someone in a small utility vehicle waiting for me outside, with my clothes bag from prelaunch in the back. They won't even let me walk to the bathhouse by myself, even though I was hiking my own trapline right up until yesterday. Now that I really understand the depth of my weight loss, though, I don't argue with them.

This fishing lodge was built for summer, not deep northern winter, so the pipes to every outbuilding but one small bath house are shut off. I step inside and go through my bag to grab something clean for the flight. My prelaunch clothes are like foreign objects to me, but I'm thrilled to have something to wear that isn't covered in soot and reeking of smoke. Someone hands me a clean towel and, with a reminder that the clock is ticking, I'm left on my own.

I strip down to my long underwear, then straighten up, and that's when I see my face in the mirror for the first time.

Oh. My. God.

Now I get why everyone is treating me like fine china that could break at any second. If I didn't know I was the only one in this room, I wouldn't believe it's my own face looking back at me. My cheeks are sunken and my eyes are huge and bulging. My head looks enormous on my spindly frame, and even through my long johns, I can see how my knobby knees and elbows jut out from my stick-like limbs. My face and hands are so blackened with greasy soot— and snot, and blood, and god knows what else—that I look like I'm wearing dark gloves. With my gray skin, oversized head, and strange eyes, I look like a B-movie alien that has been tossed into a bag of charcoal and shaken up. When I run my fingers along my prominent cheekbones, I see my hands in the mirror, and the reflection shows the deep, bloody cracks all over them.

There's a sick fascination in it, but it's incredibly disorienting to see myself this way, so I decide it's best to absorb the sight in small doses. Besides, I've probably got only twenty minutes left to scrub months' worth of filth away. I tear myself away from the mirror and climb into the shower.

It takes three shampoos before the water runs clear, even with hair that feels half as thick as it used to. Though I scrub my body all over and the dark water pours off me, my skin seems to be permanently stained gray. It will probably have to slough off before I'm my normal color again.

All I want to do is lean my head against the wall and melt into the blissfully warm water, the first physical comfort I've had in so long, but I don't have time for anything but the necessities.

I towel off quickly and shrug into a bra and underwear. The underwear dangles limply, like it's been doing for weeks, but the bra is far stranger. The molded cups stand away from my chest, and there's three inches of air space between them and my shrunken breasts. It's the only clean bra I've got, and I'm not going to the hospital without one, so even though I feel like a toddler playing dress up, I toss my long johns and sweater on and wear it like that. I'm floating in my jeans too, and don't have enough holes in my old belt to fit it to my current waist, so I tie some of the belt loops together with stray yarn I find in the bag and head out the door.

The plane ride to Yellowknife is a blur. Compared to the intensity of feelings from this morning, I feel surprisingly numb now. It's largely the shock, I'm guessing, or perhaps my wasted body had enough energy for only a certain amount of emotion today and used it all up in one go. I want to look out the plane windows and take in more of the forest and lake below, but I don't have it in me. My exhaustion catches up with me five minutes after takeoff, and I spend most of the flight slumped onto the shoulder of the medic, Ben.

I fantasized about celebrating this historic day with a juicy, rare burger and a group of people. What I get instead is a thermos of bone broth and nearly eight hours under the fluorescent lights of the waiting room until they finally call me in. Ben will always be my personal savior for letting me sleep on his lap for at least half of those hours.

My bloodwork and electrolyte levels look good (*thank you, salt buttons*). I'm not deemed to be in danger, but it's after midnight by the time I'm tucked into a hotel room in town and left blessedly alone again, with more sensory stimulation to process than I've had in weeks on end.

The electric lights and forced air heat at the hotel are disorienting but, I have to admit, absolutely dreamy. And that isn't all. I have a bathtub. *Have you seen these things? They are amazing.* A basin bigger than my whole body, that I can fill with hot water—without having to chip through ice for it, haul it, or make a fire to heat it. A dream come true.

But I can't get comfortable. Even in water, the protruding bones in my hips, butt, and shoulders rub uncomfortably against the hard porcelain. I can't relax and enjoy it until I heap towels into the tub to make a padded nest for myself. For the first two hours, I just lie there, listening to the drumming of my heartbeat in my ears. I dry off with the one small hand towel I didn't use to pad the tub and then crawl into bed. But though I lie there for over an hour, my brain won't shut down. Eventually, I draw another bath, grab the pen and hotel notepad from the desk, and sit upright in the tub, the notepad balanced on its edge. I scribble snapshot memories of my wilderness life on the front and back of every page until the notepad is filled and the sun is rising.

I would later learn that almost no one sleeps their first night back, so the few hours I got in the ER waiting room should be considered a solid victory.

72

DECIDING I AM BEAUTIFUL

y Yellowknife support team consists of two people: Ben, the medic, and Jessie, who is in charge of my care and feeding.

My skin is so cracked and dry that I beg Jessie to take me somewhere to get lotions and salves, plus a real notebook to write in, so we go to a local bookstore and then a drugstore. The bookstore is wonderful, but the pharmacy is all fluorescent lights, too many things on the shelves, and an assault of bright colors everywhere. I keep it together fairly well as I pick out my bottles of personal care products, but as we head to the checkout, I accidentally walk through the Christmas aisle. The shelves are lined with gingerbread house kits, candy canes, and boxes of cheap chocolates. I don't truly want any of them, but they're the first food of this kind I've seen in months of intense deprivation. My chest gets tight and palms start to sweat at the sight, and I have to fight down the starved animal inside of me that wants to tear the packages off the shelves and rip into them with my teeth.

"You have to get me out of here," I tell Jessie, turning my face away from the junk food.

I don't ask to be taken to town again.

For the next several days, the hotel suite is my entire world. It's clear that I'm not yet ready to be exposed to modern society. I feel like my skin is made of cellophane, like I'm totally exposed and vulnerable and every nerve ending is raw. I'm utterly fragile—physically and emotionally—needing to rest after walking from the bedroom to the bathroom and crying at the drop of a hat. I miss the peninsula fiercely but also know I couldn't make it there in this state. Now that I have them again, I can't imagine leaving food and warmth any time soon—but I also have no desire to let the rest of the world back in. Adjusting to the reality of these three small rooms is plenty, and rather than feeling trapped in them, I feel secure in my little bubble.

My life revolves around the small plate of snacks Jessie brings me every couple of hours, and Ben monitors me daily, taking my weight and vitals and closely tracking my heartbeat and digestion. Am I pooping? When and how much? Too much? Too little? Too soft? Too hard?

I don't realize at the time that these aren't just routine questions, they are incredibly important in understanding how my body is handling the return to eating. Digestive issues are common and potentially dangerous for people readjusting to food after starvation. Watching for and understanding these indicators could make the difference between healing, or ending up back at the hospital.

Water weight comes on quickly, but I still have so little muscle mass that I can't sit comfortably. I feel like Steve Martin from *The Jerk*, dragging a pen and notebook, a fuzzy sweater, and a fluffy bed pillow to sit on, whenever I leave the bedroom.

At first, I get only puréed vegetables and bone broth, but every day Jessie adds a little more substance and a little more variety to my diet. The first time she hands me a plate of real, solid food, I burst into tears. They aren't tears of sadness, nor even of joy or gratitude—which would be appropriate. It's simply utter overwhelm and confounded disbelief. *All this food? For me? And I didn't have to do anything but sit here to get it?*

Even though it's nowhere near as much food as my ravenous body is telling me to eat, it is still the most stunning display of abundance I can imagine. And to think there's a whole world of people, just outside the hotel room door, who have all this and more, several times a day, and never realize that they're blessed beyond the wildest dreams of their own, famine-honed ancestors.

Making ceremony of every meal feels vital. Jessie brings me a candle to make the room feel homey, and every time she brings me a plate, even a small snack, I turn the lights down, light the candle, and sit just looking at the food for a moment before I make the ancestor plate.

Eventually, I graduate to being able to self-administer a few select snacks. As it's so few calories and almost no carbohydrates, I get two tiny cans of V8 juice daily—*two whole cans!* Rather than drink it all at once, I heat it in a bowl in the microwave and eat my "soup" by slow, careful spoonfuls, making a feast of those five tablespoons.

With so much light and warmth and whole days to fill, I take the opportunity to explore the foreign universe my body has become. My muscles are defined and ropey, the veins protruding and wrapping around my limbs like thin snakes. I can almost see the individual muscle fibers under my thin skin when I flex. I'm utterly fascinated by the strange person looking back at me in the mirror. *Who is this wayward woman, and what has she done to herself?* Every time I stare into her eyes they well up with tears—sometimes loving compassion for all she has gone through, sometimes sadness at the state of her, and sometimes just shock and disbelief as I come to grips with the fact that this isn't a stranger in the mirror, *it's me.* Finally, as I put on water weight and some of the empty hollows in my face fill back out, I begin to recognize my own features again, though I'm still gaunt.

To think, I was socialized to be ashamed of carrying "too much weight," and of the round curves of my strong, healthy body. I feel infuriated at the society that conditioned me to judge myself so harshly back then. I was a good deal heavier in my youth than in my thirties and forties, and after spending a lot of my twenties wishing I was more slender, I would give anything to have that beautiful, round body back now. Then I realize that taking issue with this body is no different than taking issue with that one—neither attitude is gentle or loving. I look myself square in the face.

"You are beautiful," I tell the emaciated woman in the mirror. "You are absolutely perfect, exactly as you are." And the amazing thing is, I believe it. One hundred percent.

"I love you, Woniya," I tell myself. "And I'll always have your back, from here on out."

73

SEEING THE WOLF

My portion sizes increase daily, and slowly, the weight trickles back onto my frame—until I can bathe and sit almost comfortably without extra padding. I think about food every second of every day. Even as it sinks in that eating daily is something I can rely on again, I remain obsessed. I am like one of Pavlov's dogs, my stomach growling and rumbling as the clock ticks down toward my snack time. Every minute that passes as I wait for it to arrive is excruciating, and I lick the plate after every meal, never wasting a single crumb or calorie.

I can't wrap my brain around why being hungry now, when I know I have food coming, is infinitely harder than actual starvation was. I made that small pemmican ration last for months, but now I'm shocked at my lack of self-control. It's one thing going without when you're alone and have limited options. It's quite another when you're surrounded by well-fed people who have autonomy over their choices, while you, after just experiencing more freedom than you've ever known, currently have none.

As hard as it is, I know it's important and I'm grateful for the support. The transition from an all-wild diet to a modern diet would be difficult for anyone, and that's if they had been eating adequate calories of wild foods. With the level of starvation I was operating under, eating whatever my body tells me it wants right now, and in the mountainous proportions I dream of, could do serious, long-term harm to my system. Everything in the refeeding program, from the contents to the amounts, has been determined by a nutritionist working in conjunction with a doctor, and oriented toward my health and well-being.

Eventually, about a week into my refeeding program, a day comes when I can look at a full plate of food without crying over it. It feels like a loss, not a victory. I don't want to lose the sense of magic that comes with food. I don't want to eat a meal without feeling it pulse with life and hearing its calories singing to me. But it wouldn't be sustainable to stay in transcendental realms forever, so eventually the mundane seeps back in through the cracks, even though the memory of what it is to be so raw and transformed will live with me forever.

Though I don't relish the idea of going anywhere, eventually they fly me back to the production base camp in the wilderness to continue my recovery. I'm eager to be reunited with the gear that I left behind when they flew me to Yellowknife for my hospital visit, especially my willow basket of cranberries, as I miss the wild foods my system is most accustomed to. And yet, though they eventually became delicious to me on the peninsula, I can't even swallow them now. They're so saturated with smoke that it's all I can taste, and they trigger my gag reflex. Apparently, I was so well smoked out there myself that I didn't taste it.

My days at production base camp are slow and restful, and I spend a lot of them in bed reading.

One morning, Dave comes by my door and asks if I want to take a ride. He and one of the lodge caretakers are taking the lodge truck out to the runway, where the tent village we lived in before launch was set up. I can tell by the curl at the edge of his lip and sparkle in his eye that there's something up. "I think you're going to want to see this," he tells me.

I pull on my layers and join them. We are less than a quarter mile down the road when a sleek gray form pops over a bank and down into the roadbed. I crane my neck around and gasp, transfixed. It's a wolf—a beautiful gray female loping gracefully in our wheel track, right at the back of the truck. "She follows us out every time," he tells me.

When the truck slows, she hangs back. We stop and crack the doors to see her better, but she disappears instantly. When we start up again, she's right behind us in no time. She seems more secure when we reach the broad expanse of the gravel runway. She climbs a hill and watches us for a while, then after a few minutes nosing around the edge of the camp, she's off into the forest and gone.

I've finally seen a wild arctic wolf. I've checked the last box on the list of things that meant success to me.

I'm still resistant to the idea of ever going home, but as my body recovers, I know I can't postpone it forever, so I begin to prepare myself to return to the world I came from.

The still unwoven rabbit rope, the bundles of willow, and my bag of clay are like precious friends, the last remaining pieces of my wild arctic life on the peninsula. I thaw out the clay and spend the last days before my departure making rough pottery out of it, then I weave another willow basket, and sew the rabbit rope into my parka lining, reminding me that, modern food again or not, I am still part hare.

74

"CONGRATULATIONS"

Back home, my loved ones were informed and told to prepare once it was down to me and one other participant. If the other person went home, making me the winner, my selected loved one or a more available alternate would have been asked to hop on a plane to the production team's base camp at a moment's notice. From there they would have been helicoptered out to the peninsula to give me the news. None of the show staff had let on about it, but when I spoke with my mom from the hospital in Yellowknife, she asked me how I felt about being the runner-up, so I'd learned about how I'd placed on my first day back.

I've had all my recovery time to absorb and process the news that my suspicions the day before I tapped out—that it was down to me and one other participant—were correct. Upon hearing such news, there are many people who would be disappointed they had chosen to leave. I have no regrets. In fact, I'm absolutely thrilled. It confirms that my deep sense of knowing was right. That sense made the temptation to continue pushing to stay incredibly strong, and makes the fact that I was true to myself, regardless, all the more potent. I passed the test. I chose what was right, and I did it at the crux of the competition, which means that, when the season airs, all eyes will be on me and that important choice.

Throughout the long days of resting and healing, I decide that being runner-up is, in fact, totally perfect. As much as parts of me wanted to be the last one remaining, there are also parts that reject the very concept of "winning," and turning something as beautiful and powerful as a deep wilderness immersion into a competition. Being runner-up means I did as well as possible, demonstrating my skills and philosophy beautifully, but stopped just short of the crazy mind games that being dubbed "a winner" comes with in our unhealthily ego-driven culture.

Unfortunately, the runner-up leaving is what signals the end of the season. Though I would rather stay up north for weeks longer, eventually the entire production team and all the equipment is packed up and heading home, so I must too.

Standing in line to go through security in the Yellowknife airport, I'm still disoriented by the amount of movement, conversations with "normal people," and the fast pace of absolutely everything. I forget until the last minute that I have to take my belt off to go through the metal detectors. I put everything else into the trays, and then pull my belt out of its loops. As soon as I do, my pants droop down around my hips, and I catch the waistband just in time to keep them from dropping to my ankles. The line is stalled behind me as I hold up my pants with one hand, while fishing my wallet out of my pocket with the other.

"Sorry," I tell the man behind me, embarrassed to accidentally undress in front of him. "I lost a lot of weight recently."

"Oh, congratulations," he tells me.

I'm stunned. *Congratulations?* I'm not as skinny as I was when I first came out, but I've been tracking my body closely and know that I still look danger-ously emaciated. I've lost all the fat in my body, plus a significant portion of my muscle mass. I'm lucky to have stopped just short of permanent organ damage. And he's congratulating me?

Dear god, I think to myself. *This is what it is to live in a culture that worships skinny over healthy—over everything. Has he even looked at me? Has he taken in my sunken cheeks, my protruding eyes, and the deep hollows beneath them?*

Honestly, he may have, and yet he still gave me the rote, conditioned reply to an announcement of weight loss in our culture—*congratulations*.

I can't shake the impact of this one, brief comment. Having just emerged from the most potent, extreme, and beautiful experience of my life, I'm both confounded and horrified by our society. My experience in the Arctic lifted a veil, revealing the fabricated reality we have built for ourselves and the dam-age it inflicts. Almost no one I have ever interacted with in the "real world" actually understands the reality of survival or the true meaning of food.

Congratulations for almost achieving total starvation? What is wrong with you people?

At this moment, I miss my curvy, well-muscled form more than ever. I can't believe I ever felt embarrassed by my body, which, even in my twenties, was always strong and fit enough to accomplish tasks a lot of thinner girls could never dream of. Even though I'm committed to loving myself fully no matter what shape I hold, I can't wait to have some curves back and to be a proud example of a healthy woman who loves herself.

I don't answer him. I don't know what I can possibly say. I just stand aside to let him move ahead of me in line, finish emptying my pockets, and shuffle through the metal detector holding up my waistband and blinking back tears.

75

HOMECOMING

I was prepared for my time in the Arctic to be hard. What I wasn't prepared for was how devastating coming home would be. I had thought that leaving the peninsula would be the worst part, but when I was still in the Northwest Territories, even in the bustling capital, Yellowknife, I still felt connected to it. The peninsula was over a hundred miles away, but I could still walk to the shore of Tu Nedhe, the same lake that lapped against my very own rocky beach.

Watching the earlier *Alone* seasons after my invitation to the show came, I got the impression that most folks are tortured during their stay and want nothing more than to return to their life back home and their loved ones. While food, warmth, comfort, and companionship are all lovely, and I'm glad to have them, they don't make up for the loss of a way of life I've longed for since before I hit puberty. Having actually lived it for the first time, I now have a clearer picture of what I'm missing, and how impossible that kind of life is back home, where there are so few untrammeled places left.

While I never entirely accepted the modern world, I feel far less at home in it now than ever before. Once I'm back in coastal California, the northern lands I've fallen in love with seem like a distant dream. I feel the ache for them all day long, and most poignantly in the dark, wakeful hours of the night, when I have no other distractions.

It's weeks before I'm at ease in public spaces, longer before I can hold schedules and deadlines in my head clearly, and months before I'm comfortable with phones and email. All things abstract—not here in front of me, where I can reach out and touch them—take some getting used to, and I would rather not have to do so at all.

Never having felt lonely out there, I'm shocked at how isolating it is to have an experience that so few people can even begin to wrap their minds around. And that's considering the fact that my social circles are far better equipped for understanding it than most.

Harder still is the secrecy. My closest friends know something of what I've been up to—the furious preparations and my long absence made that necessary—but with most people I have to bite my tongue. Until my name is announced in the promotion of *Alone Season 6*, not long before it airs, I'm not allowed to say I was part of the show, or anything about where I've been and what I've been doing. Details about my experience and how long I was out there are even more strictly guarded. Having to actively avoid giving away any hint that I've just returned from the most powerful and transformative experience of my life is not only incredibly hard, it feels damaging to my integrity and psyche, especially because anyone can tell by looking at me that something dramatic has happened to my body

Physically, I'm utterly altered, but not in the ways I'd expected. Yes, I'm voraciously hungry and food obsessed for a long time after my return. At the same time though, the absurd decadence of modern life is incredibly obvious to me after spending months starving. While I'm horrified at the excess I'm surrounded by, I also find that I now have less ability than my peers to resist it. I'm not just eating a lot, but eating compulsively—filling my belly past the comfort point with foods I wouldn't normally choose. It doesn't help that I return just before Christmas, when cookies and baked goods are everywhere. I actually strain my esophagus once, eating so much that my stomach can't hold it all. Swallowing, and even breathing deeply, are painful for days afterward.

I'm embarrassed by my inability to restrain myself but feel powerless to do anything about it. Eventually, I stop trying to force self-control, trusting that it, like my perfectly healthy body, will return in time.

I am shocked when, for the first couple of weeks back home, I eat and eat all the rich foods I've been fantasizing about, but no weight comes on. Unable to wear my normal clothes, I go to thrift stores and buy a new wardrobe in extra-extra small. I learn later that, at first, a body in my condition uses the extra calories mostly for repair—rebuilding the withered organs as its number one priority, then healing any other damage that needs tending to. It's only after the vital systems are back to being fully functional that the body can rebuild its muscles and calorie reserves.

I'm slowly easing back into gentle exercise, when one day I notice I can't kneel comfortably on my yoga mat. My right knee hurts. Looking down, I see that it's swollen and jiggly like a water balloon, though I don't recall hitting it. I'm totally stumped, until I remember a fall I took back on the peninsula. I was carrying a heavy rock for the chimney I never managed to build. The snow was slippery, and I couldn't see my feet, then I stumbled and came down hard—hard enough to scare the hell out of me—on that knee.

I expected it to be seriously injured, or badly bruised at the very least. I expected, as a matter of fact, exactly what my knee is currently doing, but it never happened—until now. Just as my organs shrank and had to be rebuilt, and my period disappeared for a while, I believe that my body decided that dealing with the knee injury out there was too costly, so it waited until it felt safe enough to react to and heal it. The swelling lasts for a couple of weeks, and then just as mysteriously as it arrived, disappears.

Eventually, the weight does start to come back on, and then it makes up for lost time. At this point, I quickly get back to my normal weight, and then surpass it. Just as I lost a pound a day out there, I put on a pound a day for a while, even as I'm regulating my intake better and eating less. Every morning I stare at the scale, dumbfounded. *Seriously, another pound?*

Because it packs on completely differently, I still don't feel like myself, so that yet again, I don't even recognize my own body. My weight is usually evenly distributed—but no more. My arms and legs stay stick-skinny, and my butt and breasts remain flat, while my belly expands until my waist disappears and I grow a layer of padding that encircles my middle like a spare tire, dwarfing my toothpick legs and miniscule butt. This too, I've since learned, is a common phenomenon—after experiencing the kind of deprivation I did, the body guards its core first and packs extra fat around the organs.

In a few months, my shape comes back, but I hold onto the extra weight. Unlike at other times in my life, I speak lovingly to my body and praise it for its wisdom. *Darn right you want a little extra cushion these days, just in case*, I tell it. *Makes perfect sense.*

While my eating habits normalize within a few months, it takes a lot longer to shake my food anxiety. I no longer feel compelled to gorge all the time, but I need to have food near me, and I can only relax and be comfortable if I know it will only be a few hours until I eat again.

I remember clearly the day I realize that this too, has finally shifted. It's March 2019, roughly four months after my return from the Arctic. I'm on a road trip in Baja California with my dad and his wife, when I realize that I don't have any snacks with me, and I have no idea where or when our next meal will come. *And it is okay.*

76

EMERGING FROM THE CHRYSALIS

t took a year and a half for my body to find its way back to what felt normal again, but even so, it's a different normal than before. I don't yet know what the long-term impacts of *Alone Season 6* on my health might be. Today, though, just over four years later—except for my teeth, which lost all their enamel from the mineral loss combined with the acid from the cranberries—I continue to feel stronger and healthier than I did before the adventure. My chronic shoulder issues and other joint pain never returned. I'll never know whether it was the healing aspects of fasting or one more mysterious gift the land up there bestowed on me. Probably a combination.

I remained in a holding pattern for some time after returning home, healing, and reintegrating. The airing of the show and the attention that came with it were overwhelming and discombobulating. Rather than doing a third year at Weaving Earth, I chose to return to teaching. I traveled to various skills events around the western US, sharing about buckskin sewing, wild foods, wilderness survival, nature connection practices, and other subjects related to wilder living. This was how I'd been teaching for years, though, not the "new and more meaningful way to inspire a broader world of students" that I'd envisioned at the close of my second year at Weaving Earth.

Then, in spring of 2020, a little less than a year and a half after I returned from the Arctic, the coronavirus pandemic swept the globe. Suddenly, there were medical crises, supply chain issues, food shortages, and travel restrictions.

People were isolated, sheltering in place, and fearful about how they would get their basic needs met. Much of the world was getting a little taste of the *Alone* experience, and the show's popularity boomed that summer with the release of Season 6 on Netflix. In a matter of months, the pandemic accomplished what I, in decades of trying, hadn't managed—it illustrated why mastering the skills to provide for our own needs from the resources right around us is not a relic of the past but a real and present need. They aren't just ancestral ways; they are timeless ways.

As long as humans require warmth, shelter, water, and food, our lives will depend on our ability to find them, and our credit cards won't always be the answer. The beautiful thing is that this isn't a liability—it's an invitation to live a richer, more satisfying life that's in tune with the cycles of the seasons and the natural world. The skills to house, clothe, and feed ourselves are important, but connection is a survival skill too. When we listen deeply and engage with the world around us in a way that honors it and gives back, whether we're in human company or not, we are, in fact, never alone.

I was actively working on this book, making good on my promise to the land up north to share the heart of my journey there with the world, when the pandemic hit. I was seeing panic in the people around me, then got a message from a former student about how the program she'd done with me made her feel more resilient in the face of the global crisis. It gave me pause. Suddenly, millions of people were recognizing their need for the skills I teach, just as it was far more difficult to travel to share them in person.

Hmmm...

I had the skills, I had the time, and after filming my entire wilderness adventure myself for months, I had the camera training. I'd been urged by friends and peers to consider online teaching before, but not being a computer person, it had never appealed to me. Yet here was a world in crisis that needed what I had to give.

In a week's time, I pivoted from my focus on writing and began putting together online classes in off-grid, homestead, and wilderness skills. As ironic as it was to offer ancestral and land-based living skills through modern technology, I was amazed at the results. I was touching more lives than I ever had with in-person teaching, and through interactive group video calls spread out over several weeks, I could see for myself the beautiful and lasting ways the courses affected the lives of my students.

The *Alone* journey had dropped into my lap without me looking for it, and at the perfect time to answer my prayers. Likewise, the exposure and camera skills I got from the show, combined with my teaching experience and deep listening to what the world was asking of me, allowed me to expand naturally into a new form of my old calling, just as I'd dreamed of doing back in my chrysalis phase before the surthrival trip with the bobcat.

That's just one of many shifts in my world since my return. Though it's been several years now, my arctic journey still touches my life daily in profound ways. Its impacts go far deeper than the ones on my body and my career, but are harder to put into words.

It was the most powerful gift of my life, and those ten and a half weeks were the most deeply connected I've ever felt to a wild place. Though the experience helped me make peace with many hard losses and let go of some of my deepest griefs, it left me with others. To get a brief taste of the life I'd always dreamed of—one closer to that of my distant ancestors—but then to be torn away from it again, was in many ways more devastating than continuing to believe that such a life wasn't possible for me. Just as I took pieces of the land up north back with me, I left part of my heart on those icy shores. When I returned home, my soul never stopped longing for that missing piece, and I felt subtly incomplete.

How do you find your way again, when a generous land hands you a compass—a magical letter N that marks your north star—and you have to leave it behind? How do you return to the human-created world, when you've known what it is to live in the wild like a creature that belongs there and is part of it? I had tuned myself to the quiet voice of the land on the peninsula, but when I left there, the buzz of machinery and the noise of traffic muffled it and made it harder to hear. I missed it terribly.

I had anticipated this, and hauled as much as I could of that place home, desperate to bring some of its magic back with me—the baskets and clay pots, my rabbit scarf and half-finished burn bowls. Out of context though, they no longer had the same life in them and became simply *objects*. The real gifts were things that couldn't be bundled up into my luggage and flown home.

And yet, even as I mourned the loss of my wilderness life, many gifts I couldn't yet see did come home with me—the mysteries of the universe, though harder to see and feel, were still working their magic.

I came home not just *believing in* but *certain of* my abilities and my own worth, and that has changed everything. I no longer feel compelled to prove myself, to me or to anyone else. From this more empowered and relaxed place, it's easier to see the ways that my lack of self-acceptance for much of my life pushed the things I wanted away from me, rather than drawing them in. I finally feel free from this pattern.

Eating has changed forever for me, in wonderful and meaningful ways. I have a whole new relationship to the life force in the food I eat. Understanding what calories really mean to my body, I find I need less of them and am more devoted to higher-quality and wilder foods, and to dietary practices like eating seasonally and depending less on grains. Greater still—having achieved it once, I now know that there is such a thing as living on beauty and that, should I need to, I can still call upon that special type of metabolism.

My relationship to hunting and trapping has also changed. Just as the Goddess Artemis is the goddess of *wild animals* and also of *the hunt*, I no longer see the two as opposed to one another, but as mutually supportive. Having dismissed trapping as cruel for most of my life prior to depending on it up north, I went on to study with a master trapper in Alberta, Canada. I now understand that trapping can be more humane than bow or rifle hunting. With most predator populations in decline, it can also be an important tool to maintain healthy populations of prey species by preventing overpopulation, disease, and resource scarcity. Both hunting and trapping—done skillfully and with one's heart in the right place—can be an act of connection and communion. One can love something, and also kill it and eat it, and this isn't ironic; it's part of an ancient and sacred cycle.

My experience of listening to, connecting with, and eventually becoming an ancestor was incredibly powerful. I now see abundance and lack, struggle and ease, and life and death more like my ancestors likely did. All were regularly present in the lives of the wilder human generations that came before us, and I recognize now that each pair is intricately tied and neither extreme is better or worse than the other. Though not palpable in every moment, as they were toward the end of my time in the Arctic, I still feel the regular presence of the ancestors in my life.

Shortly after I returned from the north, I learned that my hearing the voices of the ancestors so strongly there wasn't coincidence. Only three months after I returned to the US, the Lutselk'e Dene of the region agreed to participate in creating a new national park in the area. The name of the park is "Thaidene Nene." The translation: "Land of the Ancestors."

I can't imagine what my life would look like today had I not responded to that first *Alone* email—had I not been willing to surrender what I thought was true about myself and trust in a knowing bigger than me and my logical mind. Like the epiphany I had by that mountain stream during my graduate research—when I realized that the shallow pond was not for me and that my spirit needed the colder, more turbulent waters—I couldn't have made peace with saying no to the *Alone* adventure and choosing what was safe, familiar, and comfortable.

Listening to the world around me and letting the journey it invited me on transform me was, as I suspected it might be, an important step in the development of the woman I was always supposed to become. Seventy-three days of surviving the northern wilderness by myself was intense, dramatic, and put me in situations where, had I not made the right decisions, death was a potential outcome—but that was what it took to make the final change from caterpillar to butterfly. In the arms of that benevolent wilderness and the life-altering process of integrating the wisdom it gave me, I was finally able to shrug off the caterpillar form of the girl who never quite believed in herself, unfurl the colorful wings of a stronger, wiser, more confident woman, and fly.

The helicopter landing at production base camp after pulling me out of the wilderness. *Photo by Dan Bree, November 2018. Used with permission.*

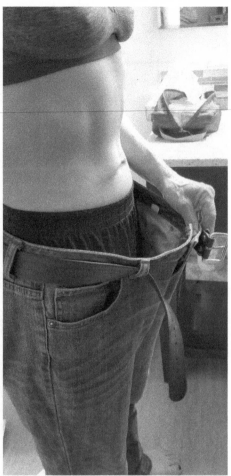

LEFT: Me during recovery in a Yellowknife hotel. This is after three days of refeeding, so I have filled out a lot with water weight but am still haggard. The skin of my hand is still stained with dirt and charcoal, and behind my hand is deep purple discoloration on my thigh, a remnant of the multiple welts I suffered from in my early weeks on the peninsula. *Photo by Jessie Collins, November 2018. Used with permission.* ABOVE: Me during recovery, wearing the pants I filled out nicely before launch. This was taken six days after the photo on the left. I have filled out more, but the difference between my body before and after *Alone* is quite dramatic. *Photo by Ben Keightly, November 2018. Used with permission.*

Shopping for a new, extra small wardrobe, in the weeks after returning to California from Canada. Still amazed at the strange reflection in the mirror but coming to terms with it.

Me busily writing on the riverside farm in Northern California where I lived for much of my recovery the summer after my return from Season 6. At this point I had gained my weight back and then some, but was healthy and thriving once again and thrilled to be writing in the sunshine.

EPILOGUE

It's 10:30 pm and I'm standing in line at Safeway, several weeks after my return from the Arctic. I'm at the point of my recovery where I'm capable of being out in public again but certainly not back to what I would consider "normal," and I have no desire to be what our culture considers normal ever again.

I'm a health food store and local co-op shopper, so buying food at Safeway at any time would be challenging for me, but in my current hypersensitive state, it is particularly so. It's far too busy and bright for me in here, and the fluorescent lights cast everything in unnatural tones I find jarring, but I was journaling in the park until after the co-op closed, and I'm out of greens at home, so here I am.

There's only one register open at this hour, so my fellow shoppers and I all funnel toward the same checkout aisle.

I look at the contents of the other shopping carts and baskets. Brightly colored sugary cereal, microwaveable deep-fried fish sticks and chicken wings, cookies, and soda. *It isn't food*, I think to myself. *None of this is food*. I stare around at the shiny packages of candy bars and chips lining the checkout aisle. Not a bit of real food in sight.

I've just come from the wilderness, where lack of food was slowly killing me. Now I'm surrounded by more calories than I could eat in my lifetime, and I'm absolutely horrified by it. All I can think is *this stuff is poison*. It's literally true. These calorie rich, nutrient poor, highly processed foods are the bane of our society. The vast majority of illnesses that so-called "civilized" people experience are due to overabundance of foods we were never meant to eat and lack of the daily activities and natural rhythms that characterized our ancestors' lives.

What would our world look like if we all knew the real value of food and gave our bodies only what would most nourish and fulfill us?

If I could give the world anything, it would be to offer each and every person an experience like I had in the Arctic. There are few things as transformative as feeling seen and held by an intact wild place, merging with the natural world around you, and coming to see yourself not as separate but as an important and valued part of it—feeling a belonging so deep that there's no such thing as loneliness.

While I wouldn't wish the extreme deprivation I experienced on anyone, I do think that there's immense value in the gift of lack. When we live for a time with less than enough, we often learn that we are far more resilient than we had ever imagined and come to appreciate more deeply the things we have, rather than focusing on what we don't.

I know most people will never have an experience like mine on *Alone*, and given the chance, most would run away from, rather than toward it. Providing an opportunity to live it vicariously, and to receive some of the same gifts, is a big part of why I wrote this book.

I'm not a survival superman. I didn't grow up with an innate understanding of my physical strength or capacity. I was a small, insecure, lonely, only child who carried ingrained beliefs about not being good enough into adulthood. I was in my late twenties before I learned to believe in my body, and well into my thirties before I firmly believed in my inherent worth.

That's why I needed to be out there, and why I needed to share the journey with you. Because in many ways, I am you, with my own challenges and struggles, and by the same token, you are me. And you can do this as well. You too are the product of countless years of human evolution and of the strength and resilience of your ancestors.

We don't often know what is inside of us until we find ourselves in a position where we don't have a choice—I know I didn't. When we get there, we can either push through or perish. The messages you tell yourself right now, today, are part of what will help you push through and bravely meet the challenges you will eventually face. The attitude you carry into them will help determine whether they break your spirit or build it up. The choice is up to you. But remember that choosing well doesn't just lift you up, it also impacts those around you and those around them, and thereby, the world at large.

I'd like to leave you with some of the most profound and life-changing lessons I brought back from the Arctic:

It's easy to feel isolated and unloved in the modern world. If we are able to let go of the perceived boundaries between ourselves and nature, and approach it in the right ways, we may find that it is right there, remembering and waiting for us, ready to embrace us with open arms.

Any day with food in it, particularly when it is enough food, is a good day. Food is not something we are entitled to, and for most of human history, our ancestors had to work hard for it and often went with less than enough. Every time you sit down to a meal, remember to look at the food in front of you with tremendous gratitude, and know that you are, in fact, immensely wealthy.

We can be nourished by a lot of things. Cultivating connection to the world around us, our human community, and ourselves, will take us a long way, as will looking for and appreciating beauty. It won't always be easy to see, but learn to pay attention to it, and when it shows up, surrender to it and let it transform you.

It's important to set small, achievable goals, and celebrate our victories. This is how we teach ourselves to believe that success is attainable, and we'll never achieve it without that belief.

Our bodies and minds believe what we tell them, so the language we use when we talk to ourselves matters. Most of us have been taught by our culture that we can never be slender enough, smart enough, attractive enough, or capable enough. Do your best to reject these teachings and tell yourself that you are enough right now. Let the messages you send yourself be ones of belonging and empowerment.

We never know what we are capable of until it's really all on the line. You likely won't ever be pushed as hard as I was in the Arctic, and I hope you aren't. Rather than waiting for an experience that proves it to you, start believing now that you can achieve the staggering accomplishments of your wildest dreams.

ABOUT THE AUTHOR

Woniya Thibeault grew up in the foothills of the Sierra Nevada mountains in Northern California. She doesn't remember a time that she wasn't drawn to and fascinated by the natural world. As a young woman, she devoted herself not just to studying biology, but to learning to be part of nature, and to cultivating the skills that countless generations of our human ancestors relied upon before modern technology made us feel separate from the wild world around us.

As of the publication of this book, she has been studying and teaching ancestral and land-based life skills for nearly thirty years. With a master's degree in environmental science and a lifetime of wilderness experience, her teaching blends an understanding of and reverence for nature with the hands-on skills for making a life within it.

As a writer, teacher, speaker, and consultant, Woniya aims to inspire and empower others to awaken their innate human skills and to live their wildest, freest lives.

Visit *www.woniyathibeault.com* for more ways to learn from her, or join her inner circle by becoming a member of her Patreon team at *www.patreon.com/woniyabuckskinrevolution*. You'll get invitations to her interactive calls, discounts on her online offerings, and the inside scoop on her projects, and you'll be part of helping to make them happen.

If you enjoyed *Never Alone*, please help it reach a wider audience by following this link or scanning the QR code below to give a written review or a star rating, and asking your local book stores and libraries to carry it.

www.amazon.com/review/create-review/?asin=1960303015

CPSIA information can be obtained
at www.ICGtesting.com
Printed in the USA
BVHW071125170523
664271BV00003B/4